which?
essential guides

MOVING
ABROAD

"Moving abroad is adventurous, but the process is fraught with pitfalls. This book will help you steer a clear path to a new life overseas."

Paul Beasley

About the author

Paul Beasley is a writer, editor and emigration specialist. He has spent the last five years working for Outbound Media on a range of publications and exhibitions that offer advice on how to move abroad successfully.

MOVING
ABROAD

Paul Beasley

Which? Books are commissioned and published by Which? Ltd,
2 Marylebone Road, London NW1 4DF
Email: books@which.co.uk

Distributed by Littlehampton Book Services Ltd, Faraday Close, Durrington, Worthing,
West Sussex BN13 3RB

British Library Cataloguing in Publication Data
A catalogue record for this book is available from the British Library

Copyright © Which? Ltd 2008

ISBN 978 1 84490 055 8

1 3 5 7 9 10 8 6 4 2

Author's acknowledgements
Paul Beasley would like to thank Mike and Alex Cole of BritsNZ, Louise and Christopher
Willis of Willis Brazolot and Co, Ian Wisdom of Canilink, Darren and Mette Hobden
of Emigreat, Louise Green of the Expat Coach, Amanda-Jo Nicholson of Govoni
International, Sarah Drane of Purple Cake Factory, Andrew Cresswell of New Cyprus
Property, Mark Williamson, Ivan Tate, Martin Darling, Lisa Kantis, Jane Hiller, Julie and
Eddy Parry, PSS Removals, Bishops Move and Robinsons International for useful
background information and insights; and Christine Stainer, David Fuller and Hanna
Lindon for research assistance.

Project manager: Claudia Dyer
Edited by: Victoria Walker
Designed by: Philip Jansseune for Walker Jansseune
Index by: Lynda Swindells
Cover photographs by: Alamy
Printed and bound by: VivaPress, Barcelona, Spain

Arctic Volume White is an elemental chlorine free paper produced at Arctic Paper
Hafrestroms AB in Åsensbruk, Sweden, using timber from sustainably managed forests.
The mill is ISO14001 and EMAS certified, and has PEFC and FSC certified Chain of Custody.

Contents

Introduction

Millions of Britons now live abroad and at any given time tens of thousands more are preparing to emigrate. This trend shows no sign of abating, especially as more of us than ever before are proving that moving overseas can be a change for the better.

From the 'Pilgrim Fathers' of America to Australia's 'Ten Pound Poms', Britons have a long history of moving abroad. However, in the last two decades, there has been a significant increase in the number of us emigrating. Government statisticians estimated that 207,000 Britons left the UK in 2006 in order to live abroad on a permanent basis; this is the largest number since the current means of record-keeping was introduced in 1991.

However, this increase is down to more than just sensationalised media coverage of 'Broken Britain' or the British 'exodus'. Neither is it completely explained by rising levels of property wealth, which enables more Britons to afford the many expenses of emigration; nor by the fact that more of us have a relative living overseas who might be able to assist with our own emigration. This unprecedented boom has primarily been sustained through government and, indeed, intergovernmental initiatives.

On the one hand, the expansion of the European Union has given its citizens more freedom to move to another EU country. On the other hand, the governments of Australia, New Zealand and Canada have increasingly grasped the potential of

immigration as a solution to skill shortages that threaten to stall their economic growth. Not only are these three governments becoming increasingly sophisticated in their promotion of immigration opportunities and their pursuit of suitably qualified workers from overseas, they have also been increasing the numbers of visas available to such workers on an annual basis.

The American government also recognises the potential economic contribution of skilled immigrants, but trails behind the other big three English-speaking destinations in terms of increasing quotas. Nevertheless, when it comes to sheer numbers the American immigration system still dwarfs all others.

Taken together, these opportunities have created a situation in which Britons have more scope to move abroad than they have ever enjoyed before.

In recent years, the British media has become obsessed with mass migration, and often runs stories explaining how Britain is in decline and why its people are increasingly desperate to escape to a country with a warmer climate and a cheaper cost of living. Often, though, the difficult and sometimes downright nerve-wracking process of actually moving abroad is missing from the media-drawn picture.

THE BUSINESS OF MIGRATION

Moving abroad is a costly business, and more companies are entering the 'migration marketplace' in pursuit of the money to be made.

Although regulation of this marketplace is increasing, it is still an industry in its professional infancy. As a result, some areas are regulated effectively, others are in the process of strengthening the necessary framework, while others have yet to introduce regulation.

Because moving abroad involves a wide and often bewildering range of processes – from immigration paperwork to the international movement of money and possessions – this patchwork of regulation presents a risk to the prospective emigrant. The fact that unfamiliar rules, regulations and processes are involved, and that these might be couched in another language, only serve to heighten this risk.

While there are dependable sources of information available to help you negotiate the process, there is also an advancing tide of advice published on blogs and online forums. Almost all of this is well-meaning, but only some of it properly anchored in a profound knowledge of the subject at hand.

The potential shortcomings of the information available, combined with patchy regulation and the opportunities this presents to unscrupulous practitioners, can make moving abroad a far riskier undertaking than it should be. This is particularly the case for those who approach the process with a reckless spirit of adventure provoked by the very nature of making such a momentous move.

MAKING THE RIGHT MOVE ABROAD

As the process of moving abroad costs thousands of pounds, and the emotional investment can be huge for all concerned, there is a lot to lose if you don't get it right from the very start of the process.

If things do go to plan you could realise your dreams of a fulfilling new life abroad. Get it wrong and you could be one of the thousands of Britons who make an unscheduled return to this country. Sometimes bad luck is to blame, but bad judgement is both easier to avoid and harder to live with.

Are you ready to emigrate?

It is important to gauge at an early stage of the emigration process whether you and the family members you are emigrating with will be able to make a new life abroad. Try to recall your own response to the events and experiences listed overleaf and consider how you may feel when placed in a similar situation while emigrating.

❝In the last 20 years there has been a boom in emigration.❞

Do you have the right temperament for emigration?

- How have you felt when moving to a different town and starting a different job? Do you approach the change positively, or anxiously? If it's the latter, moving country at the same time could put an enormous strain on you.

- How easy do you find it to meet new people – at a new job, say, or on holiday? Settling in quickly is all about meeting people, establishing a support and social network and generally just making life that little bit easier. If making new friends is a problem for you, the early weeks and months of your new life could be lonely and you may find yourself glued to the internet or phone as you desperately keep in touch with all those friends you left behind.

- If things go wrong on a foreign holiday, how well have you coped with working out what to do next? Are you forthright enough to address the problem and make yourself understood?

- How have you managed when you moved house? If the answer is 'not very well' then moving house and country could be a removal too far for you. After all, when relocating within the UK, you don't have to wait at least a month for your belongings to arrive, sell your car at the same time, pack several weeks' worth of clothing and essential possessions into a limited amount of luggage, move to a destination with a completely different culture, or have to deal with children suffering from culture shock. When moving abroad, you may have all of this and more to contend with.

- How have you coped in times of family crisis? If family relationships are important and you feel you absolutely have to be there at crucial moments, then moving overseas may make such occasions unbearable. Close family members suffering from health scares is a difficult enough situation at the best of times, but what if your sister calls in the middle of night to say that your dad has been taken ill and is in hospital? If you emigrate, you must do so accepting that this kind of situation is possible and commit yourself to cope with it. After all, without such firm commitment, your new life will be nothing more than one long look over your shoulder.

Find out more about the characteristics of a successful migrant on page 19.

Deciding to emigrate

The decision to move abroad can be taxing and is made up of a number of smaller life-changing choices, each of which is daunting enough on its own. It is essential that you take the time to work your way carefully through this series of interconnected decisions. Taking short cuts is tantamount to gambling with your future.

1

First steps

An essential first step in successfully moving to another country is a realistic appraisal of your motives and goals. This way, you can lay solid foundations for what could be some of the biggest emotional and financial challenges you and your family will ever face.

There are all sorts of reasons to consider moving abroad. Broadly speaking, these can be divided into four groups: family matters, work aspirations, the cost of living, and lifestyle and leisure. If you are to make the most of emigrating, and make the transition from the dream to the reality of moving abroad, you and any family members going with you must understand why you want to move abroad, what you can realistically expect to get out of it and how you can bring about such a dramatic change.

When considering your reasons to emigrate, start with a list of goals and put them in order of priority. It might be that some go hand-in-hand, some are incompatible and others are simply impossible to achieve. For example, you may find that your idea of the perfect lifestyle can be realised only in a location where property prices make a bigger and better home than you have in the UK unlikely. Use the list of questions opposite as a prompt to get you thinking.

" To make the most of emigrating, you must understand why you want to move abroad. "

WHY EMIGRATE?

Family matters
- Do you wish to achieve a better work/life balance or to increase the quality time you spend with your family or friends?
- Do you hope to improve the quality of your children's education?
- Are you hoping to increase your family's personal safety?
- Do you want to be closer to relatives or friends who live abroad?

Work aspirations
- Do you have professional or business aspirations that seem impossible to achieve in the UK, or that you would like to explore outside of the UK?
- What level of job satisfaction are you after?
- What are your wage expectations?
- How many hours are you prepared to work?
- What holiday entitlement are you hoping for?
- How far are you prepared to commute?

Cost of living

- Do you want to increase your personal prosperity by living in a country with lower taxes and a cheaper cost of living?
- Would you like to own a bigger and better property?
- What type and size of property are you looking for?
- What location – central business district, suburbs, rural – would suit you?
- What is a realistic budget?
- How big a mortgage are you prepared to pay?
- What percentage of your salary will you accept as disposable income?

Lifestyle and leisure

- Would you like to live somewhere with a more relaxed lifestyle?
- Do you want to enjoy the benefits of living somewhere with a warmer, sunnier climate? Or would you prefer four distinct seasons, including snow?
- Have you enjoyed one or more holidays in a specific country and want to live there permanently?
- Do you have a hobby that you could pursue more easily abroad?
- What key recreational opportunities do you want for you and your family?
- Do you want to be near to city attractions?
- Do you want easy access to beaches and parks?
- Would you prefer to live in close proximity to other Britons?
- What pace of life are you looking for?

INVOLVING YOUR FAMILY

Even if you plan to move abroad on your own, involving your family from the outset is vital for the success of your plans, not least because they may be able to give you emotional and practical support.

Most people, though, emigrate with other people – whether it's a partner, children, or both. Even if the idea of moving abroad is yours, it is vital that all those family members you intend to emigrate with also have a significant stake in the decision-making process. After all, this is the biggest move the family will ever make, and having everyone pulling in the same direction will make the experience considerably easier.

 Before you make any grand announcements to your friends and family, bear in mind that you may have your visa application turned down. If you have managed their expectations from the beginning, rather than rushing out to book holidays to visit you, they could give you valuable support from such an emotional blow.

❝It is vital that all those family members you intend to emigrate with also have a significant stake in the decision making process. ❞

11

If you intend to emigrate with your partner, ensure that they also work through their own list of motivations and goals independently of yours. There will almost certainly be some variation between the two lists, but hopefully there will be enough of an overlap to enable a consensus to be reached – perhaps after a process of compromise on both sides.

You should also consider the adaptability of your children. Questions you should address include:

- Will the move compromise their happiness?
- Should you drag them half way across the world chasing your own dreams?
- Are you sure that you have their best interests at heart?
- To what extent should you involve them in the process?

Of course, if your children are very young, they probably won't understand the concept of emigrating and will have no idea of the distance involved. However, persuading teenagers with boyfriends or girlfriends to come with you will almost certainly not be straightforward.

Nonetheless, it is important to involve your children in the process as early as possible, encouraging them to do their own research and set their own goals whilst making the benefits clear to them – such as new friends, a new hobby, or even driving at a much younger age than they could in this country. Of course, once these commitments are made, you'd better make certain that you deliver on your promises.

Family

For many people moving abroad, involving the family in the decision to migrate is not enough. Instead, providing family members with better opportunities by moving overseas is the primary reason to undertake such a process. This may be to increase the opportunities open to your children, to redress your work/life balance, or to join other family members who may have emigrated already. In fact, research by the Institute for Public Policy Research estimates than 5.5 million British nationals now live overseas permanently.

Another key decision you face is when to tell your parents, grandparents and siblings that you plan to move away from the UK. Most emigrants find that the sooner they tell their relatives of their decision to emigrate, the more time it gives them to accept and support the decision. It also increases the likelihood that they will have relatives waving them off at the airport and visiting them in their new home.

Safety

In a poll of more than 500 people published by *Emigrate* magazine in 2008, 17 per cent said that they hoped to improve the everyday safety of their children by migrating. Crime is prevalent to a greater or lesser degree all over the world and your choice of location within a particular country will have an impact on your likely exposure to crime. Bear in mind that the decision to 'play it safe' by moving to a rural community may limit other opportunities such as your family's social or cultural life.

Work/life balance

Moving abroad is often an attempt to redress the balance between increasing work commitments and dwindling time for family and hobbies. But with so much to attend to, the first few months after arrival will be anything but easy.

As with every stage of emigration, it is important not to fall prey to stereotypical thinking – that moving to Cyprus or Portugal involves nothing more than lounging in the sun, or that life in Italy is one long search for the best pasta sauce. Similarly, you must avoid assuming that only Britain expects heroics from its workforce (see Chapter 2 for more coverage of this topic). It is essential that you weigh up exactly how hard you will have to work to establish your new life abroad and whether this level of work will give you the income you want.

❝ Avoid assuming that only Britain expects heroics from its workforce. ❞

Case Study — Rachel and Steve

In May 2006 Rachel and Steve, and their son, Simon, then aged 21, moved to Perth, Australia. The couple's eldest daughter, Hanna, then 26, was too old to be included as a dependent child on the visa application. For Simon, the move only lasted three months, as he decided to stay in the UK after returning to visit his girlfriend. Despite feeling positive about the move, Rachel and Steve said they could not be completely content with their new life abroad until all of their children could also call Australia home. This dream is edging closer to reality. 'After having had another taste of the UK, Simon decided that he did want to live in Australia after all and moved to Perth while his visa was still valid,' says Rachel. Now that Simon has returned to Australia, Rachel is hopeful that she can sponsor Hanna's emigration, as her daughter will then be the only remaining family member outside of Australia.

13

WORK ASPIRATIONS

Although career progression is not one of the most common reasons to emigrate, a significant number of Britons do consider this to be one of their priorities. Indeed, in recent years many healthcare professionals and police officers have left the UK to continue their careers overseas.

Of course, when moving to another European country, you may find that working in the local labour force requires considerable ability in a second language, especially in something as technical as, say, the legal profession. In this case, you must ask yourself whether your language skills will be sufficient for a technical job with its own vocabulary; if not, are you prepared to put the work in to bring your knowledge up to scratch in order to be recruited ahead of a native speaker?

COST OF LIVING

According to the Annual Survey of Hours and Earnings released by the Offices for National Statistics in November 2007 and figures from the Land Registry, the average British house now costs almost eight times the average British wage. Council Tax bills are tending to increase above the rate of inflation every year, and rising food and fuel bills are making daily living costs spiral, so it is no surprise that many Britons want to move abroad to have an easier time making ends meet – and own a better property. But is Britain really so expensive?

According to research published in January 2008 by HSBC the answer is a resounding 'yes'. The study found that the British lifestyle is the 'third most expensive'

Case Study   Isaac

Isaac moved from Portsmouth in 2007 to a town in Reggio Emilia, Italy, to further his career and experience in engineering. Although he does not regret making the move, he admits that his inability to understand Italian created big hurdles. 'My employers are providing Italian lessons, but they only started four months after I arrived, so a lot of my day-to-day Italian is self taught. I should have insisted on more lessons from the start. There are cultural differences and translation problems, and when combined with Italy's massively bureaucratic systems, this can make things very slow to happen. I find it a challenge when people in key roles cannot speak English. We usually have to get someone to act as a translator, or I ask someone in the office to sort it out. Even outside of work, one of my big problems is finding out information. Whether it is about the local fair or something like the recent elections, a limited understanding of the language is not enough.'

in the world. It examined how long the typical British salary would last abroad if people maintained their standard of living, including eating out in a restaurant twice a week.

Britons moving to Australia and Spain would be able to maintain their current lifestyle on a lower budget. The survey revealed that 12 months' annual expenditure in the UK would last 14 months and one week in Australia and 15 months and three weeks in Spain, but only 11 months and two weeks in France.

Yet there is an obvious pitfall with this approach. When you move abroad, you almost certainly won't be earning a UK-level salary but one appropriate to the local economy. In most cases, the average salary in other countries is actually lower than the UK equivalent. It is of paramount importance, therefore, that you don't choose a destination based on a lower cost of living seen only from the perspective of spending British pounds.

❝ When you move abroad, you almost certainly won't be earning a UK-level salary. ❞

Everything looks cheap when you keep comparing the prices to what you would pay 'back home', but a far more accurate comparison would be to find out what the average wage paid for your occupation is in that area, then compare that to the prices you're paying abroad. To flesh out the picture, you'll need to factor in national and local taxes, potential mortgage repayments, utility costs, medical insurance (if applicable), car insurance, school fees, and outgoings such as fuel and groceries to determine your income after regular deductions.

Suffice to say, many emigrants find that their money doesn't go quite as far as they'd hoped, but proper research and planning can prepare you and your finances for the realities of emigrant economics.

LIFESTYLE AND LEISURE

Choosing the right destination in which to enjoy your favourite leisure activities is often a question of finding the right climate. Avid skiers find themselves gravitating towards the Rockies of North America, the Swiss, French or Italian Alps, or even the Southern Alps of New Zealand. Those planning to enjoy mountain and ocean sports in the same day may find that their choices are more limited. Due to the proximity of coastal plains to higher altitudes, the climate can often be a good deal damper than anticipated. Again, compromise may be the key.

But will you really indulge in the hobbies you dream of? Just because you move to Western Canada doesn't necessarily mean you'll become a regular skier; a home in Auckland doesn't necessarily lead to regular yachting excursions; and that long-held dream of home-grown Riesling won't become inevitable just because you move to the Rhine Valley.

Therefore, it is essential to decide not only what hobbies you hope to pursue when you move abroad but how important these pastimes are in the bigger picture. Are they important enough to tolerate a

 Free and paid for international salary comparison information is available from websites such as www.payscale.com and www.salaryexpert.com

damp climate, compromise your children's schooling, or forego the bigger house? These are the types of questions you may have to address in order to reach a balanced decision on where to move abroad.

Even if your goal is to enjoy life under sunnier skies, your choice of destination may still require more thought than you anticipated.

PROPERTY

A few years ago, climbing the property ladder when moving abroad was a strong possibility for anyone with solid equity in their UK home. But now the average property price in British migrant hotspots (such as Spain's Costa del Sol, Provence in France, Tuscany in Italy, British Columbia in Canada, California in America, and Perth and Sydney in Australia) is often more than the average property price in Britain. It's still too early to say whether rising house prices will slow the current trend of increasing levels of emigration from the UK.

CLIMATE

Most of us go on holiday during the most tempting temperatures of the year. However, these temperatures may only occur for a brief period every year, so it is important that a destination is chosen on the basis of its year-round climate rather than a small window of perfect weather.

Thorough research and exposure to seasonal temperatures typical of your chosen destination are required prior to engaging in the emigration process to ensure that you are not making a costly and easily avoided mistake.

Buying happiness

While there is clearly a strong link between income and life satisfaction, studies such as the World Values Survey (last conducted in 2005) suggest there is no direct correlation. Once you can afford life's essentials, the power of money to buy happiness diminishes in proportion to the amount of disposable income you have. As most emigrants report that they are not materially better or worse off for having moved abroad, it is just as well that a fulfilling lifestyle is about more than money.

❝The power of money to buy happiness diminishes in proportion to the amount of disposable income.❞

Good sources of basic climate data include the BBC weather website, www.bbc.co.uk/weather and the Met Office website, www.metoffice.gov.uk

Pitfalls to avoid

Some motivations for moving abroad are more likely than others to lead to success. When you are in the early stages of the emigration process, there are several incentives that you should be wary of placing too much emphasis on.

Emigration is a highly personal undertaking. There is no 'one size fits all' approach to pinpointing the right destination. However, not all reasons for moving abroad are good reasons. There are some obvious pitfalls that every potential emigrant needs to avoid.

1 We had a great holiday

A survey of more than 500 people published by *Emigrate* magazine in 2008 showed that a significant number of emigrants were originally inspired to move to a certain country after taking a holiday there. Whilst this is preferable to never having been to the destination in question, being a tourist seldom provides insights into being resident in the same location. It is essential to burst the holiday bubble before it gives you a false impression of life abroad.

- Holiday budgets are often much bigger than your typical household spending.
- Remember to consider prices from the perspective of a local wage.

- The areas with the best leisure opportunities often have the most expensive property prices, so moving to such an area might require compromising other emigration goals.
- With little or no stress, holidays are a world away from the normal routine. Ask yourself how many of the holiday activities you enjoy would be feasible on a regular basis, and whether establishing yourself in the country in question would leave you much more spare time than you have in the UK – at least to begin with.

2 It looked great on film

While such inspiration is invaluable, and may keep you going through the most demanding challenges of moving abroad, you must avoid basing your entire emigration rationale on reels of fantasy. According to a survey published by YouGov in March 2008 on behalf of the currency exchange company Foreign Currency Direct, one fifth of Britons have been influenced to move abroad by a film or television series.

 For information on how to get the most from a fact-finding trip, see pages 51-55.

3 Someone I know emigrated there

With thousands of Britons moving abroad every year, more of us now have friends or family members living overseas – and this, in itself, can influence us to follow in their footsteps. Moving to the same area as friends and family has the appeal of a ready-made support network and the security of shared interests. However, there is no substitute for taking a fact-finding trip to your favoured country prior to moving abroad.

4 Because we *can* move there

While citizens of the EU can move freely to other member states, those planning to move to Australia, New Zealand, America or Canada must qualify for a relevant permit or visa.

If you can't get a visa for your first choice destination, ask yourself whether you really want to move somewhere else. After all, it really isn't worth uprooting yourself and your family because you can move to another country; it is only worth the effort if you actually want to.

5 Anywhere but Britain

According to a BBC *Newsnight* poll conducted in early 2008, 62 per cent of working class Britons believe that life has generally become worse in the UK, while 66 per cent of middle-class Britons claim that crime in this country has increased. However, it is worth bearing in mind that those who base their emigration on push factors alone, citing reasons such as those shown in the BBC poll, may find that the 'anywhere but here' approach does not result in the grass being greener on the other side of the customs checkpoint.

For most people, the motivation is often a mixture of push factors away from Britain (such as wanting to escape from the stresses of modern society), and pull factors towards a certain country (such as a life lived under sunnier skies).

Case Study Katie and Martin

Having endured three difficult years living in Granada, Spain, and struggling with the language, Katie and Martin were left with the choice of returning to the UK or moving to another English-speaking country. 'We liked the lifestyle and the snow-capped scenery of the mountains around Granada, but really did not enjoy living in Spain because it was difficult to get anything done,' says Katie. 'However, we didn't want to return to the UK as the crime rate and health services that prompted us to leave in the first place didn't appear to be any better than they were when we left.' So they moved to New Zealand. 'We decided to try New Zealand's South Island as it has mountainous landscapes and a laid-back lifestyle, and we can provide a better future for our daughter, Mary.' Having lived in New Zealand for a year now, Katie says that the family's second move overseas has been 'much better than the first.'

Have you got what it takes?

Consider your ability to move to another country successfully. Can you really follow your dream? Do you have both the practical and emotional qualities required to complete the process?

Essential attributes

Besides an ability to understand and organise the process, you must be able to anticipate and manage different emotional states – both your own and those around you. Important personal qualities include:

- A positive-yet-realistic outlook on life.
- Patience and a commitment to achieving your goals.
- The ability to cope well with change.
- The flexibility and determination to succeed at trouble-shooting and problem solving.

Reading between the headlines: net emigration

Newspapers often fail to report **net emigration**, tending to prefer more headline-grabbing figures than are strictly accurate. Thousands of British nationals emigrate every year. However, thousands also return every year.
For example, data from the Office for National Statistics show that 207,000 left to start new lives abroad in 2006, but 81,000 returned – resulting in a net emigration figure for 2006 of 126,000.

Not everyone succeeds in establishing a happy and fulfilling life abroad, and some emigrants end up returning to the UK. This may be because of bad planning, bad luck or because they weren't up to the challenge.

Will you be happier abroad?

A survey by currency exchange company UKForex revealed that 80 per cent of respondents who had emigrated from the UK were happy with their lives overseas. The happiest people surveyed had moved to Spain, with 91 per cent of emigrants saying that they were happy or very happy with their lives there. The large majority of emigrants to New Zealand were also happy, with 88 per cent of respondents satisfied with their new lives; Canadian and Australian emigrants followed closely behind.

Jargon Buster

Net emigration The total of British nationals leaving the UK in any given year, minus those returning

19

One of the best ways of coping with such a massive upheaval is to be prepared for it. If you can brace yourself for a period of feeling unsettled, it won't come as such a shock. Remember, it is not just the physical move that you might find a challenge, but the preparation and bureaucracy before you leave too.

> ❝ One of the best ways of coping with such a massive upheaval is to be prepared for it. ❞

Case Study Patricia

Patricia finally moved to Cyprus last year after an aborted attempt to emigrate a year earlier. She lists the qualities required of an emigrant as 'a positive attitude, flexibility, a sense of humour, persistence and a good sense of self awareness.' She maintains: 'Emigrating is really about proving something to yourself, creating a sense of achievement and demonstrating the ability to take control of what you want. It is this that creates the contentment and happiness as much as the place itself.' Recognising this, Patricia advises that prospective emigrants face up to their toughest challenges, and set new goals once the initial challenges of moving abroad have been overcome.

What next?

Consider your motivations in wanting to move abroad. Draw up a list:

1 Discuss your thoughts with the family members you plan to emigrate with. Encourage them to draw up their own lists.
2 Bring your wider family and friends into the discussions – it's good to have them on your side to provide you with help and support from the outset.
3 Consider your personal attributes and emotional strengths – have you got what it takes to make the move?

When you have thought carefully about why you should go and why you are likely to succeed, it is time to decide where to go. For tips on how to get this decision right, read on.

Choosing the right country

Once you have decided that you are serious about moving overseas, you need to think carefully about what sort of location might meet your needs. Even if you already have a particular country in mind, it is worth working through a list of alternatives to ensure your initial choice fulfils your objectives.

Can you emigrate?

If you plan to work abroad, your choice of destination will often be dictated by whether you can find work there and, in some cases, whether the local immigration department will grant you a visa.

THE IMMIGRATION MAZE

One of the most baffling aspects of the whole process of moving abroad is understanding and fulfilling the necessary immigration requirements. No matter which destination you set your sights on, there will be immigration terminology to understand, challenges to overcome and bureaucratic frustrations to endure.

Each country has its own rules and regulations. For EU member countries, initial procedures may be as simple as having an up-to-date British passport. However, if foreign languages are not your forte, you may experience frustration when trying to obtain permanent residence paperwork from local government departments, where English is not widely spoken.

For Australia, New Zealand, Canada and America, many applicants find that obtaining the visa paperwork to paste into their passports is the most daunting aspect of the entire process, but that getting hold of the necessary official documents in the days after emigration is far easier to organise. Even if you opt to deal with all of the paperwork yourself, processing fees for visas and permanent residency documentation will run into hundreds of pounds, if not more. Should you call on professional help, whether to assist you in submitting an application for a visa or dealing with government offices, then your immigration bill will rise accordingly.

Moreover, the timing and the structure of your application can influence your ability to sponsor the emigration of your children, adjust your status from temporary to permanent residence, and retire in the country in question.

While European bureaucracies may have the reputation of being swathed in red tape, it is Canada and America that – in some respects – have the slowest immigration systems of the countries featured in this book. For example, those applying for a Canadian Skilled Worker visa are, at the time of writing, being told to expect a 42-48-month wait (see www.canada.org.uk for

> **"No matter which destination you set your sights on, there will be bureaucratic frustrations to endure."**

more information), while sponsoring the immigration of siblings or adult children to America can take up to seven years. For those with children at a crucial stage of development, the time it takes to obtain the relevant immigration paperwork for your two or three top choices could sway your decision one way or another.

It is therefore essential that you research the relevant immigration system before you get too excited about moving to a particular country, if only to ensure that there are no barriers to entry.

WORK

Unless you are retiring abroad or are extremely wealthy, either you or your partner, or both of you, will need to work when you move abroad.

Unfortunately, compared to seeking work in the UK, this comes with added complications. Skills, education and experience are still essential, but you might also encounter issues over your language ability and the recognition of your qualifications (including licensing issues for professions that may require a local licence, such as the legal profession).

Besides this, your skills may not even be needed in the particular area of the country you plan to move to. All of these aspects must be properly researched before a destination is decided on, or you might find that you have no means of

paying for that coveted brand new life abroad. As tempting as it is to assume that any job abroad will suffice as a starting point, issues such as personal satisfaction and commuting times don't suddenly become less important simply because you live overseas. You must therefore give these aspects as much care and attention as you would in Britain.

Bear in mind also that holiday entitlement abroad can be more restrictive than in the UK, with new arrivals in Canada and America often having to get by on ten 'vacation' days per year.

Average holiday entitlement
Days per year
France 30
United Kingdom 24
Portugal 22
Spain 22
Cyprus 20
Italy 20
Germany 20
Australia 20
New Zealand 20
Canada 10
America 10

Source: European Economic Employment and Policy Brief (No.3; 2007)

To find out more about the immigration requirements for Australia, New Zealand, America and Canada, turn to pages 156, 164, 175 and 185 respectively.

Working in the EU

Unlike nations outside the EU, working in France or Spain, for example, does not require a work permit. However, you might still need to register with the appropriate authorities. In Spain, unless you have a *número de identificación de extranjero* (NIE) you cannot be considered for a job, but in France a *carte de séjour* is not technically necessary in terms of finding employment.

Whilst this process, where required, is considerably more straightforward than for those countries outside the EU, competing against native speakers whose qualifications are more easily recognised and understood by employers is no easy task.

A potential stumbling block to finding employment within Europe is getting your UK qualifications recognised. A good first step is to contact the UK National Europass Centre; those with vocational training can also approach the European Centre for the Development of Vocational Training (see the Useful Addresses section for contact details). Proving that your qualifications are equivalent to a qualification awarded overseas will require that you obtain certified, translated copies of your diplomas and certificates – complete with original stamps and signatures.

Certain professions – such as law and accountancy – are regulated within the European Economic Area (**EEA**). Regulated professions can only be practised by those fully qualified and recognised as such by the appropriate state or professional body. Nationals from within the EEA practising medicine, nursing, dentistry, midwifery, veterinary surgery, pharmacy and architecture cannot be restricted from practising their profession in another EEA member state.

Jargon Buster

Número de identificación de extranjero (**NIE**) Identification number for foreigners in Spain

Carte de séjour Identification card in France

EEA An acronym for European Economic Area, which provides a single market for the free movement of labour and services, as well as most capital products. It comprises all the members of the European Union and the European Free Trade Association, with the exception of Switzerland

 Find out which countries are EEA members at www.ukba.homeoffice.gov.uk/eucitizens

But what if you are not practising a profession that is regulated within the EEA? In theory, your career options should be broadened by looking abroad, as having a geographically wider search area should provide you with many more opportunities to find employment. In practice, it is often only multinationals recruiting multilingual graduates that actively seek to recruit from outside of their company's home country.

However, if you have a degree of fluency in the language of the country you plan to move to and are able to 'translate' your qualifications so that they are easily comparable to those of native job applicants, you should have fewer problems in negotiating the job market.

If these scenarios don't apply to you there are, broadly speaking, four good employment possibilities:

- Working in an industry that caters directly for expatriates.
- Setting up your own business.
- Working remotely for a UK company.
- Commuting to the UK from abroad.

Catering for expatriates will require relocation to an area with an established British population (the Costa del Sol, for example) or one that is popular with British tourists. Such work would typically be in the hospitality industry, with restaurant, bar and tour group work the most obvious choices, but tradespeople such as electricians and plumbers also often find their skills in demand. Think carefully about whether this potentially narrow choice of destinations is genuinely suitable for your new life abroad.

Many expats are tempted by the thought of setting up their own business abroad. While such an undertaking would require a significant organisational challenge even for those who operated successful businesses in the UK, the idea of being one's own boss exerts a powerful pull on those hoping to take a new path.

Again, catering to British expats often presents the easiest option, at least on paper, and there are certainly plentiful success stories – from Italian property agencies to French B&Bs and Australian pool installation companies.

However, even with a relevant background in management and ownership, starting up a business in a country with different laws and perhaps a different language could tax even the brightest entrepreneurs.

Case Study Karen and David

Karen and her husband David moved from Tyne and Wear to the Algarve in Portugal in 2005. Upon seeing how successful a local shop selling famous British brands had become, they decided to set up a fish and chip shop to tap into this same market of British expatriates. After successfully overcoming a paperwork mountain, and solving problems in their cod supply chain, Karen and David opened the shop and, following a successful first two years of trading, decided to branch out by offering fish and chips from a van. 'This gives us the flexibility to provide fish and chips wherever there might be a gathering of hungry punters,' says Karen, 'such as a big event or even outside bars and clubs.' Although many of their regular customers are British, Karen and David are also making inroads into the Portuguese market. 'We had to offer free samples at first,' Karen explains. 'Now, though, we have plenty of regular Portuguese customers popping in for fish and chips,' she says.

With the advancement of the internet and the growth of online businesses, working remotely for UK companies from a home or office overseas is becoming more of an option. While such an approach would probably not fulfil the criteria of Australian, New Zealand, American and Canadian employment-based visas because the respective governments are looking to attract suitably skilled individuals to work for organisations in the country in question, more Europe-bound Britons are finding it to be a workable solution.

Before you pursue this route, though, it is important to ascertain the level of job security and how many other such employment opportunities might exist in the event of redundancy.

You must also consider tax implications. Employers usually have no problem paying directly into your bank in the appropriate currency, but whether you are liable for UK tax depends on a number of factors – including whether you maintain a home in the UK, where the rest of your immediate family live and how often you return to the UK. See page 101 for further information.

> ## ❝ Whether you are liable for UK tax depends on a number of factors. ❞

See page 101 for further information.

Case Study Christine

Christine runs her own small business on the west coast of France. 'My partner and I had discussed moving to France for a number of years,' says Christine, 'but I was worried that my jewellery design business would be compromised if I moved away from my fairly small pool of UK-based clients.' Reasoning that this potential negative could be overcome if she could persuade her clients that living in another country would be no stumbling block to her fulfilling their orders, Christine decided to finally take the plunge. 'It's been hard work, especially dealing with the intricacies of French bureaucracy, but I think it's been worth it,' she says. 'I haven't lost any regular clients, and I've even got some new ones.'

Another option is to use Europe's extensive network of low-cost air services or the Channel Tunnel to commute back to work in the UK. Although it is tempting to think of Britain being 'only an hour away' from many European destinations, you must also factor in travel time to and from the airports or train stations, as well as check-in and time spent in departure lounges. This will help you to ascertain a realistic timescale for your commute.

Moreover, you must feel certain that the key transportation services your new

For further information on income tax and capital gains tax for non-UK residents, see www.hmrc.gov.uk or call the National Advice Service on 0845 070 0040. If you are calling from abroad, telephone +44 151 210 2222.

life will rely on are here to stay, or that there are enough options to prevent you becoming overly reliant on one airline or train operator.

It is also worth factoring in some potential price rises for these key services to ensure that commuting will still be an affordable option even if it becomes more expensive.

Finally, commuting to work by air is hardly the most environmentally friendly mode of transport. Do you really want your dream life abroad to contribute to global warming?

Working outside the EU

The immigration systems of many countries, including Australia, New Zealand, America and Canada, often require the potential employer to prove that no suitably qualified citizen or permanent resident is available to take the job instead of a foreign national.

However, in order to maintain economic progress and provide services to its residents, all four of these countries accept that their labour markets require skilled workers from

Jargon Buster

International Labour Organisation (ILO)
A United Nations agency that aims to promote rights at work and employment opportunities
Alien **A non-nationalised resident or visitor to a country from overseas**

overseas – with Australia, New Zealand and Canada being particularly proactive in the recruitment of foreign nationals.

Of the non-EU countries featured in this book, America (and its immigration department) stands out for not publishing a wide range of skills in demand. In practice, this makes obtaining employment in America more difficult as, in many situations, the employer must prove that no US citizen or permanent resident is available and able to take the position instead of an **alien**.

In contrast, Australia, New Zealand and Canada publish lists of skills and professions (see Chapter 3 for links to relevant websites) that their economies are in need of. By way of illustration, healthcare professionals are highly sought after in Australia, New Zealand and Canada, but the lists range far and wide to cover many professional, management and trade positions. Suitable applicants for the relevant 'skilled visas' typically have to qualify

A survey released in 2007 by the **International Labour Organisation** revealed that although British workers tend to work the longest hours of any developed nation (25.7 per cent of us are working more than 48 hours a week), 20.4 per cent of Australians also do the same.

❝ Australia, New Zealand and Canada are proactive in the recruitment of foreign nationals. ❞

via a points test. These tests award points for education, experience and several other factors. Character (typically a police report detailing any convictions you may have) and health requirements must also be met.

In practice, though, the process is not always straightforward:

- **Job titles.** These may often be identical to those used in the UK, but this doesn't mean the duties expected overseas will match your UK job description. For example, to be officially known as an engineer in Canada you must have a degree in engineering, which isn't the case in the UK.

Case Study   Marie and Pete

Marie and Pete moved from London to Queensland, Australia, in September 2005. Prior to leaving the UK they had their qualifications validated by the respective Australian professional regulatory bodies, but were both concerned that they might struggle to find work in Australia. Initially, at least, these fears proved to be well-founded. 'One month into submitting applications with CVs and covering letters to a number of employers but having got nowhere, we thought our worst fears were being realised,' says Marie. Although the couple had a contingency plan, whereby Pete would return to the UK to work for his brother's landscape gardening business until Marie found a job in Brisbane, they didn't want to take this step unless 'they absolutely had to'. Instead, the couple attended a job application clinic to see if they could improve their CVs and covering letters. Marie and Pete subsequently adapted their CVs to a more Australian style and set about job hunting once again. Within a week of sending out her new CV, Marie was invited to an interview, and subsequently got the job.

Therefore, if you find your job title on one of these skills lists, it is important you also take the next step of researching whether the duties and qualifications expected of someone in that position correspond to your job description.

- **Qualifications.** With educational systems and trade bodies differing from country to country, British qualifications are not always recognised overseas. Thus, it is often essential to have your qualifications assessed and validated by the relevant organisation – such as Australia's Trades Recognition Authority, the New Zealand Qualifications Authority or one of Canada's Foreign Credential Referrals Offices (see the Useful Addresses section for the relevant links).
- **Exams.** Some occupations are licensed, hence you might have to sit exams to continue working in your trade or profession in your new country of residence. This is often the case for healthcare professionals.

Immigration in Alberta, Canada

Alberta is one Canadian province that is currently actively recruiting skilled workers from overseas. Their fast track programme, the Alberta Immigrant Nominee Program, is prioritising workers from a range of skilled and semi-skilled trades and professions. For further information, see www.albertacanada.com/immigration

Emigrating sensibly requires you to strike a balance between economic and lifestyle considerations. A move that is heavily weighted one way or the other has obvious drawbacks.

One issue to consider is whether you actually want to live in an area where there are suitable jobs available. It is also worth noting that opportunities available through regional immigration schemes (such as a South Australian regional programme or a British Columbian Provincial Nomination) are conditional upon the applicant being prepared to settle in the area in question. Obtaining these **regional visas** will also typically be tied to a specific job offer.

Some emigrants find that achieving the right balance is a two-stage process: make an employment-based move, then when permanent residence is secured (and access to the labour market therefore opens up considerably), relocate to the area targeted from the outset.

This approach is often necessary for those who wish to move countries and careers at the same time. As immigration requirements often demand relevant education or training and experience in a particular occupation, qualifying for a skilled visa is almost impossible in a profession or trade in which you are a complete or relative newcomer. However, by obtaining a permanent residence visa through your current

Jargon Buster

Regional visa An immigration opportunity provided by a region – whether a state, province or territory – within a country. Such schemes are used by regional governments to attract workers with particular skills

occupation, you are then free to change career paths overseas.

Studying certain courses in English-speaking countries (such as two years of full-time education or more at a post-secondary institution in Canada and some apprenticeships in Australia) can also help you fulfil their immigration requirements.

❝ Qualifying for a skilled visa is almost impossible in a profession or trade in which you are a complete or relative newcomer. ❞

For information on regional support for migrants to South Australia, see www.immigration.sa.gov.au or call 00 61 8 8204 9250.

Culture shock

Besides the possibility of using a different language on a daily basis, you will also encounter cultural differences overseas both great and small. Do not underestimate the effort required to adjust to these differences.

Your ability to adapt to the new customs which will influence your everyday life and fit in with the cultural values of your new home will play a major part in determining the success of your emigration.

For many people moving abroad, a principal motivation is that the culture of their destination appears to foster a more laid-back attitude to life, where the daily routine isn't quite so grinding, stress levels are generally lower and there's more time to enjoy life. In the long run this might be achieved, but in the short term much adjustment is required, and those unprepared for the 'fish out of water' experiences that are synonymous with the early days of emigration are set for a disorientating time.

For example, some Britons who move abroad can have difficulties adapting to aspects of the more relaxed lifestyle they were actually searching for. Often, this is because they have become accustomed to a very British sense of timekeeping and efficiency. As a result, they then struggle to contain their frustration when attending to practical matters overseas which take much longer than they think reasonable.

> ## Case Study Malcolm
>
> Malcolm, a Londoner who spent several years teaching in Andalucia, cautions those moving to Spain to expect marked differences in work culture.
>
> 'Outside the big, typically European cities of Spain, you won't find anything similar to the "Protestant work ethic" of Britain. Work is something that many Spaniards bolt onto their lives, rather than become dominated by.
>
> 'It is also worth remembering', says Malcolm, 'that in Spain it's not an insult to be half an hour late to an appointment – rather, it's quite common. You have to factor this in when attempting to attend to practical matters.'
>
> Malcolm also advises newcomers to Spain to understand the reason behind the Spanish habit of siesta, a midday break. 'There is a small town near Seville called Ecija, which means "the frying pan" – a reference to the local climate. I defy anyone to continue working in temperatures of 40°C.'

In this respect, some destinations are more challenging than others. The question you must ask yourself is: what is the appropriate challenge for you and your family? If you live in a particularly multicultural area of Britain, and if you thrive amidst the obvious cultural differences you may encounter on a holiday overseas, chances are you are already well equipped to settle in quickly – but you must also consider the abilities of anyone moving with you.

Clearly, it is important not to slip into thinking in broad stereotypical terms about a country and its culture – such assumptions can lead to disappointment and a hasty relocation. Choosing the right country to move to involves a more specific focus with a region and even a city, town or village chosen for the merits of its particular approach to life, among other things.

Whatever your decision, making a successful move abroad demands 100 per cent commitment to your cultural surroundings. Constantly making negative comparisons between your new life and 'life back home' will do you no favours.

❝ Making negative comparisons between your new life and 'life back home' will do you no favours. ❞

Local tensions

Frustration can be directed towards foreigners moving to an area in significant numbers – perhaps because it is felt that this influx is driving up property prices and taking jobs that locals should be given. With 200,000 Britons now believed to be resident in France, for example, the centuries-old rivalry between the two nations can spill over into modern life. In Bourbriac, Brittany, slogans such as 'Anglais integers, oui. Colons, non!' (English who integrate, yes. Colonisation, no!) were daubed on buildings by locals in 2005. Yet, such incidents are incredibly rare, and even cursory research and involvement in local activities on arrival should enable you to steer clear of any genuine problem areas.

Language and education

For those moving to a country with a mother tongue other than English, language is much more than just a work issue. If you are not fluent in the language in question, you will find that many everyday tasks are complicated as a result. Even if you move to an area with a significant population of British expatriates and can more or less spend your days within this English-speaking bubble, there will be times when at least a basic level of linguistic skill is absolutely necessary – such as communicating with hospital staff during an emergency.

Parents emigrating with their children might also face some tough educational decisions. The state school system of most European countries will teach pupils in the official language of that country or region.

In Spain, for example, your child might be taught in Castilian, Catalan, Euskera or Galego, depending on where you settle. For some children, being immersed in a foreign language from day one will be a daunting experience, but the younger they are baptised into bilingualism, the easier they adapt. Private lessons prior to moving abroad should help with this transition. Don't forget that you'll also need some knowledge of the language in question, otherwise you won't be able to communicate with your children's teachers, or understand what your children are saying in their new language. However, despite the potential drawbacks, learning a new language can be a rewarding experience.

Alternatively, many of Europe's bigger cities have private schools where your children can continue to be educated in English. There are drawbacks, though. Even if you can afford to send your children to private school, the resulting underdevelopment of their foreign language skills might make it more difficult for them to live and work abroad in adulthood.

Of the major Anglophone countries, only Canada might present similar issues. If you plan to move to Quebec, Canada's only officially Francophone province, then the decisions you and your family face will be similar to those outlined for European countries. Those moving to New Brunswick, Canada's only officially bilingual province, will also encounter some big educational decisions.

If you are moving elsewhere in Canada, or to an English-speaking country, you will not face such stark choices and should meet with fewer language-related issues.

Case Study — Vanessa

Vanessa, her husband Adam, and their three boys – aged 3, 5 and 7 – moved to Germany in 2007 after Adam was offered a property consultancy job in Berlin. Like many Britons relocating within Europe, the main hurdle the family had to overcome was the language barrier. 'We spoke no German on arrival, and this is still a bit of a problem for me,' says Vanessa. 'Adam is picking up the language through his job and the boys are enrolled at a bilingual school and are gently being eased into speaking German, but as I'm not working my progress has been slower.' As a result, Vanessa feels that she misses out on good deals and the best rates when arranging utilities and telecoms contracts because 'I'm not able to haggle'. However, with the family settled in Berlin, Vanessa states that the city 'is a great place to live, we've got no regrets and we're perfectly happy here'.

❝ For some children, being immersed in a foreign language from day one will be a daunting experience, but the younger they are baptised into bilingualism, the easier they adapt. ❞

Money and health matters

When it comes to emigration, money really does matter - not least because it rarely goes as far as expected. Two of the key areas to consider are housing and healthcare costs, but there are myriad other monetary considerations besides.

Many emigrants underestimate the cost of relocation. Equity in your British home can lead to a false sense of security. For example, if you have about 50 per cent equity in an average UK home (valued by the **Land Registry** at £185,000 in Spring 2008) and plan to buy an average property in New Zealand (valued by the Real Estate Institute of New Zealand at approximately £138,000), it is easy for you to assume you will be able to pay roughly £90,000 off your New Zealand mortgage and live much more comfortably there with reduced monthly outgoings.

However, you are unlikely to spend less than £10,000 on selling and buying a property, £1,000 on the immigration process and £4,000 on removals. So even before the smaller relocation costs are added in, you will have waved goodbye to 15 per cent of your emigration budget, leaving a down payment of £75,000 at most. This would leave you with £63,000 to pay off, which is only £32,000 less than the mortgage you were servicing in Britain.

But - and it's a big but - where the average wage in Britain is £23,500, the average in New Zealand is £12,600 (figures from the Office for National Statistics and the New Zealand Department of Labour). Therefore, although your mortgage in New Zealand will only be 65 per cent of your British mortgage, you will have to pay it off with an income that may be as little as 50 per cent of your UK earnings. Unless many other regular household costs are cheaper in New Zealand relative to your earnings, you will not be substantially better off as a result of your emigration.

Jargon Buster

Land Registry A government agency that registers title to land in England and Wales and keeps records on dealings such as sales and mortgages

THE COST OF MOVING

Emigration incurs many more costs than you would normally expect if you were simply moving to live in another location within the same country. Key emigration costs to factor in include:

- Research (books, internet usage, attending exhibitions).

Case Study   Paul and Fiona

Paul, Fiona and their two children emigrated to Canada in 2004. Paul admits 'Emigrating is not cheap! We paid fees to the Canadian High Commission, for an immigration consultant to check our application, for removals, estate agents and solicitors for selling our house in England. We paid the vet for our dog to receive her Department for the Environment, Food and Rural Affairs report, and then had to pay for her carrier to transport her plus the flight to Canada, then for a kennel for her to live in.

'We had to pay for our flights (for four people), our first three months medical insurance in Canada, plus our immigration medicals. We sold possessions that we couldn't take and had to pay to advertise them and, close to departure time, sell things cheaper as it was better to have some money for an item than none at all.

'In Canada, we bought a van and hired a lakefront house for a month while we house hunted. We paid lawyers' fees, building inspector fees and property transfer tax for buying our Canadian home. We paid house insurance and car insurance. We had to pay to take a driving test and replace our licences. On top of this, we had to live on the money we brought with us as we had no income for the first couple of months until I found a job. These are the things that I can remember, there may be more.'

Overall, Paul estimates that the cost of emigrating was 'probably over £20,000, and that does not include buying cars or replacing items, just the costs, fees and charges related to relocating our lives to a different part of the world.'

- Selling your house (and possibly not achieving the asking price).
- Moving your possessions overseas (£3,000-£5,000).
- Moving your pets overseas (at least £350 per pet before paying for a flight).
- Possible tax on pensions and investments (this could easily run into thousands).
- Flights (could be anything from £50 to £750 or more per person, depending on the destination, which airline and class is booked, and how far ahead of the departure date the reservation is made).
- Accommodation on arrival.
- Property rental (at least £500 a month).
- Property purchase costs (agency and mortgage fees, etc).
- Car rental.
- Car purchase costs.
- Health insurance.
- Contingency fund in case of unemployment.

Those moving to countries outside the EU must also factor in the following:

- Visa fees (could range from £100 to £10,000, depending on the type of application).
- Immigration assistance (typically costs between £1,000 and £5,000, also depending on the type of application).

To help estimate some of your emigration costs, see the free estimate tools of websites such as www.moveme.com or www.reallymoving.com

Taking your pets with you

Generally speaking, it is possible to take pets over three months old overseas, but certain breeds of dog such as pit bulls will not be admitted. A combination of signing up to the Pets Travel Scheme, vaccinations, microchipped identification, blood tests and, in some cases, quarantine is generally required. However, it is important that you check the requirements for the country you plan to move to.

HEALTHCARE

Easy access to adequate healthcare is of primary importance, particularly if you or a loved one has ill health or you have reached retirement age. Emigration to several non-EU countries, including the US, Canada, Australia and New Zealand, is prohibited in some cases on the grounds of ill health that is either serious or highly contagious, or likely to be a massive drain on state resources.

While healthcare in the countries most popular with British emigrants is generally considered to be of a good standard (France and Germany, for example, spend significantly more of their GDP on healthcare provision than the UK does), services are not always provided free of charge.

Therefore, it is essential that you check on the national and regional rules surrounding healthcare (which will differ from the healthcare available to tourists), take account of any insurance payments necessary in your emigration budget and build in a contingency plan just in case the rules suddenly change.

This, and the provision of any specific healthcare requirements, should certainly play a part in deciding where you move abroad.

66 France and Germany spend more on state healthcare than the UK. **99**

Case Study **Anne-Marie**

'In general, the cost of living in Florida is much lower than that which I used to experience in the UK,' says Anne-Marie, a business visa consultant who emigrated with her husband Paul. 'Some individual bills can be - or at least seem - higher in the US. Health insurance is one example which springs to mind immediately.' However, Anne-Marie is not convinced by the view that healthcare costs are higher across the Atlantic. 'Though it is understandable to feel that health insurance is free in the UK, my feeling is that if you compare the 11 per cent National Insurance payment paid from every individual's salary each month in the UK with a contribution to the cost of a health insurance plan here, there is often very little difference between the two expenses. In mine and Paul's case we actually pay less here towards our medical cover as a percentage of our earnings.' During 2007, the couple paid $330 a month for their health insurance.

35

Healthcare provision can change

Initial healthcare provision for British citizens living in other EU countries is typically covered by reciprocal agreements between the various governments involved. To access this provision, you normally need to be in possession of the appropriate form available from the Post Office or the Department for Work and Pensions (see below).

Economically inactive Britons under the state pension age going to live in other EU countries can obtain an E106, which typically gives them health cover for two years. It is worth noting, though, that agreements can be amended or even scrapped. In 2007, proposed changes to the French healthcare system seemed set to lead to those E106 holders being barred or expelled from the French healthcare system.

However, following the intervention of British health ministry officials, the French government removed the controversial aspect of the reform. Now, only those economically inactive British citizens under the state pension age who moved to France after 23 November 2007 must take out private health insurance until they reach state pension age or have been resident in France for five years.

One of the following three forms should provide you with free healthcare cover in another EU country, at least for an initial period of residence. How long it lasts will depend on whether you could still get UK short-term Incapacity Benefit if you claimed it. When this period ends, the UK cannot give you any more healthcare cover. When you start work in your new country of residence, the cover outlined below ceases to be applicable.

Access to health cover for non-workers in the EU

EHIC The European Health Insurance Card replaced the E111 in 2005 and covers you for any medical treatment which may become necessary in an EEA country and Switzerland. It is only applicable for temporary visits abroad. You can get an EHIC by contacting the Prescription Pricing Authority (see www.dh.gov.uk/travellers or call 0845 606 2030) or by obtaining an EHIC application pack from the Post Office.

E106 The E106 provides you with up to two years healthcare cover under the same terms as nationals of EU, EEA states and Switzerland, if you are under the state pension age and either looking for work or retired. You can get this form by contacting the Department for Work and Pensions (see www.dwp.gov.uk or call 0191 218 7777).

E121 The E121 provides you with access to health cover if you are in receipt of a UK state pension and moving to an EEA country or Switzerland. Contact the Pension Service within the International Pension Centre for form E121 (see www.dwp.gov.uk or call 0191 218 7777).

Lifestyle and environment

A common denominator among Britain's prospective emigrants is the desire to live in a warmer, brighter climate. This objective often goes hand-in-hand with the goal of enjoying more of an outdoors lifestyle.

If you plan to move to a destination hotter than the UK, ask yourself whether you could stand working in the more extreme seasonal temperatures. Lazing on the beach in sweltering heat might be all well and good, but what if you have to labour outside through the heat of the day or even work in an office without air-conditioning? Living in a drier, sunnier country can also be something of a double-edged sword: it might improve the health of some, but greater exposure to the sun also brings with it potential downsides, not least potentially greater water costs and increased risk of health issues such as skin cancer.

Those moving to a country with lower temperatures than Britain won't necessarily escape lightly. After all, driving in snow and ice is not the easiest of tasks, and the thought of working outdoors during a harsh winter is enough to make even the hardiest character think twice.

Climate change

If choosing the right country to move to wasn't difficult enough, the planet's rapidly changing climate introduces added complications. It would be foolish to ignore the potential impact on the climate and landscape of your short-listed destinations. This is a far from cosmetic issue, as climate change could undermine the benefits of moving to a certain destination, and herald challenges and costs that leave you regretting your decision further down the road. The following questions should at least be considered:

- Will rising sea levels damage the coastline near your proposed new location?

Climate change

For further information on the possible impact of global warming on the destinations you may be considering, see:

Union of Concerned Scientists at www.climatehotmap.org

Intergovernmental Panel on Climate Change at www.ipcc.ch

New Scientist at http://environment.newscientist.com

BBC at www.bbc.co.uk/news and click through science/nature to special reports

- Will falling river levels jeopardise the local water supply, and send rates spiralling?
- Will a higher incidence of flooding put your new house at risk?
- Will melting glaciers reduce opportunities to enjoy winter sports?
- Will global warming result in an influx of immigrants driven from their home countries by changing geography and dwindling resources?

❝ Now is when your long-term planning should be at its sharpest. ❞

Case Study | **Peter**

For the first five years of his life in Alberta, Canada, Peter worked in the building trade – and still vividly remembers some of the more testing conditions. 'The cold weather does have an impact on how you do your job,' he recalls. 'For a start, it tires you out quicker as you use more energy to keep warm, and although it was sunny much of the time, it is still quite miserable to be working in temperatures of -20°C.' Despite this, Peter looks back with fondness on his time spent outdoors on building sites.

You can't predict everything, of course, especially the political consequences of climate change. Yet, to use this as an excuse not to consider some potentially fundamental points is to fall prey to short-term thinking exactly when your long-term planning should be at its sharpest.

Wildlife

No matter which of the featured countries you move to, your change of habitats signals a change in surrounding flora and fauna, too. While for the most part this is nothing to be alarmed about, those unsettled by the proximity of poisonous spiders and snakes must think very carefully about the suitability of some countries, for example, Australia.

Thought must also be given to the affect the new environment will have on pets such as cats and dogs. The following questions should be addressed by pet owners:

- Will it be safe for them?
- What impact will the presence of unfamiliar and potentially dangerous wildlife have on their usual behaviour?
- What effect will a markedly different climate have on their health and well-being?

Decision time

If you are having trouble deciding between two or more countries, or have your sights set on just one but want to make certain that it measures up to your expectations or, indeed, that you haven't overlooked a better option, the following exercise should help you clarify your thoughts.

Take a blank sheet of paper and write yourself a direct statement at the top of it, such as 'We are considering a move to America because...' Fill in everything relevant you can think of underneath this statement. Do the same for the opposite statement. Repeat this for every country still under consideration. The result will be a list that resembles the box below.

Although it may not give you any definitive answers, it will help clarify pros and cons for you and, if you are emigrating with others, will help highlight areas for discussion.

 If you do plan to move to a warmer climate, take suitable precautions to protect your health. Cancer Research UK's skin cancer prevention campaign, SunSmart, provides lots of useful tips on how to protect yourself from the more harmful affects of too much sun. See their website at www.cancerresearchuk.org/sunsmart

❝ Consider what affect a markedly different climate will have on the health and well-being of your pets. ❞

Weighing up the pros and cons

'We are considering a move to America because...'
- A more relaxed lifestyle appears possible there.
- Many of its states enjoy a warmer climate than the UK.
- We want to live near sandy beaches.
- We believe it has a lower cost of living.
- It is English-speaking.
- It is close enough to the UK for travel times to be less than one day.

'We are concerned about the following aspects of a move to America because...'
- Its property market appears to be unstable.
- We have heard it is difficult to apply for visas.
- As parents, what we've heard about the crime rate concerns us.

What next?

At this stage, your decision-making process should have reached one of the following points:

1 You have a clear idea of your motivations and which country you want to move to.
2 You have worked through your motivations and now have a shortlist of countries.

3 You have identified your motivations but have no idea as to which country is right for you and your family.

Whichever point you have reached, the exercise on weighing up the pros and cons should help you tell the possibles from the improbables. Then it's onto the research to sort the facts from the wishful thinking.

The rules of research

Once you have a shortlist of potential destinations, the next step is to build on your knowledge of the countries under consideration. While your instincts are important, the more information you arm yourself with, the more likely it is that your ultimate decision will be the right one. This stage of the process is crucial.

3

Determining boundaries

Define clearly from the outset what each of your emigration goals is and what information you need. This is essential when ascertaining whether your goals are realistic.

In all likelihood, you already have some knowledge of one or more overseas countries, whether through first-hand experience or through information and impressions gained via a variety of sources. However, it is unlikely that you already know enough to make an informed decision about the viability of a destination as a new home for you and your family. To achieve this, you will have two different tasks to complete:

- Researching subjects you have no prior knowledge of (for example, immigration rules).
- Finding evidence to support what you think you already know (for example, whether the climate in a certain location is ideal for the life you hope to lead).

Some of the information required will be easy to come by, but other information – especially for countries where you are not fluent in the language – may take time to track down. Be prepared to conduct some preliminary research on other destinations as well, if only to make sure your first choice is the right one. Clearly, it's better to encounter surprises at this stage than after you've invested thousands in taking a fact-finding trip – and, indeed, moving abroad.

 You may experience a strong temptation to make the move as quickly as possible, but this is effectively gambling with your entire future.

Preliminary research

How much time you should spend on your preliminary research depends on how much you already know about the country in question, and the quality of that knowledge. Those starting with no prior knowledge could easily spend several weeks collating all the necessary information, especially if they have to wait for responses to questions asked of both official and unofficial sources. Subjects such as climate should require no more than one evening searching the internet, but issues such as immigration and work might require extensive research and even visits to exhibitions. Suffice to say, before you take the next step you should have addressed all of your research goals as fully as is possible. Make sure you do this before making the financial outlay required to visit the country in question.

Researching regulations

It is imperative that the starting point for your research is the immigration regulations of the country in question, as it would be demoralising to find out that you are unable to qualify for a visa after spending several weeks of research into other aspects of the country. This is doubly important for non-EU countries, where immigration regulations are more wide-reaching.

You could do this research yourself, or you might wish to enlist the help of an immigration expert. If you want to complete an initial assessment you will typically be charged between £10 and £100 by the immigration lawyer, agent or consultant carrying out the assessment, although some companies do offer this service free of charge. This process should provide a clear indication of whether you can obtain a visa, or if there are any issues regarding which family members can accompany you.

If, subsequent to the assessment, there is any doubt about your eligibility for a visa, or you have concerns about the knowledge of the expert in question, do not hesitate to get a second opinion.

What do I need to find out?

The researching stage of moving abroad could potentially be an open-ended, never-ending endeavour, with every scrap of information hunted down and collected.

Define clearly from the outset what each of your emigration goals is, what essential information you need to ascertain and whether these goals are realistic. For example, you may hanker after a warmer, sunnier climate, but without losing the distinct seasons we enjoy in the UK. In this case, your research goal is to find information on temperature, sun hours, rainfall and humidity – for both your target destination and the UK as this will enable you to make a valid comparison.

This type of information is purely factual, and while essential, is not enough on its own to provide a solid foundation for moving abroad. You should also seek the following information to demonstrate the feasibility of your goals:

- Personal experience.
- Second and third-hand accounts.

> ❝ Researching could be an open-ended, never-ending endeavour. ❞

To find out more information about who you can ask for help with immigration paperwork and rules, see Chapter 4.

Starting with one of your short-listed countries, the exercise you completed at the end of Chapter 2 may have left you with the following:

I am considering moving to Australia for the following reasons:

- It has a hot climate.
- It offers a laid-back, beach-based lifestyle.
- It will be better for my children.
- I will be financially better off.
- It is English-speaking.

Such objectives can now be broken down into subject headings for your research. For example, an assessment of the lifestyle in one of your candidate countries should also consider its people and their culture, while financial matters need to be divided into issues such as property costs, earnings and living costs.

However, these headings must also be supplemented by other key subject headings. For those heading out of the European Union, the most important of these additional headings is 'immigration' as this will determine whether you can qualify to start a new life in the country or countries now in your sights. It is also essential that you consider potential negatives, such as the distance of the country in question from the UK, and any fears you may have about the country or countries in question – such as extreme weather. Taken together, these research topics should enable you to gain a rounded picture of the destinations being considered.

Your research categories could look like this:

- Climate.
- Lifestyle, leisure and culture.
- People and attitudes.
- Health and well-being.
- Employment.
- Education.
- Childhood.
- Financial matters.
- Language.
- Immigration.
- Transit time.
- Fears.

Once you have identified your research categories, define your goals for each one. With 'employment', for example, you could record your goals like this:

Emigration goal: To move to a destination where I can continue in my current occupation, but work fewer hours and still afford the cost of living. **Research goal:** To identify up to three destinations within the country under consideration that would offer such an opportunity. **Information required:** Facts such as potential employers, average wages for my occupation, average hours worked, and typical annual leave entitlement, as well as first-hand experience and testimony from trustworthy sources.

It is important that you devise an efficient system for recording and storing the fruits of your research, otherwise you'll lose track of your progress in a blizzard of paperwork.

Sources of information

Relevant information is available from a wide range of sources, but not all of it will be accurate. Bear this in mind as you work through your research, and prioritise finding the most dependable, up-to-date information you can.

Where to find information

- **Official sources** - such as government and statistical websites.
- **Unofficial sources** - for example, printed media and property websites. Be aware that this might only be a partial view presented as comprehensive, and might be designed to encourage you to buy a certain item or service. For example, a property investment company will gather together evidence supporting its view that you should buy property in a certain location. Just remember that it's the company's job to make this sound impressive, but it's your job to verify the sources of the information used, search for data that contradicts the view expressed, and look for alternative locations that might be equally suitable.
- **First-hand experience** - including direct and relevant personal experience of a destination. However, remember that although having taken a holiday to a potential emigration destination is better than not having visited at all, it is no substitute for a fact-finding trip.
- **Second-hand information** - this includes experiences related by others, perhaps through family, friends, or acquaintances (both social and professional). When evaluating this

information, ask yourself how well you know, generally agree with and trust the people in question.

- **Third-hand information** - comprising personal experience related by others about people they know or have heard about. This could take the form of stories and accounts told to you about people you don't know directly. Stories in emigration publications and on websites also fall into this category. In this case, ask yourself if the writer's intention was to promote a lifestyle, or present a balanced view of moving and living abroad.

❝A holiday taken in a potential emigration destination is no substitute for a fact-finding trip. ❞

INTERNET

Government immigration websites

With borders open to EU citizens, and little in the way of immigration requirements, it is unsurprising that countries within the European Union offer little in the way of official government-run immigration websites.

Of those that do exist, the most useful is

undoubtedly the website of the French Embassy in London (www.ambafrance-uk.org), which briefly covers key basics such as visas, moving, retirement, social security, taxation, driving, further reading and an excellent section on the French education system.

In contrast, the immigration departments of the Australian, New Zealand, Canadian and American governments all have useful websites. After all, Australia, New Zealand and Canada are actively looking to attract migrants who can offer the country the skills or investment its economy needs. It therefore follows that the websites in question mix factual immigration information with a gently promotional approach to presenting the benefits of moving to the country in question.

These websites provide overviews of the requirements for each visa class or category, a self-assessment tool for the most popular skills-based visa, downloadable application forms, and a range of introductory information about the location, climate, people, employment opportunities, relocation process and various regions.

Immigration websites

America – www.uscis.gov
Australia – www.immi.gov.au
Canada – www.cic.gc.ca
Cyprus – www.police.gov.cy
Europe – www.euimmigration.org
France – www.ambafrance-uk.org
New Zealand – www.immigration.govt.nz
Portugal – www.acime.gov.pt

Emigration websites

The emigration market is well-served online, so it is certainly worth surfing before you spend money on printed publications. You could start your online search with the small selection listed in the box below, although there are many more also worth looking up.

Online emigration information

www.emigrate2.co.uk – regional and city profiles, personal stories, blogs and immigration advice.
www.telegraph.co.uk/global – links to relevant news stories, as well as health, education and financial advice.
www.britishexpats.com – active members can answer your specific questions about locality and living costs.
www.angloinfo.com – an extensive forum, information on moving abroad and a directory of English-speaking businesses overseas.

While online forums are a fantastic resource for getting a range of questions answered about the process and experience of moving and living abroad, they also provide a podium for those with an axe to grind. Therefore, it is essential that you bear this in mind when logging onto a forum, otherwise you may end up with an imbalanced impression of living overseas. It is also fair to say that many answers provided are not comprehensive nor provided by experts. However, some forums are better than others, so ensure that any forum you use offers balanced advice. To avoid being misled, check and double check all information provided. There are plenty of other websites featuring useful information, many focused on just one region or city.

Of course, before taking the information at face value, you should ask yourself who the website is serving. Some such websites are run by property agents whose ultimate goal is to encourage you to buy property, so it is important to bear this possible bias in mind.

Weather

If you're searching for information on climate, www.bbc.co.uk/weather, is one of the most useful tools available. Here, you can search for the average annual conditions of all the countries featured in this book, and can also access mean information for several of the major cities. The Met Office's website, www.metoffice.gov.uk contains weather information on every region in the world. This includes a summary of past weather and a regional climate overview.

Country profiles

The BBC website also provides country profiles, where information such as current affairs, politics and the media is provided. Similar information is available on the website of the Foreign and Commonwealth Office, www.fco.gov.uk, and many useful statistics can be found at www.oecd.org (Organisation for Economic Co-operation and Development).

Websites such as Spain's National Statistical Institute (www.ine.es), France's National Institute for Statistics and Economic Studies (www.insee.fr) and Italy's National Statistical Institute (www.istat.it) provide useful data on their respective counties. The websites, Facts about Germany (www.tatsachen-ueber-deutschland.de), Deutschland Portal (www.deutschland.de) and the federal government website (www.bundesregierung.de) give a range of information on Germany and German government policies. Other web addresses can be found in the country profiles on pages 113 to 207.

❝ The emigration market is well-served online. So it is certainly worth surfing before you spend money on printed publications. ❞

Flights

If researching flight times and prices, websites that enable searches of many airline schedules at once (www.skyscanner.net or www.ebookers.com, for example) will indicate what choice and frequency is available. This information could prove to be invaluable when deciding how quickly you can return to the UK from abroad, or British-based family members can visit you, in the event of an emergency. It will also help you decide if your plans to visit the UK on a regular basis are financially viable and whether your British-based family will be able to afford to visit you regularly.

Schools

If you are emigrating with school-age children, you will find lists of schools on the relevant department of education websites. Further research could take you to specific school websites and onto forums to ask about schools in a specific area. Those setting their sights on Australia, New Zealand, Canada and America may find the website www.ratemyteachers.com useful, while one of the best single online sources of information about schools and schooling in Europe is probably www.angloinfo.com. Those of you with children who are about to enter higher education could visit www.topuniversities.com, where you'll find information on the world's top 500 universities (ranked overall and by subject).

Involving your children

Getting your children involved with the research process can, if properly managed, be a great way to stoke their enthusiasm. For example, with a degree of supervision relevant to their age, your children could research schools online and focus on extra-curricular activities that they have no opportunity to pursue in the UK. They could also research potential new hobbies, interesting facts about wildlife, and the latest teen celebrities and fashions.

Jargon Buster

Job board An online listing of job vacancies, often published by newspapers or by dedicated websites such as Monster

This will enable them to have an active stake in the process of moving abroad and focus them on the personal benefits of taking such a step.

Economics and employment

There are a variety of sources for statistics that will help you build up a picture of inflation levels, Gross Domestic Product and key labour market sectors in any given country. For example, *The Economist* website (www.economist.com/countries) contains 'country briefings' among other information which can be an invaluable resource for assessing the ongoing economic health of the country you plan to move to. This is particularly useful when considering employment opportunities abroad. Another website worth visiting is the CIA World Factbook (www.cia.gov/library), which lists primary industries along with a breakdown of labour forces by occupation – handy when you're gauging whether your skills could be needed in a certain destination.

For those moving to Canada, the website www.workingincanada.gc.ca is a brilliant tool as it enables you to find information about wages and employers in specific areas. For New Zealand, www.immmigration.govt.nz is almost as useful, and contains a handy list of prices for everyday items to enable you to compare living costs to the UK; the equivalent Australian and Canadian websites also provide advice on the subject of living costs.

Beyond this, the official statistical websites for these countries, along with America, provide average wage data per region and, sometimes, per sector – hence can prove to be insightful when researching your own potential level of remuneration abroad.

A great starting point for research into European labour markets and employment opportunities is the website www.europa.eu.int/eures, which also features a job search tool where parameters such as sector, trade or profession, country and region can be set so you can access the information that's most relevant to you.

Another European Commission website worthy of attention is www.europa.eu, which provides a downloadable guide – *Europe in Figures*; here you'll find a cost of living comparison.

Also useful as a comparative tool is the annual cost of living survey conducted by Mercer (www.mercerhr.com). In total, 50 cities worldwide are compared, so you can assess whether, for example, New York is a more expensive city to live in than Sydney. Although there is a charge to obtain the full survey, an overview is available for free.

Job searches can also be conducted via international **job boards** such as www.monster.com and www.jobserve.co.uk, or with individual recruitment agencies that specialise in the geographical area you are interested in.

Depending on the site or agency, you may or may not be given specific salary information up front, but if you have access to the contact details of the recruiting company, this is information that you can find out.

Property

Although buying a property overseas can sometimes be complicated by a struggle to find reliable information, there are plentiful sources.

For price information, some countries – such as Spain – have government-run statistical departments which collate the latest data, although prices tend to be stated per square metre. For other countries, the best option is the figures published by real estate associations. Beyond this, websites such as www.rightmove.co.uk/overseas and www.worldofproperty.co.uk feature thousands of properties for sale, from which a broad picture of property pricing can be gleaned. Be aware, though, that average prices stated by websites such as www.globalpropertyguide.com and the Spain-focused www.kyero.com are based on the average price of properties for sale on the web, not on an actual national or regional average.

❝ Buying property abroad can be complicated by a struggle to find reliable information. ❞

PUBLICATIONS

Publications including magazines and books can be divided into two camps:

- Generalist magazines that cover a range of destinations.
- Specialist publications that cover a specific country only.

Established introductory-level magazines include *Living Abroad* and *Emigrate*. These combine case studies with a variety of lifestyle stories and more in-depth information. *Emigrate's* monthly sister-titles – *Emigrate Australia, Emigrate New Zealand, Emigrate Canada* and *Emigrate America* – provide more detailed information on the specific countries and focus on areas such as 'People & Places', 'Visas & Advice', 'Jobs & Money', and 'Homes & Relo'.

Other periodicals on antipodean destinations include: *Outlook Australia, Outlook New Zealand* and *Australia and New Zealand Magazine*.

Merricks, the publishers of *Australia and New Zealand Magazine*, also produce a range of magazines for European destinations, such as Italy, Portugal, France and Greece.

Alternatively, a number of country-specific books on living and working abroad are available.

> ❝ Many property agents are British expats who've moved overseas and set up a business. ❞

EXHIBITIONS

A very effective way of gathering a range of information is to attend an emigration exhibition, though these tend to cater mainly for Australia, New Zealand, Canada and America.

Most exhibitions present the opportunity to speak directly to government

Emigration exhibitions

Working In - www.workingin.com
Emigrate - www.emigrateshow.co.uk
A Place in the Sun Live -
www.aplaceinthesunlive.com

immigration departments, visa lawyers and consultants, removals companies, financial experts, employers, and property and relocation service providers. The latter are often run by Britons who have moved abroad and can answer specific regional questions, as well as conveying the roller-coaster experience of emigration. You may also get the opportunity to attend presentations featuring government representatives and a range of emigration experts.

Furthermore, immigration specialists often hold city-based seminars, usually working in tandem with other specialists. While much information can be gained from such seminars, should you use the event as an opportunity to enlist the help of an immigration expert, bear in mind that there will be little or no choice. Suffice to say, when moving abroad it really does pay to shop around.

Although it is fundamentally a property exhibition, *A Place in The Sun* also offers a seminar programme featuring presentations such as 'Emigrating to Europe'. A reasonable proportion of the property agents exhibiting are themselves British expats who've moved overseas and set up a business, so there is the potential for you to ask them about their own experiences as well.

Fact-finding trips

A fact-finding trip should focus on relevant and clearly defined objectives and should be treated as an essential task to carry out to the best of your abilities, not a holiday in disguise.

Fact-finding trips, especially to countries outside of Europe, might seem like an unnecessary expense, but considering that even emigrating to another European country could cost you a five-figure sum, investing in a research trip first could convince you of the value of moving abroad or, alternatively, help you realise that it is not right for you and your family.

Seeking assistance

The process of organising a research trip can appear baffling, so much so that you opt to enlist the services of a **relocation agent**. Those heading to one of the four non-European destinations should have plenty of choice. In broad terms, relocation agents operating in America, Canada, Australia and New Zealand should be able to assist with the following:

- Planning an itinerary – if you supply them with your emigration goals they should be able to suggest a range of locations worth visiting.
- Arranging good quality, fully furnished, self-catering, short-term rental accommodation, sometimes with residents.
- Organising a rental vehicle.
- Meeting and greeting you at the airport.
- Tips and advice about what to research while you're in the country.

Case Study **Janet**

Janet adopted a 'see how I get on' approach to emigrating – which didn't include taking a research trip – when she moved to South Australia in 2001. 'The main influence on my decision to emigrate, was wanting to get away from the crowds,' says Janet. 'South Australia was the least densely populated part of Australia at the time. Had I realised that densely populated in Australia has a very different meaning than it does in the UK, I would have probably chosen another destination to start with.' Reflecting on her experiences, Janet says: 'You never really know what a destination is like until you get there – you can't learn it from a book or brochure, which is why it is worth visiting beforehand.'

❝Emigrating could cost as much as a five-figure sum. ❞

If your relocation agent is an estate agent, he or she will also be able to take you to view a selection of homes so that you can see the different styles, sizes and what you get for your money. However, you must check that this advice is being offered independently of any one developer or development that the agent might be promoting at that time.

𝄖𝄖 Always give yourself more time than you think you will need. 𝄖𝄖

If taking a fact-finding trip to a European destination, relocation assistance is more likely to be offered by smaller, family-run property agencies. These often have employees who have emigrated from Britain and can share their first-hand knowledge and experience with you.

Organising a fact-finding trip

There are six key questions posed by the process of organising a fact-finding trip.

1 **Who should go?** Ideally, you and everyone who is emigrating with you – after all, it is their move as much as yours. But depending on your answers to the question below, you might find that it's a case of how many of you can afford the time and cost of such a trip.

2 **When should you go?** Work commitments and school terms will play a big role in answering this question, but seasonal considerations – for example, wanting to visit when your preferred destination is experiencing mean, minimum and maximum climatic conditions – should be considered as well.

3 **Where should you go?** This depends on how many destinations you have left on your list of possibilities, their locations within a country relative to each other and transport links between them.

4 **How long should you go for?** You don't want to rush, so it is important that your itinerary is not overly ambitious. Always give yourself more time than you think you will need. Transit time aside, you might find that one day suffices to explore a small town, but a week is required to explore a fairly large city. For destinations outside of Europe, it is often more cost-effective to take a longer trip than two or more shorter trips – therefore, paying for only

one return flight per person. If, for example, both Australia and New Zealand, or Canada and America, are still under consideration, then a trip of four weeks in total split between the two countries will be a cheaper option than taking two entirely separate trips. If you are taking children with you, you should also allow time for activities tailored to their needs.

5 What should your objectives be?
Your precise objectives will depend on whether you are deciding between different countries, different regions within a country, or checking that your chosen destination is as good in reality as it looks on paper. For example, you might want to investigate employment opportunities and the cost of living, or simply get a good feel for a place. For more ideas on what your objectives could include, see the information on fact-finding trips overleaf.

6 How much will it cost? By this stage, you should know who is going, when and where you are going, and for how long. Armed with this information, you can now plan your budget by researching the cost of flights, car hire and fuel, accommodation, travel insurance, food and various other expenditures. As it is advisable to keep a record of the places you've visited, if you don't own a camcorder consider buying or borrowing one. When all of these costs are estimated, you may have to review exactly how many of you can go on the trip and for how long.

> ❝ It is advisable to keep a record of the places you've visited. ❞

If you are visiting Europe, resist the temptation to take a trip organised by a property company as a means of saving money. Typically, you'll only see what the property company subsidising the trip wants you to see – and this will not offer the breadth of research and experience required of a fact-finding trip.

Questions to ask yourself

- **What are my chances of finding suitable employment?**
Decide on which employers are worth targeting and, where possible, make contact with them before going on the research trip. See if you can arrange a meeting with them. The purpose of this meeting is to see whether your job prospects are good, but if the employer subsequently offers you a job then it is a massive bonus.

- **Where do my family and I want to live?**
Find out about rental and property purchase prices and explore some neighbourhoods you think will be in your price range and commutable from the area you are likely to work in. This will involve checking out local facilities (healthcare services, supermarkets, recreation), as well as leisure opportunities nearby that you and your family would be interested in. Ask yourself if these faculties are accessible during the evenings and weekends, or whether occasional trips of longer duration are more realistic.

- **What does the cost of living appear to be?**
Researching potential earnings is a good start, but you'll need to find out about mortgage rates, taxes, utilities, transport, medical insurance, entertainment, educational and grocery costs as well. Talk to locals about their own opinions on the cost of living as this will help you get a rounded picture.

- **If you are emigrating with children, what is local schooling like and how much does it cost?**
You need to find a school where your children will fit in, enjoy the curriculum and any extra-curricular activities. You should also check on the timing and structure of the examinations, and the reputation of the qualifications – both nationally and internationally. Visit schools relevant to your children's ages and speak with the teachers and, if you get the opportunity, ask to speak to pupils' parents too. Also consider the timing of your planned emigration. It can be helpful for your children to enter the education system at the start of an academic year. This will boost their chances of adjusting to the syllabus and making friends.

- **What do British families living locally think of the area?**
Many British families living abroad offer 'homestays'. This is a great opportunity to answer a broad range of questions and experience residential living, as opposed to staying in tourist accommodation.

- **How will the working routine feel?**
  Get up at the time you'd need to in order to go to work in that country and drive or catch a train to where you think you might be working. This will enable you to assess issues such as commuting times. Furthermore, it will ensure that your fact-finding trip doesn't give you a false impression of the destination.

- **What are the people like?**
  Are they happy to talk to you? What is their attitude toward immigrants? Are they proud of their country?

- **What is the climate like?**
  Is it appropriate for your health and lifestyle aspirations? If you are a tradesperson, ask yourself if you'd be able to work outside during all the different seasons, and whether the climate is in fact too hot or cold for the outdoor lifestyle you were envisaging.

Money-saving tips

There are ways to reduce your fact-finding costs without compromising the value of the trip.

- **Flights**
  If you are prepared to travel outside of the school holidays, take connecting flights, and avoid flying on a Friday, Saturday or Sunday, your savings could be substantial. If visiting the Southern Hemisphere, remember that December to February is summertime and therefore the most expensive time of the year to visit. For those planning more than one fact-finding trip, check frequent flyer schemes. By always flying on the same airline, you can accrue air miles and save money on future flights.

- **Travel insurance and car hire**
  Using price comparison websites such as www.travelsupermarket.com and www.which.co.uk is a good way of seeking out the cheapest online deals.

- **Communication**
  If travelling alone, and therefore needing to make regular calls back home, you could buy a cheap mobile phone abroad and pay-as-you-go; use your UK mobile (remember that North America uses a different bandwidth) and buy prepaid cards abroad; or sign up to a voice over internet protocol (VOIP) provider such as Skype or Vonage. VOIP technology allows you to make telephone calls via the internet for little or no charge.

What next?

Once you have finished gathering information on a particular destination, the next step is to assess the data.

1 Working through your key areas of research will enable you to weigh up the pros and cons you now have evidence for.

2 If you plan to emigrate with members of your family, remember to include them in the assessment exercise – their interpretation of the information you have gathered may differ markedly from yours. If they were unable to accompany you on a fact-finding trip, but you've returned armed with DVD footage, photos, recorded commentary and notes, now is the time that these efforts will pay dividends.

3 Regardless of whether you plan to emigrate with others or on your own, it is useful to analyse your findings with trusted friends or relatives. People you can rely on to give you an honest and constructive answer should help you evaluate what to do next.

Even if your research has given you a solid understanding of the procedures necessary in order to wrap up your affairs in the UK and settle comfortably abroad, you may still wish to seek professional help in some areas. Chapter 4 outlines the best ways to find help and how to get the most from it.

Getting the best help

From immigration and financial advisers, to currency exchange experts, lawyers and estate agents, there are a wide range of people able to offer you assistance when moving abroad. This chapter gives advice on how to find the best experts to help you and how to get the most from your money.

Finding a professional

Deciding on which country to move to leads to other crucial decisions, such as determining how much professional assistance you need in order to relocate successfully. Getting these decisions wrong can be costly, so make your choices with care.

How much professional help you require, and indeed can call upon, is greatly influenced by which country you plan to move to. For example, there is little in the way of specific professional assistance available to help you apply for a resident's permit in another EU country, largely because it is something most people can manage themselves. However, the far more complex immigration laws in place in Australia, New Zealand, Canada and America have resulted in a range of companies offering competing services. Furthermore, transporting your possessions to a country in the EU is something you could probably do yourself, but if you are heading to Australasia or North America, you will almost certainly need to employ a removals company.

Ultimately, it is up to you to understand exactly what services you are enlisting, for what price, and what recourse you have should the assistance fall short of the expected standard. You must also ask yourself what the person giving you the advice stands to gain if you accept it and employ them. After all, the cost of getting it wrong could run into the thousands, and, in the case of buying property and businesses abroad, tens of thousands.

It is always worth remembering that it is also your job to find out what, if any, regulations apply to the professionals you enlist, where and when these regulations apply, and how active the regulating body is in punishing unprofessional conduct. Don't assume what you know about UK rules applies overseas.

Beware also that some people stray outside the limits of their role. An example of this would be a recruitment consultant in one of many provinces of Canada, who asks you to pay them for finding a job: this kind of practice is illegal. Moreover, be sure to check that such a fee is not inexplicably added to another part of the bill, such as dealing with your immigration paperwork. Some recruiters in Australia and New Zealand are also known to charge the job seeker fees, even though they are often paid by the employer as well. Ask any recruiters you use to explain their payment policy to you, and if you think it's unfair, take your business elsewhere.

Making a choice

The internet, relevant publications and exhibitions are all good starting points to gather a list of companies that could help you. Once you have a shortlist, take the following steps.

Step 1 Check credentials. Visit the website of the association or society with jurisdiction over the company in question. When you do consult with companies, let them know that you have investigated the licensing requirements – this will send a clear message to them that you know your rights.

Step 2 Consult a range of competitors. Although it is far more time consuming, consulting companies in person will give you a better opportunity to appraise them. A true professional would not become flustered when you ask hard questions.

Step 3 Ask the right questions. Find out how much experience the company in question has in dealing with the specifics of your situation, such as a particular destination within a country or a specific type of visa. Also question the value of their experience – they may have years of experience of working in the industry in question, but is that experience really relevant to your situation? If you encounter a language barrier, make use of friends or contacts who are fluent speakers of the language in question, or employ a translator who works locally but is not connected to the company.

Step 4 Compare costs. Where a fee is charged you should research whether it seems reasonable compared to charges made by rival companies. Check when the fees are to be paid, and how – this can sometimes reveal suspicious practices.

Step 5 Look at the timing. You may have found the perfect company but want to use their services during peak season (such as summertime for removers). Any delays this entails could have a knock-on effect on your plans, so seek assurance that the services can be carried out exactly when you need them.

Step 6 Seek recommendations. This can be done through your network of friends and family, or via an internet forum. Professional recommendations (for example, your American business consultant recommending a lawyer) are not without value, but treat them with caution. A recent industry award is also a good sign of professional service.

❝ It is up to you to understand exactly what services you are enlisting and for what price. ❞

For further information on how to hire a removals company see the website of the British Association of Removers, www.bar.co.uk or the Fédération Internationale des Déménageurs Internationaux, www.fidi.com

1 Is your profession regulated?
2 What consumer protection is in place?
3 What credentials do you have?
4 If you have credentials, what was involved in obtaining them, and when did you obtain them?
5 What tasks do these credentials permit you to carry out on my behalf?
6 Do you have a specialism within your field?
7 If so, for how many years have you been specialising in that particular area?
8 How much do you charge, what is the breakdown of these charges, and when do you charge?
9 Why do you charge more or less than your competitors?
10 Can you provide me the services I need in a timely fashion?

❝ There are plenty of non-corporate relocation services available. ❞

RELOCATION AND REMOVALS

Although you could do most of the tasks yourself, you will undoubtedly benefit from the assistance of professionals in both relocation and removals.

If you are moving abroad because your employer is relocating you, it is likely that your employer will hire a corporate relocation services firm to help you. However, if this is not the case, there are plenty of non-corporate relocation services available too. For further information on these services, in addition to other issues concerning relocation, see Chapter 6.

Moving home can be a gruelling and stressful exercise at the best of times. Add to this the complication of shipping your belongings overseas, not to mention dealing with the paperwork that this involves, and you might be better placed to hire the expertise of an experienced international removals company.

There are plenty of issues to consider before you employ a removals company, however. These range from how to find a reputable company, to working out what you should and should not take with you. These topics and more are examined in more detail in Chapter 5.

Immigration paperwork

Differing immigration regulations can make the process of obtaining a visa or a permit appear dauntingly complex, but with qualified professionals to help you, this stage of moving abroad should not be a stumbling block.

If you plan to move to another country in the EU, or are going to employ a professional to submit your application for a destination outside of the EU, you will still need a degree of knowledge. This includes an understanding of where to be, at what time, and with what paperwork. If you plan to submit your own application for an Australian, New Zealand, Canadian or American visa, you will need a more profound knowledge of the requirements and bureaucratic procedures necessary. You will also need to be diligent in checking your paperwork.

THE EUROPEAN UNION

The good news is that those moving from the UK to another EU country do not need to qualify for a visa to enter the country in question. The bad news is that, when it comes to the documentation you do need, European bureaucracy is famously slow, often requiring what would appear to be unnecessary repeat visits or shuttling back and forth between different departments.

Although it is not legally necessary to obtain a resident's permit in some countries, in practice such documentation can prove to be invaluable. The countries in question can be divided into three groups:

- Those which do not require documentation.
- Those which do not officially require documentation, but in practice it could be advantageous.
- Those countries which do require documentation.

> **Although it is not legally necessary to obtain a resident's permit in some EU countries, in practice such documentation can prove to be invaluable.**

For the specific requirements of each country, turn to the following pages: Spain 116, France 126, Portugal 133, Italy 139, Germany 145, and Cyprus 150.

Who can help?

Although negotiating European bureaucracy isn't exactly straightforward, the fact that EU nationals do not have to qualify to live in another EU country limits the money to be made from assisting in this capacity. Therefore, unlike Australia, New Zealand, Canada and America, there are no professions dealing specifically with this role. Nonetheless, limited help is available. Depending on your choice of destination and whether you need to obtain certain residency paperwork, you might need to call on the services of a translator, and in some cases help with form-filling and submitting applications can be obtained. If you are moving to Spain or France with your family and decide to apply for a *permiso de residencia* or *carte de séjour* respectively, you will need your marriage certificate and the birth certificates of your children translated; in some cases, a translation of a job offer or employment contract is also required.

❝ Limited help is available in Europe. ❞

There are several good places to start your search for a translator:

The European Union of Associations of Translation Companies (EUATC) works with national translation bodies to introduce a standard for quality and consistency of service. The EUATC website, www.euatc.org, has links to the national translation associations of France, Spain, Portugal, Germany and Italy – from which you could find a well-qualified translator.

The Chartered Institute of Linguists aims to establish and maintain high standards, and has around 6,500 fellows, members and associate members. You can search by specialism (for example, law and property) and country at www.iol.org.uk.

British Chambers of Commerce in Europe have member directories, with translation being among the membership categories. Although chambers of commerce are primarily created to serve British business interests abroad, some companies listed also cater for individuals needing residency paperwork translated.

For those who'd rather hand over as much of the form-filling as possible, there are two options:

- Employ a licensed representative.
- Employ a company offering such services.

Those moving to Spain have the greatest choice, those moving to Portugal are also reasonably well catered for, while those moving to France and Italy will find their options to be a little more limited.

OUTSIDE THE EU

The immigration systems of Australia, New Zealand, Canada and America are essentially divided into four identical categories; skilled, business, family and humanitarian.

- **Skilled.** This is for those with skills in demand. In America, this category is called 'Employment-Based'; in Australia, it is the 'Skilled Stream'; in Canada, skilled and business visas are grouped together under the 'Economic Class'; and in New Zealand it is the 'Skilled Migrant Category'.

- **Business.** Business is for those with investment funds, business ownership or management experience. These are typically known as 'Investor' or 'Entrepreneur' visas.
- **Family.** This area is for those with spouses or common-law partners who can apply for their immigration. Dependent children, parents and grandparents are some of the other relationships that can benefit from a family immigration programme.
- **Humanitarian.** Humanitarian visas offer protection to people who fear persecution or who may be at risk of torture or cruel and unusual treatment or punishment, and are unwilling or unable to return to their home country.

It's worth stating at the outset that you do not officially need professional assistance in order to make an immigration application to Australia, New Zealand, Canada, and America: you are legally entitled to do this yourself. However, if you hate filling in forms, have a tendency to be slapdash, or have doubts about your ability to qualify – perhaps because of a criminal record, for example – hiring a professional might be advisable. Certainly, those facing more complicated applications, such as for business visas or skills visas that require overseas employment first, must think long and hard before going it alone.

A wide range of companies exist to provide these services for you, indicating that many people are happy to pay for a professional to deal with the bureaucracy for them. Nonetheless, consulting with a professional from a position of complete ignorance could put you and your money at risk. The less scrupulous practitioners might be tempted to overstate the difficulties involved in the hope of talking you out of money you really didn't need to spend.

Bear in mind that even those who can help will sometimes say no. Workload aside, this could be because they only take on clients they feel 100 per cent sure will qualify for a visa. Conversely, a small number of immigration professionals will attempt to establish a reputation by taking on difficult cases, and may decide not to assist you on the basis that your application is too straightforward.

This raises the following question – how much do you need to spend? Application fees payable to government immigration departments range from hundreds to, in the case of some business applications, thousands of pounds. Fees for immigration professionals follow a similarly sliding scale, ranging from approximately £1,000 to £5,000, but with full application-to-citizenship packages and business fees generally falling between £8,000 and £12,000.

❝ You may not officially need professional assistance to make an immigration application. ❞

For further information on how to contact the British Chambers of Commerce in Europe, see the Useful Addresses section on pages 211 to 215.

Who can help?

Although similar, the regulations covering professional assistance in Australia, New Zealand, Canada and America are by no means identical. Here's who can help:

- Australia – Migration lawyers and migration agents.
- New Zealand – Immigration advisers.
- Canada – Immigration lawyers and immigration consultants.
- America – Immigration attorneys and business consultants.

Specific details on the roles of immigration professionals in Australia, New Zealand, Canada and America are detailed in the respective sections of Chapters 8 and 9. However, some elements are common to all. For example, it is worth checking to ensure your professional adviser is covered by **professional indemnity** insurance. Most professionals have this cover and many such as lawyers, accountants and financial advisers are often legally obliged to have it. Other professionals, such as architects, consultants, advertising and PR agencies also often opt for it. Although it protects the company selling you the service in question, professional indemnity insurance also protects you and gives you a platform from which to seek recompense. The governing bodies of many industries also require companies to have professional indemnity insurance as a condition of membership.

Immigration changes

Immigration departments tend to make changes on an annual basis; other major changes tend to be made following a change in government. By way of illustration, between June 2007 and March 2008, Australia overhauled many of its skilled visas. Canada announced, but did not immediately introduce, changes to its skilled visa programme and brought out a brand new work-related visa. New Zealand changed the financial requirements of its investor visa and tinkered with its 'Skilled Migrant Category' (see pages 156, 185 and 164 respectively for more information). Sometimes, changes are made retroactively, undermining an application that had already been submitted. Always check the latest regulations and criteria.

Jargon Buster

Professional indemnity A type of insurance (also known as 'errors and omissions insurance' in some countries), that protects a business against compensation sought by a client claiming it has made mistakes or has been negligent in some or all of the services provided

 Under New Zealand's Immigration Advisers Licensing Act, immigration advisers will now be subject to regulation. See pages 169-170 for more details.

Financial advice

Moving your money abroad, choosing a local bank and managing financial assets such as a pension requires careful consideration in terms of how you do it, when you do it, and who you do it with. Good professional advice at this stage could literally save you thousands.

CURRENCY EXCHANGE

Wherever you are moving to, you will need to arrange for your UK money to be exchanged into the local currency of your destination. As this amount will almost certainly include the money from the sale of your UK residence, savings, investments you've cashed in, and perhaps even the sale of a business, you are likely to be exchanging tens if not hundreds of thousands of pounds.

But it's not quite as simple as exchanging your money into dollars, euros or other currencies and having an exactly equivalent amount waiting for you in your new currency. Exchange rates fluctuate, and even a small weakening of the pound against the currency you are exchanging your money into can have a big impact on your spending power. There are two main ways to minimise these exchange rate risks:

- Watch the markets closely, then transfer money via a bank when the time is right.
- Use a foreign exchange (or 'FOREX') specialist.

If you take the first option, you'll need to have the money ready to transfer at the right moment (which is sometimes easier said than done), as well as investing considerable time in learning about currency markets. Even when you do exchange the funds, you might find that you are only offered the tourist rate rather than the rate at which banks trade currency between themselves, and will probably be charged a fee to transfer the money overseas. Before making the exchange, it is worth talking to the bank that you plan to use to see if they can offer you a better rate than the one advertised.

If you take the second option, there are plenty of companies available to help you, and you can often secure a better rate than the best offer from a bank.

Foreign exchange companies make their money by shaving off a miniscule margin from the actual exchange rate. In essence, then, it is a commission service, but even with this factored in the rates can still beat those offered by the banks. A study conducted by the DQM Group for exchange company HiFX and published in *The Sunday Times* in January 2008 revealed that it offered rates of between 0.01 and 0.06 better than the best bank rates. Although this doesn't sound like much, if you were exchanging £60,000 the saving would be anything from £600 to £3,600. However, for very small amounts – usually under £5,000 – you are unlikely to receive anything like the best rate.

So, how do you decide which company to use? Currency exchange companies are not registered by the Financial Services Authority (FSA) at present, so checking for credentials is not possible.

However, all funds made available for transfer by a customer should be transferred by the currency specialist into a **client trust account** with a bank. This protects the customer's funds through the bank's accordance with FSA regulations. When choosing a company to help you change currency, the following points should help:

- Check on the websites of companies dealing in currency. Some will publish their rates online; to get information from those that don't, you'll probably have to register – which is normally free.
- To work out whether the rate you have been quoted is a good one, think in terms of percentages. For example, you should be able to get an exchange rate within one per cent of the interbank rate, the rate at which banks exchange money between themselves. Gather quotes from several currency exchange companies to see which one offers the smallest percentage deviation from the interbank rate.
- Request information on additional charges for providing the service and how long they take to transfer money on their clients' behalf.

- Find out if they have dedicated immigration staff, how long they have been in business, and how many big corporate clients they have. The more they have, in theory the more money they are transferring, and this might result in better rates for private clients such as you.
- Ask if they have indemnity insurance for their staff.
- Check if they have a client trust account and, if so, which bank it is with.
- If you are still undecided, seek recommendations by visiting online forums or emigration exhibitions – there are usually several such companies present.

Jargon Buster

Client trust account An account maintained at a bank for the purpose of holding client funds

Spot trades Buying the currency at the current price, and paying for it immediately

Forward trades Fixing an exchange rate in advance of currency purchase, usually for up to two years. Typically, you pay a 10 per cent deposit but don't pay the full amount until you make the full transfer

Limit orders An advance agreement to an upper or lower exchange rate whereby the currency purchase is triggered as either limit is reached

Spot trade is the fastest of the three options in terms of making your liquid assets available in another currency, and if you have the flexibility to get the timing right then you could secure a good exchange rate.

Forward trade is a convenient option for those who need to sell their assets first (a house, for example) in order to raise the funds to transfer.

Limit orders give you the flexibility to achieve a more attractive rate of exchange than is available when you sign the contract, but it does tie your money up in the meantime.

You must also consider your overseas banking arrangements and the timing of your property purchase overseas.

BANKING OVERSEAS

Unless you are being relocated by a multinational company or you employ an estate agent who also offers relocation services (see Chapter 6 for more information), choosing a bank abroad is your decision alone.

In some cases, you can opt for a bank familiar from the UK high street, or an overseas bank that makes a play for migrant business. For those intent on shopping around, there is much more to consider than interest rates. The key differences between banking in the UK and abroad are listed opposite.

- **Terminology.** In the UK we have banks and building societies, but you'll find commercial, co-operative, credit unions, thrifts and various other names for banks overseas. Generally, though, these function like a typical UK bank or building society, and accounts will either be current (also called 'checking' and 'transaction') or savings accounts.
- **Cheques.** These are not used so widely abroad (with the exception of France). This is partly because many countries don't use cheque guarantee cards.
- **Charges.** Many overseas banks charge for banking transactions, such as direct debits, withdrawals and processing cheques, regardless of whether you are in credit. America and France are exceptions to such high-charge transactions. In addition, be aware that penalties for unauthorised overdrafts and bounced cheques can be much more severe overseas than it is in Britain.
- **Insurance.** Some banks in Canada and America belong to organisations that offer 'deposit insurance' – if the bank goes bust, deposits of up to $100,000 are insured.
- **Assorted products.** Banks abroad sometimes sell a wider range of products than simply offering financial services. If you need to buy a bicycle in Spain, for example, a bank may be the answer.

The European Central Bank publishes information about interest rates offered by banks and other financial institutions in EU countries on its website: www.ecb.int

INDEPENDENT FINANCIAL ADVICE

In the UK, professional help with asset management falls to Independent Financial Advisers (IFAs), which are regulated by the Financial Services Authority (www.fsa.gov.uk – here, you'll find regulated advisers listed, along with their disciplinary records). It is a criminal activity to give advice without being regulated. A condition of being regulated is that an IFA must carry indemnity insurance, without this he or she would be breaching a condition of their regulation. Advisers who give advice without being regulated cannot obtain indemnity insurance. An unregulated adviser is therefore putting the consumer at risk – as the consumer has no protection. Furthermore, advisers must have passed specialist exams to carry out **technical analyses** before they can recommend the transfers of benefits from, for example, final salary schemes. The difficulty with moving abroad, though, is that an IFA in the UK is only qualified to advise on UK investments, not overseas investments, and an IFA from outside the EU is not permitted to give financial advice in the UK.

European financial services regulation

The European Economic Area took steps to harmonise the regulation of investment services across all member states by introducing the Markets in Financial

Instruments Directive (MiFID) in November 2007. Firms covered by MiFID are authorised and regulated by the country in which they have their registered office. Once a firm has been authorised, it will be able to use a MiFID passport to provide services to customers in other EU member states. Thus, a UK IFA could advise on investments in Spain. A more confidence-inspiring approach is to work with a UK financial services company that has an office overseas staffed with financial advisers qualified in that particular country. In theory, such a company should possess knowledge on the various rules and options of both countries in question.

Although termed 'independent', many financial advisers are paid solely through commissions from financial institutions. In this case, you must question how 'independent' your adviser is.

The Which? website contains independent advice on how to find a qualified financial adviser you can trust, www.which.co.uk/advice/financial-advisers

Shop around and see if you can find such a company for your destination.

Financial services outside of the EU

It follows that weighing up the pros and cons of moving financial assets, such as a pension, to a country outside the EEA requires an assessment of the tax regimes of both the UK and the destination. In which case, the solution is to work with one or more people who can advise, individually or collectively, on either end of the move. This could take one of three forms:

- A person or group with the requisite investment knowledge of both countries in question. A UK IFA who emigrated recently and has since become a financial adviser overseas would fit the bill.
- A UK IFA who works with an overseas IFA who understands the dynamics of migrant finances.
- An international firm with expertise in the jurisdictions applicable to you.

Case Study Len

In January 2007, Len moved to Nova Scotia in Canada. He used financial experts to move his money to Canada but also managed to make savings by taking care of some things himself. 'I found the process of exchanging money quite stressful, not because it was difficult but because the potential savings or losses are huge', says Len. 'I began to monitor the exchange rate in summer 2006 knowing that small changes can pay dividends when you're exchanging tens of thousands of pounds'. Having set exchange rate goals, Len then instructed his currency specialist to make the exchange at the right time. However, Len decided to leave his UK pension in place for the time being. He explains: 'In April 2006 there were changes to the rules surrounding pension transfers between the UK and various countries, including Canada'.

10 questions for IFAs

1 What are your financial planning credentials?
2 How long have you been offering financial planning services?
3 Do you have a disciplinary record with a professional or regulatory governing body?
4 Do you have experience of financial planning for Britons moving to my country of interest?
5 Will you provide financial planning advice for me, or will it be one of your colleagues?
6 Do you have an office or partnership elsewhere? If so, how are your representatives there regulated?
7 Do you have a minimum fee?
8 How are your fees structured?
9 Do you receive financial incentives for recommending certain financial products?
10 Do you provide a comprehensive written analysis of my financial situation and your recommendations?

Buying property

At some point in the emigration process, you're almost certain to enlist the services of a property agent. Tapping into the knowledge of the right property agent could save you time and money.

ESTATE AGENTS

If you are buying a home in Spain, Italy or Germany, you might be tempted to search for your own property, thereby avoiding the need to pay agents' fees that could be up to 5 per cent of the cost of the property. (Note that the seller typically pays the agent's fees in France, Portugal, Cyprus, Australia, New Zealand, Canada and America). However, it is worth remembering that a good agent knows the local marketplace, which companies or developers are trustworthy and those you should stay away from.

How to find a good estate agent

Many estate agents selling overseas property to British buyers belong to the Association of International Property Professionals (AIPP). This organisation has its own code of conduct, insists on member companies having indemnity insurance and offers consumer advice and insights. In a survey conducted by the AIPP in 2007, 69 per cent of respondents said that they were worried about being given unreliable or misleading information when buying property abroad, and 94 per cent said that they'd feel more secure if overseas property companies had to follow

professional guidelines and face disciplinary action if they did not.

Wherever you are searching for a property, responsible agents should be willing to prove their credentials. Indeed, it is typical to see relevant certificates displayed on the walls of estate agencies.

Nonetheless, don't allow yourself to be convinced by the waving of any official-looking documentation under your nose. Instead, clearly establish what membership, licensing and accreditation the agency in question has, and do your own background checks on the protection afforded by all or any of these things.

For example, there are three official French estate agency bodies – the *Fédération Nationale des Agents Immobiliers,* the *Syndicat Nationales des Professionels Immobilier* and the *Union Nationale de L'Immobilier.* Although they must hold a *carte professionale,* a French estate agent doesn't need to be a member of all of the official bodies, nor have a fidelity bond (*pièce de garantie*) – which provides a financial guarantee that in the event of the agent absconding, you will get your deposit back.

Membership of the appropriate body is no guarantee of quality service, although it does give you an obvious channel through

Property-buying frauds

Selling property is an obvious way for fraudsters to make good money. Here are a few known scams to look out for:

- **The agent offers to hold your deposit while the sale goes through, but disappears with your money.**
- **The agent inflates the sale price agreed with the seller, and pockets the difference.**
- **You are sold a property that is not technically for sale. This can happen in rural parts of some countries where the owner appears to have abandoned the property, but the title deeds will still be in their name.**
- **The property owner offers to sell you property in a way that avoids tax and red tape, but then disappears with your money.**

agent, there are a potentially bewildering array of local laws, procedures and differences to contend with. Here's a list of the key points:

- **Terminology and language.** Besides the obvious differences in language, the fact that types of property are named differently even in English-speaking countries can be cause for confusion.
- **Size.** The standard British listing of a property by number of bedrooms is not followed overseas; instead, properties are often listed by size in square metres. As a general guide, a 50 square metre property may be equivalent to a one-bedroom apartment, while a four-bedroom detached house may be approximately 150 square metres.
- **Features.** Different features may be relatively standard in different countries. For example, many Canadian homes have huge basements, many New Zealand homes have no central heating, and many Spanish homes have tiled floors.

which to make an official complaint. You also need to be aware of any partiality in the dealings of the agents in question, such as them catering to a certain market sector or, only dealing with a limited number of developers.

Good advice from a professional estate agent can be the difference between you realising your dream and meeting with disaster. Spending so much money at once is a huge step, so ensure that you take every precaution possible, never, ever buy sight unseen, and don't rush in – even when you're being made to feel that this is your one chance to secure your dream property.

When you do engage the services of an

What an estate agent is called overseas

France – *agent immobilier*
Spain – *agents de fincas*
Portugal – *mediador autorizado*
Italy – *agente immobiliare*
Germany – *makler, immobilienmakler* or *wohnungsmakler*
Cyprus – estate agent
Australia – estate agent
New Zealand – real estate agent
Canada – real estate broker or realtor
America – real estate agent, realtor or realtist

- **Listings.** Details of properties for sale in Canada, America and Australia are advertised on a country-specific Multi Listings Service (MLS), a useful online location to start your property research.
- **Mandate.** In North America, agents can either act on behalf of the seller, or the buyer, or both; in Europe, the agent typically fulfils the role of a British estate agent, assisting the seller. By law, American and Canadian estate agents should disclose who they are working for. In France, agents might have a mandate to sell the property exclusively, or simply be given permission to be one of potentially many agents selling the property.
- **Contracts.** Preliminary contracts often allow for the insertion of conditions and clauses. Bear in mind, though, that signing on the dotted line abroad can in some cases be more binding than in the UK.

Once you've found an agent you trust, their usefulness to you will be greatly influenced by your ability to brief them properly. Armed with a realistic budget and research on some possible locations, you can now put together a list of property criteria to help the agent fulfil your requirements. As with your primary reasons for wanting to emigrate, you might find that some of your property criteria are more important than others, enabling you to present your requirements to the agent in terms of flexible and non-negotiable elements.

MORTGAGES

Apart from the lucky few, buying a home abroad is likely to involve sourcing a suitable mortgage. This is something that you can do yourself by researching the various mortgage lenders in your destination, or you can employ a professional. Whichever route you take, there are some key differences between British and overseas mortgages that you should take note of:

- Mortgages are either granted on the basis of a **multiple** of your salary, or a percentage of your **net monthly income** (in Europe, this typically ranges from 30–33 per cent).
- The maximum **loan-to-value** mortgage is usually lower in Europe than it is in the UK (typically 60–80 per cent as opposed to 85–90 per cent).
- Loans are available in some countries to make up the shortfall between the mortgage and the purchase price (this is the case in Canada and Germany).
- Lenders' valuations can be less than the purchase price, therefore the mortgage may not be sufficient. This is often the case in Portugal and Germany (see pages 136 and 147 for more information).
- Terms in most EU countries are typically 15 years, as opposed to the 25-year standard in the UK and the 25 to 30-year terms common in Australia, New Zealand, Canada and America.

For further information on buying property see the Which Essential Guides, *Buying Property Abroad* and *Buy, Sell and Move House.*

- Terminology varies (for example, in New Zealand, a repayment mortgage is known as a 'table mortgage' – see page 168 for details).
- The range of available mortgages differs (for example, **pension** and **endowment-linked mortgages** are not available in France, Spain, Italy and Cyprus); in fact, repayment mortgages are the norm in the EU.

If you are going it alone, specialist magazines and websites cover the mortgage markets in many countries. These include *Your Mortgage* magazine in Australia or the 'Home Finance Center' pages of the *New York Times* website. National newspapers also often carry thisinformation on the best rates. These should arm you with enough information to go direct to lenders in your new country. Even within one country, many lenders will have their own subtle variations on how they calculate mortgages and cap borrowings, so obtaining a range of quotes is an essential part of the process.

Although some estate agents offer their own mortgage packages, these tend to be limited in number. Therefore, when looking for help with a mortgage in your new country, you must call upon an established mortgage broker.

Mortgage brokers

A good broker should be able to advise you on how much you can borrow and the mortgage products which will best suit your circumstances. This should save you considerable time and, hopefully, money. Throughout the procedure your mortgage broker will liaise between you and the lenders in question – this may prove to be a solution

---

If you decide that you need assistance to help guide you through the mortgage maze, the credit crunch of 2008 should be sufficient warning that the mortgage industry can be beset by misselling.

Jargon Buster

Multiple Mortgages calculated on the basis of your income. For example, in the UK, you might be able to obtain a mortgage that is three times your annual wage

Net monthly income What's left of your monthly income after regular outgoings (such as taxation) are accounted for. So your maximum mortgage might be based on your ability to meet your monthly mortgage repayments with 30–33 per cent of your net monthly income

Loan-to-value The ratio of the mortgage loan amount to the property's appraised value or selling price, whichever is less

Pension-linked mortgage An interest-only mortgage where the borrower usually pays a monthly amount into a pension fund. When the borrower reaches retirement, the cash lump sum repays the outstanding balance on the mortgage

Endowment mortgage The monthly payment is used to buy stocks and shares. The hope is that when the term of the mortgage comes to an end the endowment policy will have increased to a level where it can be used to repay the original loan – and perhaps provide surplus cash

to any linguistic shortcomings you may have. Bear in mind, though, that a broker usually makes his or her money by receiving commission from the lending organisation, so it is imperative that you feel they are giving you the right advice rather than looking to maximise their takings. The regulation of mortgage brokers is somewhat patchy. For example:

- **Regulation.** Some associations (especially those in America and Canada) fulfil more of an educational than a regulatory role. In other countries, the role of the broker is underdeveloped and is not well regulated. This is currently true for Cyprus.
- **Professional indemnity insurance.** Some professional associations insist upon the broker taking out professional indemnity insurance as a condition of membership (this is the case in Australia and New Zealand). Some brokers have professional indemnity insurance but are not necessarily members of a national-level association (this is common in France and Spain).

With this in mind, therefore, it's important to avoid assuming that any official-sounding association of mortgage brokers will afford you an effective level of protection. One alternative is to opt for a UK-based overseas mortgage specialist, in which case you can check whether they are registered with the FSA, as well as obtain further details on your rights with respect to mortgages and investment advice, in the consumer information section of www.fsa.gov.uk. But, as with choosing any professional service, you must ask yourself if their level of expertise is really appropriate to your situation.

Mortgages: What to do and what not to do

What to do:

- Compare rates and prices by shopping around and getting a range of quotes from accredited brokers. If a lender or broker gives you the hard sell on why you should use them rather than a competitor, walk away.
- Ask what association the broker belongs to, and whether a condition of membership is professional indemnity insurance. If it is, you know that the broker is covered against any compensation claims – hence, in the event of perceived wrongdoing you are more likely to get your money back.
- Check thoroughly that the costs and loan terms are what you originally agreed to.
- Take the utmost care working out how much you think you can afford to borrow. It's better to err on the side of caution than fall foul to a cavalier approach to finances borne by the excitement of your new start in life.

What not to do:

- Sign contracts or documents without checking them thoroughly.
- Lie about your financial situation in order to get a loan.
- Let yourself be convinced that you need to borrow more money than you know you can afford to repay.

The purchase process

Buying a home abroad is a similar, but rarely identical, process to doing so in the UK. Once you have decided on your budget (provisionally arranged with a mortgage lender), and found a property you like within budget (either with or without an estate agent) you now have two further steps to take in order to take legal possession of the property.

Firstly, you must negotiate a price and draw up a contract with the seller or the seller's agent and formalise the fundamental points of the contract into a legally binding agreement. At this stage – and particularly before you sign on the dotted line – it is advisable to take independent legal advice to ensure that the contract is fundamentally sound.

The second stage, which involves checking that the title deeds are in order, arranging the registration of the title, recording the sale, and that land tax, council and water rates have been paid by the previous owner, is known as 'conveyance' in the UK. This is handled by a solicitor – normally a lawyer who specialises in conveyance.

In most countries, using a specialist conveyancer – whether they are called a solicitor, lawyer or a notary – is obligatory. However, you can opt to process the necessary paperwork yourself in Australia and New Zealand, while in America hiring a lawyer to complete the property transaction is common practice but not essential. Notaries aside, there are often no set fees for conveyance, so it pays to shop around.

What a conveyancing solicitor is known as abroad

Solicitor or **conveyancer:** In Australia only a solicitor can be enlisted in Australian Capital Territory, Queensland and Tasmania; a conveyancer is also known as a settlement agent, land broker or land agent.

Lawyer: Used in Cyprus, New Zealand, America and Canada (excluding Quebec).

Notary: Used in France (*notaire*), Spain (*notario*), Portugal (*notario*), Italy (*notario*), Germany (*notar*), Canada (Quebec only - *notaire*).

What is a notary?

Notaries are public officials qualified in civil law. In many cases the seller will probably suggest that a notary handles conveyance, and is involved in the initial drafting of contracts, too. Notaries do not act in an advisory capacity, hence it is essential that their input is not considered to be a substitute for independent legal advice. Notaries' fees are fixed by the relevant government on a sliding scale according to the value of the property (from 1 per cent for a simple transfer to 5 per cent or more for a more complex case).

Surveys

Pre-purchase surveys are much more common in the UK than they are in Europe, Australia, New Zealand, Canada or America. Although the property-buying process can move more quickly in some countries than it does in the UK, leaving less time to attend to such matters, many locations have specialist surveyors you can call upon. For further information, see Chapters 7-9.

Deposits

In most cases, deposits are only refundable where conditions in the preliminary contract were not met by a specified time. Your lawyer must ensure that the wording of the contract clearly shows how the deposit is being offered. Moreover, in some cases, you could be sued for breach of contract – and end up paying a hefty sum in compensation.

Never hand over deposit money directly to the seller, and only to the estate agent if they are fully bonded. Instead, it is advisable to lodge the monies with your own lawyer or with the conveyancing specialist handling the sale.

What next?

The types of professional assistance available to you and the jargon used by their business can vary greatly from country to country. Spend some time on your homework before you employ someone and make sure you understand what you want from them. Work through this checklist:

1 Check credentials and references. Do you believe the professional in question can deliver what you are looking for?

2 If you are thinking of taking on an overseas professional, compare their services to what you might expect to get back home. If this falls short, consider whether this might be due to differences in law, customary working practices, or both before you dismiss them.

3 Check out whether a UK-based professional, perhaps a member of a trade association you know of and trust, can provide you with what you need at a reasonable cost.

4 Try to keep on top of as much of the process as you can so that you can intervene the moment things don't appear to be going to plan.

Once you have negotiated the potential pitfalls of employing a professional to help you with the areas that you cannot complete alone, it will be time to wrap up your UK affairs. For further details on what might appear on your 'to do' list, turn to Chapter 5.

The Conference des Notariats de l'Union Européenne represents notaries in France, Spain, Portugal, Italy and Germany, as well as several other countries. Its website, www.cnue.be, has links to the national bodies.

Wrapping up your UK affairs

Having already taken several significant steps in preparation for moving abroad, you'd be forgiven for thinking that the hard work is over. Think again. From selling your house to organising your finances, disposing of some possessions and arranging removals for the rest, not to mention pet predicaments, wrapping up your UK affairs is a challenge not to be underestimated.

A clean break?

When wrapping up your UK affairs, it can be tempting to cut all ties as soon as possible, making a clear commitment to your new life abroad. However, you might also want to consider how to return.

If you do plan to make a clean break, selling your house, striking yourself off the electoral register and closing your bank accounts makes it much more complicated for you to return to the UK should you need to.

How many ties you can leave in the UK depends on whether you can afford to keep your British property, where you're emigrating to and what distance you're covering. Those moving to Europe, for example, will have lower costs and a shorter distance to travel home. With this in mind, give some serious thought to the question of how many loose ends would be appropriate for you to leave behind.

Selling your home

More often than not, moving abroad is funded by the sale of your UK property. How easy or difficult you find this task will be greatly influenced by the prevailing market and the type of chain your buyers are involved in. It is worthwhile giving yourself as much time as possible to complete, so start thinking about putting your house on the market a good

> **66** More often than not, moving abroad is funded by the sale of your UK property. **99**

Case Study **Melanie and Dan**

Melanie's husband Dan, a software developer, moved to San Francisco, America, in June 2007, while Melanie stayed behind to oversee the selling of the family house. Unfortunately, this has proved to be more difficult than anticipated. 'Our house was put on the market at £358,950 and then after having had no viewings we dropped the price to offers over £340,000' explains Melanie. However, this was only the start of the discounts. 'We rejected an offer of £325,000, then £320,000, but we've had no interest since then so the estate agents have advised us to drop the price to £300,000.' This 'loss' of nearly £60,000 has already had an impact on the life the couple thought they would be able to lead in America.

 For information and advice on renting, letting, buying, selling and moving home, see the Which? Essential Guides *Renting and Letting* and *Buy, Sell and Move House*.

year before you plan to emigrate.
(See the timeline on pages 82-83.)

It is also worth seeking advice from the professionals. Your local estate agent should have a good idea of what sells quickly in your area, as well as the other houses that yours may be in competition with. Ask if there are any cosmetic changes you can make that will improve your chances of selling the house. Spending a bit of time and money repainting a few rooms may pay dividends in the long run when your house is sold before an identical one down the road with shabby interiors.

Clearly, how long it takes you to sell your property could have a severe impact on both the timing of your move abroad and how big your relocation budget is. Whatever the economic conditions are when the 'for sale' sign is put up outside your property, you have three broad options:

- Only consider offers close to your asking price.
- Do everything you can to sell your house quickly.
- Let the property until you feel you can achieve the price you want for it.

As with most emigration dilemmas, there is no right answer. If you are undecided as to how to proceed, take a few minutes to write down the pros and cons of each option for you and your personal situation.

For those absolutely desperate to sell, there are specialist companies that will buy almost any property – and fast. The strength of this approach is that you release the funds tied up in your house, there are no estate agency fees and you don't have to pay an indefinite number of additional mortgage repayments. However, you are only likely to get 75–90 per cent of the market value – and this fact alone often puts all but the most desperate off making such a decision.

❝ It is worthwhile giving yourself as much time as possible to complete. ❞

If you would like to hang onto your UK home, a key question is whether you will be able to afford the process of relocating to another country without access to the funds tied up in your property. Of course, a sluggish UK property market might take the matter out of your hands. Even so, if you need the money from selling your British home in order to pay for your emigration but are unable to sell up or raise the funds elsewhere, consider whether the timing really is right for you to move abroad.

Letting your home

Another option in these circumstances is letting your home. If you do take this option, points you should consider include:

- **Defining your market.** Who is your typical tenant likely to be, how long will they rent for and how much are they likely to pay?
- **Assessing alterations.** Will your property need to be decorated or adapted for your typical tenant?

- **Advertising.** How and where will you advertise, and for how long?
- **Assistance.** Will you enlist the help of a friend or relative to oversee the lettings, or employ a property management company to handle the letting for you? If the latter, how much of your potential rental revenue are you prepared to spend on this aspect?
- **Taxation.** What implications will there be to where and how you get taxed, and will letting out a UK property result in you being defined as 'ordinarily resident'
- **Income.** Will the rental income you receive for your property be in excess of the costs of both your mortgage and maintenance? If not, consider whether it will be worth your while letting it.
- **Feasibility.** Will your property be attractive to the rental market? If your house is a sprawling country home, you might find it more difficult to let than a city-based home located close to transport links and therefore convenient for renters such as students and first-jobbers.

Selling your car

Besides selling houses, another item that can potentially take months to sell is a car. As with houses, you can sell it to a specialist company at a price lower than the market value. Further options include internet auction sites, such as eBay, specialist second-hand car trade magazines, classified ads with your local newspaper or a paper that specialises in classifieds in your region and car dealerships. It is also worth asking around your friends and family – someone you know may jump at the chance of buying your car. Whatever your approach, make sure you factor in enough time to sell your car and get a clear idea of how much you will raise from the sale.

For details on how ordinary residence is defined, and the implications of tax on rental income in the UK, obtain leaflets IR20 and IR40 from the tax office, or visit www.hmrc.gov.uk. Tax residence is also discussed in more detail in Chapter 6.

Getting the timing right

Picking the right moment to make your move abroad is no easy task. In addition to ensuring you give yourself enough time to organise your affairs, you will need to factor in variables such as selling or letting your house and fulfilling employment contracts.

No matter how organised you are, the final weeks before departure can all too often turn into a mad dash through a seemingly endless list of things to do. If you start notifying the relevant companies and authorities too soon you'll end up boxing yourself into a corner, with the power cut and everything packed.

Clearly, it's best that your planned departure date is not too optimistic. Although you might want to book flights in advance to capitalise on any savings to be made, it is also important that this doesn't give you a severe organisational headache. The watchword here is 'flexibility'.

You might find that not everybody is supportive of your emigration. This is only natural, not everyone will share the same views or desire as you. Try to put any negativity out of your mind. Remember, as long as you are clear as to your motives, and have put the necessary groundwork in, you should make success more likely than failure.

Case Study | Sarah

Sarah found that the permanent residence visa she'd applied for took longer to be processed than anticipated. 'The last part of the process was a whirlwind experience,' she says. 'I had my immigration medical on 22 February, and handed my passport to the Immigration Division of the Canadian High Commission in London on 20 March. I was able to pick my passport and visa up on 4 April – just in time for me to catch the flight to Vancouver I'd booked for 7 April.'

A useful online tool for planning the tasks you'll have in the final few months of living in the UK is www.moveme.com. You simply type in your departure date and it automatically creates a calendar, with tasks listed on the appropriate date. Tasks can be moved, added or deleted at will, and there are even letter templates to help you whizz through all of the official correspondence you'll be mailing.

When working out the logistics of moving, one good tip is to write a detailed 'to do' list. Start with your planned departure date and then work back listing what you need to do and the date you need to complete this by. For an example of how to do this, see overleaf.

COUNTDOWN TO DEPARTURE

When you have decided on an approximate departure date, you can start working backwards to plan the timing of everything you will need to do before you leave.

One year to six months to go

- Check that your passports don't need to be renewed. If you are moving outside of the EU you should check six months before you expect your visa to be ready.
- If possible and applicable, check on the progress of your visa. Is it likely to be ready when you are?
- If you plan to take a pet abroad, look into what inoculations, paperwork and quarantine procedures are necessary.
- If you are more than four months away from UK state pension age, you can ask the Inland Revenue for a forecast of what UK state pension you can expect to get. Use this information, along with any occupational or pension scheme statements, to get advice from a financial professional with experience of migrant matters on whether to maintain a pension in the UK, or move it abroad. For more detailed information on sorting out your UK pension and investments, see pages 84-85 overleaf.
- If you plan to sell your house or let it through an agent, invite quotations from three agencies.
- Check your employment contract – how much notice do you need to give?

Six months to three months to go

- Notify the school and local authority of your children's final day of attendance.
- Open a bank account in your destination.
- Unless you are moving your own possessions or selling almost everything you own, organise for three removals companies to visit your house and provide a full written estimate of the costs involved. Book your chosen removals firm.
- Start to sort through your belongings. Organise what you want to sell and what you want to take with you. If selling, explore options such as online auctions, car boot sales and classified ads, and prepare your goods accordingly.
- Make a list of all the paperwork you might need on arrival overseas, and take the necessary steps to collect anything you might not have.
- Organise any specific travel or health insurance you may need.
- If you are staying in rented accommodation, inform the landlord or the rental agency of your departure date.

Three months to one month to go

- Start filling packing boxes with any possessions that don't need to be wrapped by the experts, and clearly label them.
- Notify your local council that that you are moving abroad. This may trigger a council tax refund.
- If you haven't already done so, give your employer official notice of your resignation.
- If you haven't yet bought property overseas, arrange a place to stay on arrival so you can pass on an address to the various UK organisations and companies you need to inform of your move. Alternatively, provide a forwarding address.

- If you are taking one or more vehicles overseas, obtain leaflet V526 from the Driver and Vehicle Licensing Agency (www.dvla.gov.uk). If you are not taking your vehicle overseas, prepare it for sale and place the necessary advertisements.
- Check to see if family or friends will be providing the transportation to the station, port or airport. If not, book other transport.

One month to two weeks to go

Notify the following organisations of your impending move:
- Tax (ask your tax office for form P85 – which will help HM Revenue & Customs decide how you should be treated for UK tax purposes after you leave).
- Social security.
- Legal and financial services (such as insurers, accountants, banks, credit card companies) your local GP and dentist.
- Clubs and organisations you belong to.
- Publications you subscribe to.
- Any local businesses you have an account with.
- If you want to keep your right to vote in British elections, obtain Overseas Elector's Declaration form RPF37 from the local electoral registration office.
- Notify the Post Office, provide a UK address for any remaining mail and ask about their international redirection service. This is calculated per surname, not per person, and costs from £14.85 for one month to £74.75 for 12 months.

Final week
- Check that all the documentation you are taking with you is complete.
- Arrange for the appliances you are taking to be disconnected by professionals.
- Check tax and social security contributions for a possible rebate (for further information, visit: www.direct.gov.uk/en/MoneyTaxAndBenefits/index.htm).
- Cancel all regular payments made from your bank accounts.
- Pay outstanding bills.
- Finish packing your belongings.
- Ensure neighbours and local authorities know that a large vehicle will be parked on your street for an hour or two while your possessions are loaded.
- Say your goodbyes.

Departure day
- Take final utilities readings and request final bills.
- Request final bills from your telecoms and television companies, as applicable.
- Leave keys to your property with your estate agent, rental agency, or family, friends or neighbours, as appropriate.
- Provide stamped addressed envelopes so that the residents can forward any mail addressed to you that is not sent on by the Post Office's redirection service.
- Ensure that all important documents and emergency numbers are accessible.

Finance

Taxation and pensions almost seem the antithesis of the excitement provoked by the possibilities of emigration. However, neglect the financial nitty gritty, and you could run short of funds.

TRANSFERRING YOUR ASSETS

Moving abroad will undoubtedly raise some potentially complicated financial issues – what should you do with UK-based savings and pensions, for example, and what are the tax implications of owning a British rental property when a resident of another country? Many of these questions are best addressed by a financial adviser (see Chapter 4 for tips on how to choose the right professional for your purposes), but this section will give you an idea of the issues at hand.

TAX

Becoming a resident of another country also means your income will be taxed from there rather than the UK. France, Spain, Portugal, Italy, Germany, Cyprus, Australia, New Zealand, Canada and America have 'double-taxation' treaties with the UK, so you won't be taxed twice on any income derived from assets remaining in the UK. For further information on the tax implications of living abroad, see Chapter 6.

PENSIONS

Pension planning is a complex business, especially when you become liable to the tax system of another country. The following information will introduce you to the key issues involved and help you decide what you must do next.

Preparation

In preparation for your move abroad, you should collect information on all of the pension schemes you are currently contributing to. If you are more than four months away from UK state pension age you can ask the Inland Revenue for a forecast of what state pension you can expect. If you have occupational or personal pension schemes, you should already be receiving regular statements.

Take this information to a financial adviser (see Chapter 4 on how to get the best professional help) to help you get a clear picture of what your pension income abroad is likely to be, and to address the following questions:

- Can you continue to contribute to your UK pension schemes from overseas – and, if so, what are the tax implications?
- Can you claim a pension overseas?
- Will you receive the same benefit from them as you would if you had stayed in the UK?
- Should you keep your pensions in the UK, or transfer them to an investment scheme in your new country of residence?

Continuing contributions

If you are still of working age, ask your adviser about continuing to pay voluntary National Insurance contributions while living overseas in order to receive the full UK state pension. Note, though, that this option is not available to those moving to Australia, New Zealand or Canada as your pension will be frozen at the point that you emigrate – you will neither be able to make further contributions, nor will the value of the pension increase in line with the prevailing interest rate. Effectively, then, its real value decreases over time as inflation makes the cost of everything else relatively more expensive.

You can remain in any UK-approved occupational or private pension as long as the scheme's rules allow. However, you will only receive tax relief on your contributions to these private pensions in the five years following your move abroad. After this point, it is unlikely that continuing with your UK pension will be the most tax-efficient option.

Claiming your pensions

Once you reach retirement age, you can claim your UK state pension in any European Economic Area country, as well as America, and will get the same income as you would if you had stayed in the UK. This is because the UK has social security deals in place with these countries.

Assuming you have notified the Pension Service of your new address, you'll be sent a claim form about four months before you reach the UK state pension age. The form will also have space for you to state your insurance and residence in other countries.

If, by this point, you have paid sufficient contributions into a scheme in your new country, you should also be eligible for a pension there as well.

You should also be able to receive payments from personal and occupational pensions when you reach retirement age abroad. However, you must check the following:

- Whether your annuity company pays into an overseas bank account.
- If overseas money transfers are free of charge.
- Whether it pays in the local currency.

If your pension is paid in sterling, it will need to be exchanged for the local currency – exposing it to the prevailing exchange rates, whereas pensions paid directly into a foreign bank in the local currency reduce the risk that you'll lose out if sterling is in a weak position against the local currency at the time the payment is made. Note that some currency exchange specialists now offer free regular transfers to your overseas bank, so this is worth investigating further.

Moving your pension overseas

You may consider cashing in your UK pension and moving the funds to the country you have moved to. However, before you do anything to such an important investment as your pension, it is worth seeking professional advice. Early redemption penalties, taxation and differing interest rates will all have an impact. It is worth checking with an expert to ensure you do not end up worse off than if you had left your pension alone.

Removals

Unless you are transporting your own possessions, or just travelling with personal luggage, you will need to use a company that specialises in international removals.

Deciding on whether you need professional removals assistance is a question of destination, time, number of possessions, and confidence behind the wheel of a large van. If you are moving a significant distance you should consider selling everything and buying anew when you've moved abroad or hire an international removals company to move your possessions for you.

Step 1 **Check that your chosen removals firm is a member of the following:**

- The British Association of Removers (BAR). This association has an advance payment protection scheme, which offers certain guarantees to the consumer.
- The *Fédération Internationale des Déménageurs Internationaux* (FIDI) which, through its FAIM (FIDI Accredited International Mover) accreditation, is the quality assurance standard for the international moving industry.
- The Overseas Moving Network International (OMNI).

Step 2 **Ask for quotations from three appropriately accredited firms.** If they suggest that you don't need a quotation, eliminate them from your shortlist. If your goods are being shipped, this will be either as a full (sole use) steel shipping container load, or as a 'part load' or 'groupage'.

If you are taking the second option, estimates are based on the number of cubic metres your possessions need, and you may find that this number differs quite drastically from company to company. Unless you are moving only a few hundred miles (to northern France, for example), expect to pay £3,000 to £5,000 to move the possessions of a three-bedroom house – but considerably more if you are taking your car to North America or Australasia.

Removals companies recommend that the most efficient method of moving your goods is to have your own sole use

Jargon Buster

Advance Payment Protection Scheme
A scheme, run by the Overseas Group of the British Association of Removers (BAR), insuring customers against a loss of money or possessions, should the removals company they have employed cease to trade

Removals terms

Full (sole use) container load
Your possessions are transported in a 20ft or 40ft steel shipping container. Although the more expensive option, there are two advantages:
- **Exclusivity** – No one else's possessions are transported in the same container.
- **Speed** – The container is brought to your home, loaded with your possessions and shipped as soon as the next available container ship sails to your destination.

Part load or groupage
Your possessions are transported in a container along with those of others. The advantage of this option is that it's cheaper, although your belongings might take longer to be shipped if the removals firm has to wait to fill the container with other goods.

container (unless this is too much space for your needs). The sooner you get an estimate for the shipment of your goods, the more chance you have to adjust the inventory to ensure that it will all fit into one container.

Cars

The question of whether or not to take your car overseas is not always a straightforward yes or no answer. Even if you are simply taking your car to France, there are a number of bureaucratic issues to negotiate in order to legally register the vehicle.

In some other European countries, there are compliance tests for your vehicle and possible modification – and in all EU countries featured in this book bar Cyprus,

cars are left-hand drive, not right. You must also consider whether there will be access to sufficient spares in your new country to make the importation of your car a sensible decision. This issue is magnified if spares also need to be shipped to say, Australia or New Zealand, where the shipping costs will be the highest. Those moving to America and Canada must have their cars tested to ensure they reach the relevant safety standard; if not, modifications will be required. This expense, and the fact that vehicles are often much cheaper abroad, can make the whole issue something of a non-starter. In these cases, you might decide that only a cherished vintage car is worth the hassle.

 See Useful Addresses on pages 211–215 for contact details for the British Association of Removers, the *Fédération Internationale des Déménageurs Internationaux*, and the Overseas Moving Network International.

Insurance

Insurance is typically offered by international removals companies at 3 per cent of the value of the goods being shipped – so make sure you agree with the valuation. There are cheaper deals available through independent commercial brokers that offer marine insurance, especially if you are prepared to risk less comprehensive coverage.

However, bear in mind that a removals company will not want its reputation tarnished by refusing to pay a valid insurance claim, whereas if you use a broker you don't have such a card to play. Either way, the company offering the insurance must be registered with the Financial Services Authority (FSA), or offer the insurance of a company that is. This can be checked at: www.fsa.gov.uk

Choosing a removals company

Timing could be your deciding factor. You normally need to give removals companies at least a month's notice of your departure date. If you are moving during the summer, some companies may not be able to provide you with their services exactly when you want them. However, once the date is booked, experienced companies are often flexible enough for you to delay your move due to problems such as not selling your house or not receiving your visa when expected.

The removals company you contracted in the UK is responsible for every stage of your removal until your goods have been installed in your new abode. For goods that are shipped, the company will either have an overseas office or use a

10 questions to ask a removals company

1 Are you a member of the BAR Overseas Group and have FAIM accreditation?
2 Which removals company will be dealing with our possessions in the destination, and what accreditation do they have?
3 How will my possessions be transported?
4 How big will the van be and should I contact the local authorities to let them know when and where your vehicle will be parked?
5 Do you provide packing materials? If so, at what cost?
6 How much preparation will I be expected to do myself?
7 Do you dismantle furniture and take down curtains free of charge? If not, what is the charge?
8 Can I pack everything myself – and will this save me money?
9 Is there an additional charge for packing fragile and oddly shaped items?
10 Can I provide my own evaluation for insurance purposes?

destination partner – effectively another removals company based in the relevant country – to handle the importation and unpacking. It is essential that this partner has the correct level of expertise and belongs to the appropriate association (this could be a national-level organisation as well as FIDI, or OMNI, or both).

IMPORTATION DUTIES AND PAPERWORK

Your removals company should advise you on how to negotiate Customs when bringing your possessions into the country. Different countries have different requirements concerning duty and documentation.

Duty

EU

No duty or taxes will be payable on your imported possessions.

Australia, New Zealand, Canada, America

No duty is payable on goods that have been owned and used abroad for 12 months or more preceding the owner's arrival into the country. In Australia, new items bought within 12 months of importation must be declared to customs. In addition, duty and a Goods Service Tax (GST) will be charged at the relevant rate. In New Zealand, new items may be liable for duty and GST depending on the type of item. In Canada, all new items, or single items with a value over $10,000 will be subject to duty calculated on their value. Proof of purchase will be also required.

Documentation for household goods

EU, Australia, New Zealand, Canada, America

In all of the countries listed above, apart from Canada, you must attach a photocopy of the photograph and visa pages of your passport to your inventory list. In Canada, customs officials will want to see your actual passport. In addition, you will need to submit a Customs declaration form in some countries. Check this with your removals firm. In Australia this is called a B534 Customs form. In Canada it is the B4E declaration form. In America, you will need the Customs form 3299 Declaration for Free Entry of Unaccompanied Articles, the supplementary declaration form RC-159 and a Power of Attorney must be completed before your departure from the UK.

Personal and Retail Export Scheme

In some cases you can buy new goods in this country without paying the VAT, as long as you don't take delivery of the goods in this country (and they are delivered directly to your removers instead) and you complete the relevant forms. This applies to cars for those moving within and outside the EU, but only to other goods in the latter case. For further information, visit: www.hmrc.gov.uk

What to ship

Practical and emotional factors collide when deciding what items to take with you overseas. It will always be difficult to leave behind items that you have a strong emotional attachment to, but you must try and be as objective as possible when choosing what to take with you. For most items, you may want to make a simple decision: take it or leave it. In most cases, 'leave it' will mean selling the item, giving it away, or throwing it away.

However, it may be worth considering storing items and shipping them later. This might be useful if you plan to rent a small apartment while searching for a larger home. If you can't store items with friends or family, bear in mind that there will be a cost implication that should be factored into your budget.

It is also worth remembering that the more items you have shipped overseas, the greater the cost will be. At a certain point, you have to ask yourself if it would be better to sell some large items you were thinking of taking with you, which in turn saves money in shipment costs, then replace these items in your new destination. When considering what furniture you would like to ship, think about whether your furniture will suit the climate and surroundings of your new home. Think about how easy it will be for you to buy new furniture too. Perhaps it would be simpler or cheaper for you to ship your old belongings after all?

In order to make an informed decision on this subject, you'll need to estimate how much money could be raised by selling certain items, and how much they will cost to replace in your new country of residence. You could then calculate the difference in shipment cost by asking the removals estimators to provide two quotations – one for the items you are definitely taking and a second for those plus the items you are unsure about taking. These figures must be calculated relative to your likely earnings and cost of living abroad, taking into account that the exchange rate you use to estimate the cost of replacing items will almost certainly fluctuate.

It's also worth considering that anything you have shipped to your destination could take a day or two (parts of France), to more than a month (removals to New Zealand, Australia and parts of Canada and America can take more than a month to arrive). Unless you are moving into fully furnished rental accommodation, buying certain items upon arrival might make life easier than waiting weeks for your appliances to arrive.

But there are other practical issues to consider. Once you know what you want to take, ensure that you make the best of your chosen removals company's expert knowledge about which items you should pack and which you should leave to them. Some countries have stringent requirements covering how to clean items and to what standard. For example, the Australian Quarantine Services and the New Zealand Ministry of Agriculture and Fisheries carefully check that items likely to have come into contact with soil and vegetation are properly clean; extra costs will be incurred for any additional cleaning necessary.

Electrical items

When thinking about whether it is worth taking electrical items abroad, there are three factors to consider: electrical supply, plug type and television standard.

- Most appliances are built to tolerate current at a certain percentage above or below the rated voltage. Furthermore, some smaller items are often built to work with a dual currency, and can be switched between the two. Converters and transformers can also be bought for some items, such as laptops, but this can turn out to be expensive.
- With more than ten types of plug and socket in use in the world, it is almost certain that you'll have to change the plugs on any electrical items you take. If you're moving to Cyprus, you should escape this chore.
- There are three main TV standards in use throughout the world, but there are several types of each of these. A difference might not incapacitate your set completely, but could certainly limit its usefulness. Some modern sets have multi-frequency converters, which means that they can be switched over, but most do not.

Paperwork

Along with your packing inventory, which will be supplied by your international removers and should be copied twice for customs purposes, you'll need to gather together a range of other documents to take with you. These will help you obtain the necessary clearances, approvals and identifications you'll need shortly after arrival abroad.

Here's a list of the most essential documents you should take. It's a good idea to have two photocopies, preferably at least one of them in your hand luggage:

- Passport (valid for at least six months).
- Colour and black and white passport photos with white background (for identity cards or registering with social security etc).

- Proof of address, such as title deeds to your home or rental property, driving licence, or utility bills.
- Proof of funds – bank statement or mortgage statement, if applicable.
- Work contract, if applicable.
- Private health insurance policy, if necessary.
- Driving licence.
- Details of insurance history – number of years insured, no claims history, and details of any claims history. This might help you obtain a better car or home insurance deal than would otherwise have been the case.
- Glasses prescription, medical and dental records.
- Education certificates and schooling records for your children, if applicable.
- Birth and marriage certificates.
- Prescription or letter from your doctor about medication you are taking with you, if applicable.

Besides taking documentation overseas, there could be some merit to leaving copies of much of the above paperwork in the UK, especially if you still have a vested interest in the UK. You could do this with a trusted family member, friend or solicitor. Furthermore, should you retain assets in the UK, ensure that your will is up to date and left in safe hands – this could be with your solicitor or even a specialist will registry.

Health insurance

If you are bound for another EU country, you will have access to the same free healthcare as permanent residents of the country in question, providing you obtain form E106 from the Department for Work and Pensions. The E106 entitles the holder to free healthcare for up to two years, but will become null and void as soon as you register with the country's social security system.

If you are moving to America, you must obtain health insurance before you emigrate. With Canada, whether you need health insurance depends entirely on which province you are moving to.

Taking your pet

Moving your pet overseas certainly isn't cheap. The cost of vaccinations and micro-chipping could run to several hundred pounds, kennels run by professional pet transport firms cost £10-13 per night

Pet checklist

Before leaving the UK, your dog or cat must usually be:
- **Micro-chipped (a 'tattoo' suffices in a small number of countries).**
- **Vaccinated against rabies at least 21 days before entering another EU country. This doesn't apply for Australia, New Zealand, Canada and America as the UK is considered to be rabies-free. But your pet will need other vaccinations if you are bound for Australia see the Australian Quarantine and Inspection Service, www.aqis.gov.au**
- **Blood tested to confirm that the vaccination has taken effect.**
- **Covered by a pet passport.**

per animal, an International Air Transport Association-approved wooden or plastic air travel container will cost approximately £50-100, the cost of the flight will add hundreds of pounds more, and there is VAT payable on European destinations. If you'd rather do-it-yourself in an attempt to save money, bear in mind that the correct vaccinations and timing are crucial if you are to avoid your pet ending up in quarantine.

There may also be limits on the age of pets that can be imported (typically, they have to be at least three to six months old), and the number. Only Australia insists upon a quarantine of imported animals, which lasts for 30 days and costs approximately A$13.50 to A$18 per day. See the Australian Quarantine and Inspection Service (www.aqis.gov.au) for further information.

Packing your personal luggage

If you have job interviews to attend, ensure you are taking enough smart clothing with you, and if you have a job lined up ask the HR department of your employer what is considered to be suitable work attire there.

With lots of organising and sorting out to attend to, casual clothing suitable for fairly physical tasks will be a welcome addition as well. Of course, the closer your destination is to the UK, the sooner the rest of your possessions will catch up with you, so the question of what to pack is less pressing. Nonetheless, if you are flying out to your new life overseas, overweight bags will attract a surcharge from airlines, and excess baggage could cost between £50 and £100 per bag.

Child's play

Long journeys can be tough and incredibly boring for children. Taking the time to ensure their comfort and entertainment (perhaps something as simple as a small bag of new toys, crayons and colouring books), could make all the difference to their experience – and yours.

Emotional times

Friends and family, both adults and children, will often experience heightened emotions as your departure day looms. For those moving to Australia, New Zealand, Canada or America, the physical distance will make your emigration seem like even more of a rupture to those you are leaving behind.

However, it is essential that you continue to hold fast to your reasons for wanting to move abroad – if you can do this you have a greater chance of explaining to your family and friends that you believe you are making the right decision.

When planning the departure day itself, ask yourself if a big family send off at the airport is really such a good idea. Yes, it would no doubt be convenient to get free transport

For further information on carriers authorised to handle pets, as well as information on the pet passport scheme, and regulations per country, visit www.defra.gov.uk, the website of the Department for Environment, Food and Rural Affairs (Defra).

to the airport, but a collective outpouring of emotion just before you head towards the departure gate will sap your emotional strength at a time when you need as much fortitude as you can muster.

If you approach your relocation sensibly and considerately, you should be able to maximise the highs and minimise the lows you encounter when you are wrapping up your UK affairs.

Environmentally-friendly emigration

Emigration doesn't have to be a case of stamping your carbon footprint down hard. There are a number of steps you can take to make the emigration process as eco-friendly as possible. See box, right, for some green thinking.

Green tips

- **Choose a removals company making a concerted effort to go green. Such a company might use recycled packaging, fuel-efficient vehicles, and recycle both its own waste and yours in a way that minimises the environmental impact.**
- **Sell appliances that are relatively energy-inefficient, and buy low-energy appliances abroad.**
- **Fly green – some airlines offset their carbon emissions and some fly partially bio-fuel-powered planes.**
- **Alternatively, take the boat. Many cargo ships also take a limited number of passengers. This is neither cheap nor quick, but by some quirk of fate you might even be on the same ship as the rest of your possessions.**

What next?

Working through the issues raised in this chapter should enable you to wrap up your UK affairs in a sensible and timely fashion. Think about:

1 The issues that will affect the timing of your planned departure.
2 How much of a clean break you want to make.
3 What steps you need to take to sort out your finances prior to moving.

4 Arranging for your possessions to be moved or disposed of.
5 Strategies for coping with stress and possible heightened emotions.

Of course, when you reach your destination you'll have to unwrap your UK life and start turning it into one compatible with the country you'll then be calling home. Turn the page to understand what's involved in relocating successfully.

Relocation

With your UK life packed up, it's time to start all over
again in a country you might not know well. The reality
of the relocation process is often slow and uncertain,
so it is worth bracing yourself for what can be the hard,
uneasy effort of settling in.

Arrival

No matter which country you are moving to, the initial immigration processes you will be asked to complete on arrival are similar.

Regardless of whether you are moving within the EU or leaving its boundaries, you will have passport checks. In addition, if you are moving to a country outside of the EU, you will have customs forms to sign and a **landing card** to complete.

On arrival, if you are moving to a non-EU country, you will have your visa stamped. In some cases, proof of funds will be sought, so it makes sense to have with you recent bank statements to prove to the border agents that you have the means to fund yourself and your family upon arrival.

If your destination is outside of the EU,

America places great importance on a landing card. Its arrival–departure record card (I-94) is an essential part of the immigration procedure. After all, it is the date that customs officials stamp on this card – and not the duration stated on your visa – that determines whether you can enter the US and how long you can stay there.

you must fill in a customs declaration. In addition, if you are moving to Cyprus and are using a removals firm, they should supply you with a packing list or inventory. If you are emigrating with your partner, or children, or both, the head of the family can make a joint declaration for the rest of the family. Australian, New Zealand, Canadian and American Customs in particular expect a detailed list of the items you are importing.

There is usually a limit to the amount of currency (in cash or traveller's cheques) you can import without declaration. For most countries, this is 10,000 of the local currency, but there are exceptions. See the country profiles in Chapters 7-9 for further information.

GETTING STARTED

One of the most challenging aspects of being a newly arrived immigrant is finding reliable help with day-to-day matters. As with most aspects of moving abroad, the amount of assistance you can call upon differs greatly from country to country. Certainly, there is plenty of information available, but those moving within the EU may find that much of this information is stuck behind a language barrier. Moreover, not all of this information is as useful as it should be – even official sources of information can be out of date, and some acquaintances are more knowledgeable than others.

The following lists the sources of support and information that you might be able to call upon.

- **Immigration departments.** The Australian, Canadian and New Zealand immigration departments provide regionally-focused settlement support. This can range from a helpdesk number, to short-term accommodation, or having a person assigned to help you negotiate many of the unfamiliar everyday routines. In Quebec, new arrivals who speak English can attend a short session on integration. The US provides a downloadable guide and lists sources of assistance on the website www.welcometousa.gov, although most support is offered to immigrants whose limited English language proficiency could compromise their chances of settling successfully.
- **Town halls, visitors bureaux, tourism offices, chambers of commerce,** libraries and British embassies or consulates. You will find most of these are located in major cities and can all be a useful source of information on local services.
- **Clubs and organisations.** If you are moving to an area popular with British expatriates, chances are that there is a British-orientated club nearby that can help with information about schooling, healthcare services and many of the practical arrangements new arrivals face.
- **Expatriate websites.** Many Britons abroad use online communities with well-subscribed forums to ask questions, keep in touch and make social arrangements. Among the most established sites are www.angloinfo.com, www.britishexpats.com and www.expatforum.com.
- **Friends, family, neighbours and colleagues.** Many emigrants find the local population to be extremely helpful, so even if you don't have friends and family to help you settle in, you are not necessarily on your own.
- **Relocation services.** The services of relocation agents are available in many areas – either for a fee or as a complementary part of another service, such as estate agency. See overleaf for further information.

❝One of the biggest challenges is finding help with day-to-day matters.❞

RELOCATION SERVICES

The relocation process can be one of the most underestimated challenges of moving abroad. Although this is an area you can deal with alone, many people seek help. Tasks that seem almost second nature in the UK – such as arranging bank accounts, utilities, mobile phones – can suddenly take on a daunting aspect overseas. Despite this, relocation is a much-underserved profession. In fact, only if you work for a big international company which is going to the expense of relocating you to another country might you receive the services of a relocation consultant. Those dealing with the relocation of key personnel and, in some cases, whole companies, should belong to the European Relocation Association (EuRA), which was launched in 1998. In the spring of 2008, EuRA started carrying out the first audits of companies aiming to earn its seal of quality.

If you are not receiving help from corporate-focused relocation agents, there are various companies that offer help, usually for an hourly fee, for everything from finding you a house to picking you up from the airport and helping you fill in the necessary paperwork. There is no representative body for such services. Although some of the assistance offered is similar to that given by a relocation agent, the comparatively piecemeal basis of this assistance means that it is far cheaper and considerably less comprehensive than a corporate-sponsored relocation.

In addition, some estate agencies double as unofficial relocation consultants, often for no charge. The commercial sense of this is in building up customer loyalty in the hope of selling a property to you at some point. After all, if you settle easily in their area, you may want to buy a house there and may well choose to do so from them. This strategy is much more prevalent in Australia and Canada than it is elsewhere.

 For further information on the European Relocation Association, visit:
www.eura-relocation.com

Red tape

Once you have a roof over your head, if only temporarily, one of the first items on your list will be registering your presence with various government departments.

Exactly what official steps you should take after arrival depends entirely on the rules of the country. Even EU countries have their own ways of dealing with such matters, often within a specific time. For further information, see Chapters 7-9, or contact the immigration department of the country in question.

The following checklist summarises what you need to do shortly after your arrival:

- If relocating to the EU, you will probably need to apply for a resident's permit. You may also have to register with the local authorities.
- If you're moving to America, you must notify United States Citizenship and Immigration Services of your new address within ten days of arrival.
- Contact your local embassy or consulate and register your residency with them.
- Apply for a tax number.
- If you plan to work, notify the department of social security.
- Register with the national health service (if applicable).
- Sign up with a local doctor and dentist.
- Contact the driving licensing authority (if applicable).

Other key points to consider when applying for residence in the EU are listed opposite.

- **You are only given a set period of time in which to register or apply for residency paperwork.** In Germany, you must register within a week of taking up residence in a private dwelling, but other EU countries allow 30, 90 or 120 days to apply for the appropriate permit. A fine may await those who fail to observe the time limit, or have not registered at all.
- **You'll need a range of documents.** This includes your passport and passport-sized photos (Germany excepted). The documents you need may also include completed application forms, fees, proof of residence, birth certificates, marriage certificate, a record of good conduct provided by the police, evidence of financial independence and employment, or both, bank account details and health insurance.
- **Becoming a fully-fledged resident of an EU country is typically a two-stage process.** First, you qualify for a residence permit. Then after a qualifying period – usually three or five years – you can apply for permanent residence. This could afford you further benefits, such as complete access to social security and healthcare.

 Although it isn't mandatory, registering with the British consulate in your destination is a good idea so you can be found more easily in an emergency.

Case Study — Sally

In April 2002 at the age of 23, Sally emigrated to Marbella, Spain, to work for an international real estate company. Six years later, she has set up her own marketing business and owns a house in a town a few kilometres inland. Although happy with life abroad, Sally still marvels at the peculiarities of Spanish bureaucracy.

'From April 2007 Spain stopped issuing residency cards to EU nationals. The irritating thing is that the old residency card doubled up as ID and, at credit card size, was ideal for producing with your credit card to make transactions. The new certificate does not, so you have to have other ID on you to make credit card purchases – such as a passport if you're British, or a driving licence. Neither are documents you really want to carry at all times.' She continues: 'Applying for residency is becoming more and more of an arduous task these days. Marbella's main police station, the place to apply for national insurance numbers and residency permits, if you live on this part of the Costa del Sol, literally has queues of people waiting for up to four hours.'

Sally's advice is to 'get someone else to do it for you, like a *gestor*. Yes, it's likely you'll have to be seen in person at the police station but for around €100 a *gestor* will make sure your form is filled in correctly, you have all of the paperwork you need, they'll go to the bank, pay the fee and stand in the queue for you.'

TAX AND SOCIAL SECURITY

Obtaining a tax and social security identification number is one of the most important steps to take in establishing your presence overseas. In some cases it is vital to enable you to tick off other things on your list – such as opening a bank account.

However, France, Spain, Portugal, Italy, Germany, Cyprus, Australia, New Zealand, Canada and America all have their own unique tax and social security procedures, some of which differ quite markedly from the UK.

Some countries operate social security and national health systems in a similar way to the UK, but most don't. In some countries, employers register you for social security, but others will require you to do that yourself. And in some, you will need to register for a number that will act as both a tax and a social security reference. For details on specific countries, see Chapters 7, 8 and 9.

In some cases, registrations have to occur in a certain order. For example, in America and Canada you'll need the equivalent of a national insurance number in order to start work, while in Italy a tax number is needed before you apply for a job, buy a house or register a car. Attempting to do things in the wrong order could result in return visits to government departments and could be costly. In Australia and New Zealand, if you get a job before you obtain your tax number a higher rate of tax will be deducted from your initial pay packets (much like an emergency code in the UK).

Therefore, when arriving in your destination you must find answers to the following four questions (see box) in order to register both you and your family with as little fuss as possible.

For further information on the work of Spanish *gestores* and how they might help you, see page 116.

Registering for tax and social security

- How many government departments will I have to register with?
- What paperwork will I need in order to do this?
- Is there a certain order in which the registrations must be carried out?
- Is there a certain time limit in which I must or should complete the registrations?

Tax residence

Tax residence is defined through a number of factors, such as property ownership, the amount of time you have spent in the UK and abroad, and your employment situation. From a taxation perspective, emigrating is effectively moving from one tax residence to another. Depending on your circumstances, you could be considered tax resident in two countries simultaneously.

If you inform the Inland Revenue via form P85 that you are moving abroad permanently and can provide the necessary documentary evidence, you will typically be considered not resident or 'ordinarily resident'.

However, if you continue to own a property in the UK and the case you have made for your impending permanent residence abroad is not convincing enough, this could complicate matters. Nonetheless, if your property is rented on a long-term let, you won't be considered to be tax resident in the UK; if it isn't, you may have to be absent from the UK for a complete

tax year to be considered not resident in the UK for tax purposes.

The UK has double taxation treaties in place with the ten main countries featured in this book.

Retiring to the EU

EU citizens have the right to live in another EU country without working. Although a whole range of issues must be taken into account, the two key points to research most carefully are proof of funds and healthcare arrangements.

No matter which EU country you are moving to, you must prove that you have sufficient income – whether monthly pension payments or otherwise – to support yourself and your dependents. Proof of your retirement income may include:

- UK pension statements
- Bank statements
- Investment income statements.

Double taxation agreements

A double taxation agreement or treaty is an agreement between two countries whereby people who have income from both countries avoid paying tax twice on it. This also applies to income from pensions. Not all countries have such agreements, however, and details can also vary between countries. For further information contact Her Majesty's Revenue & Customs. In addition, the Department for Work and Pensions publishes a guide to social security agreements with 28 EEA countries and 16 other countries on its website. For details, see www.dwp.gov.uk

❝ Emigrating is effectively moving from one tax residence to another. ❞

Claiming benefits abroad

Britain has social security agreements with all European Economic Area (EEA) countries, and – in a more limited form – with New Zealand, Canada and America. These agreements cover some or all of the following:

- Continuing to pay National Insurance contributions, principally for the purposes of a state pension.
- Jobseeker's Allowance.
- Incapacity Benefit.
- Statutory Maternity Pay.
- Statutory Sick Pay.
- Medical services.

However, these agreements differ in content so it is essential you understand what benefits you could receive abroad and for how long. This will influence how soon you should register with the healthcare services in question, take out private healthcare insurance, or both.

❝Once you are a resident of another EEA country, are employed or self-employed and start contributing to the national social security scheme, you should be able to receive social security benefits. ❞

Agreements with EEA countries

Britain's social security agreement with the EEA countries means that your benefit rights are protected abroad so long as you:

- Are employed or self-employed.
- Have been employed or self-employed and have paid enough contributions in a given period to be eligible to receive benefits.
- Are a student studying or receiving vocational training leading to an officially recognised qualification – although, in this case, only limited rights arise.

Payments available from UK

Some benefits will be available to you in other EC countries if you have paid enough into the UK social security scheme. You can claim the contribution-based part of the Jobseeker's Allowance (JSA) for up to three months after leaving the UK, although you must have been registered as looking for work in the UK with a Job Centre or Job Centre Plus and receiving JSA for at least four weeks before you moved abroad. You must also follow your new country's rules about looking for work. This benefit will be paid by the employment services in your new country of residence.

Maternity Allowance and short-term Incapacity Benefit are also payable, as is long-term Sickness Benefit, but you will

To find out about Britain's social security agreements with other countries and the UK's social security programme, visit: www.dwp.gov.uk

only get UK Child Benefit if you remain employed by a UK employer.

Other benefits, such as Unemployment Benefit and Statutory Sick Pay are only available if you have worked for a UK company abroad, and are limited to a set period.

Payments available from your new country

Once you are a resident of another EEA country, are employed or self-employed and start contributing to the national social security scheme, you should be able to receive social security benefits. Sometimes, you need to have been paying social security contributions in your new country of residence for a certain period before you qualify to receive benefits. This is the case in Spain, and also applies to Australia, New Zealand, Canada and America.

Agreements with America, Canada, Australia and New Zealand

Britain's agreements with the four non-EU countries featured in this book are much more limited in scope (covering Statutory Sick Pay and Statutory Maternity Pay), and generally only apply if you are working for a UK employer for a limited duration.

Driving licences

If you drive a vehicle in the UK, chances are you'll want to drive abroad as well.

Rules concerning driving licences vary from country to country. Some allow your UK licence to be valid for a certain period of time, at the end of which you need to obtain a new licence. Others allow you to exchange your UK licence. Ensure that you check the regulations thoroughly before departing for your new country of residence.

Even though it isn't technically necessary, in practice an International Driving Permit (IDP) could be advantageous to you. If applying for an IDP by post, do so at least two weeks before your departure date. Alternatively, selected Post Offices will process IDP applications made in person.

Note that if you have a special occupational driving licence (such as for driving an articulated lorry), you will need to take a test in your new destination in order to obtain a new licence.

> **❝ Even though it isn't technically necessary, in practice an International Driving Permit (IDP) could be advantageous to you. ❞**

To find out about the International Driving Permit, visit: www.direct.gov.uk/motoring or the AA (Automobile Association) at www.theaa.com/getaway/idp/ and the RAC (Royal Automobile Club) at www.rac.co.uk/web/know-how

Healthcare

Very few countries offer free healthcare as comprehensively as the UK. With both your health and your bank balance to consider, this is one aspect of the relocation process you must not overlook.

Healthcare in the EU

If you have not already researched and organised any necessary healthcare cover before your move abroad, this is something you must address as soon as possible after your arrival.

Within the EEA, the **E106** provides you with up to two years of cover for necessary treatment in the EEA at the rate the locals would pay until you have become a resident or started work and signed up with social security (whichever happens first). The E106 must be obtained before you leave the UK from the Department for Work and Pensions.

You may find that private health insurance, which is popular in many European countries, is necessary as well. This is because public healthcare in many European countries is not fully subsidised – meaning that if you receive treatment you will have to pay a portion of the cost.

 As healthcare can be costly, it is imperative that you investigate the situation in your chosen country before you leave the UK – it is your responsibility to ensure that you have healthcare cover.

Healthcare outside the EU

Outside of Europe, reciprocal health agreements, such as that covered by the E106, do not exist. In Australia and New Zealand you are covered for state-provided healthcare as soon as you become a permanent resident, but you should register nonetheless. In Canada, you can register with some provincial and territorial health authorities on arrival and therefore be covered immediately, but for other authorities you have to wait three months and must therefore take out private medical insurance in the meantime (see page 188 for details).

In America, there is no general public

Jargon Buster

E106 A certificate issued by the Department for Work and Pensions entitling you to an extension of the European Health Insurance agreement cover for a period of up to two years

E121 Like the E106 form, this is available from the Department for Work and Pensions, but is for people in receipt of a UK state pension

Healthcare arrangements

EU citizens are entitled to healthcare cover throughout the EU on the proviso that:

- If you are under retirement age you obtain form E106 from the Department for Work and Pensions and register your presence with the relevant healthcare authority overseas. Note that an E106 is only valid for two years, so if after this point you have not reached retirement age you will need to take out private healthcare cover.
- If you have reached retirement age you need to obtain form E121 from the Department for Work and Pensions and register your presence with the relevant healthcare authority overseas. Form E121 is available to you for as long as you are claiming a state pension.
- Some public healthcare systems in other EU countries do not offer the comprehensive cover provided in the UK, so it is essential that you research what treatments you can expect to receive free of charge in your new country and make private healthcare insurance arrangements if necessary.

healthcare service, hence unless your US employer is dealing with this you must organise your own private healthcare insurance.

Finding a doctor

The type of healthcare provision in your new home country will determine what steps, if any, you must take to select and register with a general practitioner. Exactly what you must do depends upon the system in place. However, one or more of these scenarios will apply to you when you relocate overseas.

- A specific doctor will be allocated to you once you've registered with social security and visited the local offices of the national healthcare system.
- You will have a choice of GP, but do not have to register and are free to see any GP.

- You will have a choice of family doctor, and will have to register with one.

As in the UK, most countries have both public and private healthcare services. If this is the case, and you do not have private healthcare insurance, check that the doctor you want to consult is affiliated with the public healthcare system.

If you are moving to a non-English speaking region and wish to find a healthcare provider that speaks English, the British Embassy website can be a useful place to look. Alternatively you could employ a translator to help you. Further information on finding a translator can be found in Chapter 4.

❝ Check whether your doctor is affiliated with the public healthcare system. ❞

Banking and property

Although buying a property will almost certainly be your biggest outlay abroad, even the smallest purchase will require you to make the necessary banking arrangements.

BANKING

Even though it is advisable to take a UK bank or credit card and a combination of cash and traveller's cheques when you move abroad as it may take days if not weeks to obtain your new cards, you will soon have to open an account in your new country.

Although in many cases you cannot open a resident's bank account until you have the necessary visa, permit or card to show, waiting until you've emigrated to open a bank account can be the more complicated option. For example, if you move to New Zealand and open an account without first obtaining an Inland Revenue Department number, you'll be charged resident's withholding tax – and this could make your first few weeks in New Zealand that bit more difficult to afford.

If you haven't opened a bank account before you actually move abroad you will have to attend to at least one other item on the checklist of things to do on arrival before you can do so. In some cases, this is as simple as having proof of address (title deeds, a signed lease or a financial statement or utility bill with your address on it usually suffices), but in other cases you will need to have obtained at least a tax or social security or insurance number first. However, if you open a bank account from abroad before you become a resident then this situation is avoided.

ACCOMMODATION

The issue of whether you should rent or buy a property on arrival is one of the biggest decisions your new life abroad will face.

Clearly, there is no one piece of advice that is applicable to all situations. Therefore, you must weigh up your emotional needs with a level-headed assessment of the best financial course of action – an assessment that may well be based upon a prediction as to where exchange rates and property prices are heading.

 To find a UK lawyer specialising in International or EU law, contact the Law Society. See www.lawsociety.org.uk or see Useful Addresses, pages 211–215, for further details. For information on property, see the *Which? Essential Guide* to *Renting and Letting*.

Renting property

If you do not know the area you are moving to, renting property offers the opportunity to test out living in a certain area to see if local schools and amenities are suitable and whether any commute is tolerable.

Fewer financial ties to your new life abroad might also prove to be beneficial. Good preparation should help minimise the risk of your new life not working out as you had hoped. However, unforeseen circumstances or challenges could result in you wanting to return to the UK. In this case, not having a property to sell could be a blessing.

There are also financial considerations to account for. Renting first in a property market that is showing signs of deflation could prove to be a sound financial decision. However, renting in a market that is booming could cost you money on two counts – renting the property and having to pay much more for a property when you do decide to buy.

Fluctuations in the exchange rate will also impact on your decision on whether to rent or buy. You might wish to rent a property until you are able to receive a more favourable rate of exchange – giving you a greater amount of local currency from your original pounds sterling budget. If you do plan to sit tight and watch the exchange rates make sure that you also watch the housing market. If house prices rise faster than the exchange rate, you could still lose out.

Case Study | Louise and Rob

Louise and her husband Rob moved to the Costa del Sol, Spain, in 2005. Feeling that property was overpriced at the time, they lived in rented accommodation for their first two years in Spain.

However, by late 2007 property prices were beginning to decrease, so the couple decided it was a good opportunity to drive a hard bargain. After they enlisted the services of an estate agent, the couple were shown a property they loved, but could not quite afford. Negotiations followed, and because of the prevailing market conditions, the couple managed to get €80,000 knocked off the asking price.

Buying property

Although it is important to find somewhere to live, there can be both financial and emotional costs to either buying property hastily or renting for too long.

It is certainly tempting to buy a property as quickly as possible. After all, having a place to call your own to furnish and decorate as you see fit could help you feel at home. If you have children, this sense of stability might be beneficial to them as they settle into their new life abroad.

Ideally, though, you should only buy a property when you know the area in question well and can define exactly what location and price range is suitable. You might believe that thorough fact-finding trips to the area have enabled you to

Relocation

107

pinpoint the neighbourhood that's right for you, and therefore feel that buying a property fairly swiftly after your arrival is not a risk at all.

If you are moving to an area of a country where property prices are surging ahead, buying sooner rather than later also makes financial sense.

When you do decide it is the right time to buy a property abroad, it is essential that you research the buying process in your country of residence. Although every country has its own unique property transaction procedure, compared to the UK there are not necessarily any more pitfalls when buying a home abroad.

Arranging utility connections

Once you have bought a property, or have moved into rented accommodation, you'll need to ensure that the necessary utility companies are notified and contracts are in place. There are several ways you can go about doing this. If you have bought a resale property, you can generally take over the existing electricity supplies from the previous owners. You should organise a meter reading (check with the individual company whether they are happy for you to supply this, or if they want to send someone out to take a reading). You could also find a utilities company through price comparison websites, business telephone directories or asking advice from your neighbours. Different countries and even regions will have differing degrees of choice, but it normally pays to shop around. You may also have different energy options. For example oil and wood is used for heating in many countries and not all regions have access to gas. Remember that if you are buying a new property or the utility supplies have been disconnected, you may have to pay a reconnection fee. Be aware of differences in billing too. In Spain, for example, you effectively have to estimate how much electricity you think you will need. Although it is tempting to underestimate this amount, it could result in the power cutting out!

Get connected

Utilities to consider arranging include:
- **Electricity**
- **Gas**
- **Water**
- **Telephone**
- **Broadband internet connection**
- **Television (subscription, satellite or cable)**
- **Refuse collection**
- **Recycling collection.**

Settling in

Besides the important practical side of setting up your new life abroad, there are also more emotional considerations to take care of. Doing what you can to feel at home as soon as possible is of the utmost importance. Educational and employment needs are a crucial part of this process.

EDUCATION

If you have children of school age, you will need to find them a suitable school in your new home city, town or village.

Depending on their age, educational ability, where you move to and how much money you have to spend on their schooling, you could have a choice of sending them to a state school, private school or an international school.

When choosing a school for your children, consider the following points:

- **Where you live could determine your child's choice of schools.** Research catchment areas carefully before committing to a property purchase.
- **School starting and finishing ages, as well as terms, can vary.** As a result, your child may have to enter an academic year that is either higher or lower than their age dictates. Think about what will be best for both their educational and social development.

- **If you are moving to a country where English is not the first language, check to see if you have a choice of schools.** Some schools may only teach in the native tongue, others only in English. Although your child may struggle at first if immersed into an education conducted in a foreign language, the long-term gains could be considerable.
- **Religion may play an important part in your choice of school.** However, some countries – and some regions – offer more choice than others.

❝ Your children could attend a state, private or international school. ❞

 The Council of International Schools is a worldwide association of schools and post-secondary institutions. For details, visit: www.cois.org

COPING WITH CULTURE SHOCK

In addition to practical considerations, it is equally important that you cater for your emotional needs as well.

In the first few days and weeks of your relocation, it is natural to feel disorientated. After all, you are getting used to a society from scratch, and everything from social conventions to a lack of your favourite gravy granules in the supermarket can provoke a sense of what is called 'culture shock'.

During this period, it is inevitable that you will want to keep in regular communication with your friends and family back home, but you must also devote some time to establishing a new network of friends.

Therefore, it is essential that you and the family members who've moved abroad with you make an effort to meet the neighbours, join social and sporting clubs, get involved with community life and do some of the things you promised yourself you would do when you emigrated.

Ways to minimise culture shock

- Try to be as open-minded as possible. Avoid negative comparisons with the UK.
- Walk before you can run – don't put pressure on yourself by trying to overcome culture shock in an unrealistically short period of time.
- If moving to a country with another language, make a concerted attempt to learn it.
- Explore the local area, and start to build up a network of favourite places.
- Give yourself every opportunity to forge friendships with neighbours, colleagues or fellow students.
- Visit local groups and clubs to see if they might be suitable.
- Try local foods and start adjusting to local produce, brands and flavours – there might be some you love.
- Seek out people with whom you can find a shared experience such as other British people living locally.
- Set up your own 'Brits Abroad' club.

Some British emigrants like to throw themselves into the unique opportunities that their new country of residence affords them, while others prefer to socialise with British people living locally. In fact, some emigrants even set-up their own 'Brits Abroad' clubs.

Neither approach is better than the other – it is a question of working out what's right for you. Although you have new social customs to observe, many

❝ In the first few weeks, it is natural to feel disorientated. After all, you are getting used to a society from scratch. ❞

emigrants find their new neighbours and colleagues to be open and friendly, so make the best of the opportunities that present themselves.

It might be through such endeavours that you discover a new goal to focus on. The emigration process will have given you something to focus on and will have organised your thoughts and free time for months, if not years. Once you've successfully completed the relocation process, you might enjoy having new goals to strive for.

EMPLOYMENT

Unless the specifics of your situation mean you had to obtain employment as part of your immigration procedure, or your partner is the breadwinner, one of the first goals you must set yourself is finding suitable employment.

After all, being unemployed in the UK can make you feel that you don't have a stake in society, and these feelings will be exacerbated when you're settling into a country that you have not fully got to grips with.

Ideally, you will have already done the groundwork and your choice of destination will have been influenced by your economic opportunities there. In this case, you will have already done the following:

- Assessed the labour market in your new destination.
- Researched potential employers and likely salaries.
- Had your qualifications evaluated.
- Taken any steps necessary – such as obtaining licences or further qualifications – to boost your employability.

- Tailored your CV to the style prevalent in the labour market in question.

If you have not completed the list above, the sooner you can undertake these tasks the better.

❝ The emigration process will have occupied your free time for months, if not years. ❞

Of course, the new culture you will find yourself immersed in also extends to the workplace, and anything from a radically different management style to an increased emphasis on multitasking could pose new challenges for you – and

Case Study   Emily

Emily describes her move to Portugal in 1996 as a series of plans to tick off. 'We had to find a rental property, get a car, get our children into schools and find jobs'. She explains that although this period was very busy, her 'to do' list gave her a strong sense of purpose. Once these tasks were completed, however, Emily felt a huge sense of loss. 'I was too busy to think about what I was doing. Once I had more time, I think I became quite depressed. I missed my sisters and parents desperately.'

However, in spite of her darker moments, Emily believes that moving abroad has been worth all the effort.

perhaps induce feelings of culture shock. Even if you have found employment with an identical job description to the one you left in the UK, you will probably still find some significant differences. If you are prepared for this from the outset, you will find it easier to settle in and get used to your new way of working.

Either way, even if you feel you have solid contingency funds, it is best not to dip into these any more than is strictly necessary. The overall cost of living will almost not be as cheap as you'd hoped, and the longer you delay a return to work the harder it could become – both in terms of your employability and your willingness.

Just as settling into a new school will greatly increase a child's chances of feeling at home in their new environment, so entering suitable employment could be a significant step in helping you feel your new life abroad is falling into place.

What next?

The periods shortly before you emigrate and immediately after are the busiest you will have to face. Tasks to complete range from the practical to the bureaucratic and will include dealing with the emotional strain of settling in to a new culture.

The exact nature of these issues and challenges depends upon your own attributes and circumstances and – crucially – your destination of choice.

However, a checklist might read as opposite.

- Complete the bureaucracy of Customs, Immigration and other related departments, such as Social Security.
- Ensure you are covered for appropriate levels of healthcare.
- Organise your finances and find somewhere to live.
- Settle into your new local community.

The next chapters look in greater detail at some of the countries in Europe and from the other continents.

Europe

Europe as a continent comprises 47 countries. Of these, 27 are also members of the political and economic alliance, the European Union (EU). The EU is the world's biggest trading power. When it comes to personal prosperity, Europe offers the highest concentration of economically developed countries anywhere in the world.

Spain

Spain owes much of its popularity with British expatriates to its sandy Mediterranean coast, its warm, year-round climate and relaxed lifestyle.

Factfile

Area: 504,030 square kilometres
Population: 45.2 million
Capital: Madrid
Number of British nationals resident for a year or longer: 761,000
Gross Domestic Product (per head): US$29,900

OVERVIEW

In addition to a pleasant climate, affordable cost of living and high quality of healthcare, Spain also boasts colourful fiestas, art and architectural riches, distinctive food and wine, a laid-back sense of timekeeping, and short travel times to and from the UK.

When the Balearic and Canary Islands are taken into account, Spain is almost twice the size of the UK, with a landmass which is divided into 19 autonomous regions including Andalusia, Catalonia and Valencia.

After having lived in the UK, you may find that Spain's general approach to timekeeping comes as a surprise. In fact some expats have reported that it's impossible to appreciate how obsessed Britain is with punctuality until you have experienced how relaxed Spaniards can be about turning up when agreed.

MEDITERRANEAN SPAIN

This region stretches from the Costa Brava in the northeast to Gibraltar in the south; it also includes the Balearic Islands.

The beaches, climate, property developments, golf courses and marinas of the Costas are a British migrant magnet. Today even the hotter, drier Costas of Murcia and Almeria have become built-up as, Britons in particular, take advantage of the affordable property on offer.

Despite this increasing foreign presence, Mediterranean Spain has great cultural strengths. The cities of Malaga and Sevilla, in particular, host some of Spain's most traditional fiestas.

The area is also home to Barcelona, the country's second-largest city but very much the beating heart of Catalonia – a fiercely independent region with its own language (Catalan).

Barcelona

Barcelona, with its *modernista* architecture popularised by Antoni Gaudi, is Spain's cultural cutting edge. Its colourful life is best exemplified by Las Ramblas, a café-lined pedestrian thoroughfare that skirts the Gothic Quarter and connects the city centre with the seafront.

Barcelona's diverse economy provides its 1.6 million residents with plenty of opportunities. Offering a strong industrial base, the city also has strengths in construction, tourism and clothing, but air transport, research and development, public administration and healthcare are also important sectors.

CENTRAL SPAIN

Central Spain is situated on a plateau rising several hundred metres above sea level and is flanked by mountain ranges. This location means it is dry all year round but cold in the winter and sometimes incredibly hot in the summer. Central Spain is home to the historic cities of Toledo, Segovia and Madrid, the Spanish capital. Madrid is the heartland of Castilian culture and language – Spain's official language.

Madrid

Madrid has a population of 3.1 million, a figure which includes the largest foreign-born population in Spain. The city is Spain's financial powerhouse. Its economic strengths are retail, construction, wholesale trade, hospitality, property activities, and transport, but it also has a comparatively high number of businesses specialising in publishing and graphic arts, technology, the manufacture of metal products, furniture and food.

Supplementing its economic clout and sprawling, industrial character, is a range of world-class leisure activities – with art galleries, flamenco and bullfighting events of particular note.

Due to its inland location high on a plateau, Madrid is a stiflingly hot city in the height of summer, so *Madrileños* seek shade and siesta in the middle of the day – a break that gives them the energy to keep eating and partying until the early hours. The Sierra de Guadarrama, an hour away from Madrid, provides a complete change of scenery.

ATLANTIC SPAIN

This northwestern corner is by far the most verdant area of Spain. It is also home to two distinctive cultures: Basque and Galician.

Geographically speaking, the Costa de la Luz (situated between the Costa del Sol and Portugal's Algarve) and the Canary Islands (which are located off the northwest coast of Africa) are also part of Atlantic Spain. However, with less rain and warmer summers than is typical of northwestern Spain, these two areas have more in common with Mediterranean Spain.

POPULAR DESTINATIONS

The Costa del Sol and Costa Blanca bask in temperatures that rarely drop below 20°C for most of the year, boast miles of sandy beaches, and are extensively developed for overseas property buyers and holidaymakers alike. These two Costas offer something of a home from home for many British expats. There are British pubs serving Sunday roasts and showing football matches, cafés serving all day breakfasts, expat newspapers and clubs, English-language schools, British estate agents, British tradespeople to call upon, even cricket and bowling clubs, and more than enough golf courses.

Many of these English-speaking communities offer a range of employment opportunities for those who have little or no knowledge of Spanish. From teaching, to construction work, to setting up a business that caters specifically to British holidaymakers and expats, there are plenty of opportunities for those seeking employment or self-employment.

IMMIGRATION

Spain no longer issues residency cards (*targetas de residencias*) to EU nationals, who may live and work in Spain using their EU passport. Those making a permanent move to Spain should apply for a residency permit (*permiso de residencia*) at a national police station (*comisarias de policia nacional*) with an immigration office (*oficina de extranjeros*). Although this isn't compulsory for those who are economically active, in practice having a permit can help with other bureaucratic matters.

Before you apply for a residence permit, you should obtain a *certificado de empadronamiento* or *padrón* from the local council offices, which proves you live in Spain. You'll need your passport and utility bills showing your address. You then need to take this certificate to the national police station with the following:

- Original and copy of completed and signed application forms.
- Three colour passport photos.
- Passport and copy of personal details.
- Proof of address – title deeds to your property, rental contract, or utility bills.
- Proof that you have paid the permit's fees, which must be paid via a bank.

- A medical certificate (*certificado medico*) from any Spanish doctor.
- A certificate of good conduct (*certificado de antecedents penales*) from your local police authority in the UK.
- If you are married, a certificate related to your marital status, translated into Spanish.

❝ There might be several weeks between applying for and receiving residency paperwork. ❞

In addition, your dependents require passports and photographs. Retirees will also require proof that they belong to a private health insurance scheme valid in Spain, or proof that they are entitled to treatment by the Spanish public health system, as well as evidence of sufficient funds (for example, receipt of a regular income such as a pension).

There might be several weeks between applying for and receiving the above paperwork, but you should be given a temporary document to use in the meantime.

If you don't already have a foreigner's identification number, a *Número de Identificación de Extranjero* (NIE), you'll get one at the same time. An NIE is the Spanish equivalent of a National Insurance number; it is needed to purchase property, open a bank account and arrange credit terms.

Don't fancy dealing with the paperwork yourself? One option you have is to employ a company set up to assist foreigners with such matters. British Chambers of Commerce websites are a good starting point, as companies offering relocation and translation services sometimes also provide help with residency paperwork. Free advice might also be available through a property agent who uses their first-hand knowledge of bureaucracy in the country in question as a competitive advantage; expat clubs in the area and country-specific web forums are also possible sources of help and support.

DRIVING

Due to reciprocal agreements, UK photocard driving licences (*permisos de conducciónes*) are recognised in Spain, but must be stamped and registered at a provincial traffic headquarters (*jefatura provincial de tráfico*). However, exchanging your UK licence for a Spanish one makes dealing with the Spanish transport police easier in the event of any inspections or infringements.

HEALTHCARE AND SOCIAL SECURITY

Those who live and work in Spain must pay into the Spanish social security (*Seguridad Social*) system. Contributions (*cuotas*) are calculated as a percentage of your taxable income. If your employer doesn't register you, you must apply to the local social security office with passport, proof of residence, birth certificate, and marriage certificate if applicable. You may need to get these certificates translated first. You will then receive a health card (*tarjeta sanitaria*), which you must present to your local health centre in order to register there.

Public health benefits under the national health system (*Instituto Nacional de la*

Customs and money

The maximum amount of cash and traveller's cheques you can bring into Spain at any one time without declaring it is €6,000.

"Social security contributions are calculated as a percentage of your taxable income. "

117

Salud) include general and specialist medical care, hospitalisation, subsidised medicines and basic dental work.

UK pensioners moving to Spain can receive their UK pension in Spain and will be entitled to receive the same level of free medical treatment as Spanish pensioners. This is provided that you obtain form E121 from the Pensions Service and take it to the local office of the *Instituto Nacional de la Seguridad Social* (INSS) with your residence card and passport. You will receive a *tarjeta de afiliación* card and be assigned to a medical centre (*ambulatorio*).

The INSS provides benefits such as healthcare, industrial injury, unemployment insurance, pension, invalidity and death benefits. To qualify, you must have been employed in Spain for a limited period and have reached a minimum level of social security contributions. If you are self-employed, you must register with the INSS as an *autónomo* (a self-employed person).

Healthcare provision in Valencia

The Valencia provincial government has introduced a law (*Ley de Aseguramiento Sanitario*) which aims to control free access to the health system in the autonomous region of Valencia. Those most affected are retired expats who do not have an E121 or E106 or who do not pay Spanish social security contributions. These people are advised to take out private health insurance. In addition, the Valencia government has confirmed that the new law has scope for new conditions to be introduced. For the latest information on developments in Valencia, see the website of the British Embassy in Madrid, www.britishembassy.gov.uk/spain

EDUCATION

Spain's state education system is conducted in Castilian, but depending on the region, classes are also taken in Catalan, Basque and Galician. If you prefer your children to be educated in English, private and international schools are typically situated in the biggest cities and those areas with a large expat population.

School years

- Pre-school (*educación infantil*), ages 3-5 (optional, though 9 out of 10 attend).
- Primary school (*escuela primaria*), ages of 6-12.
- Secondary school (*secundaria*), ages 12-16. Becoming a graduate (*graduado*) of secondary education is a minimum requirement of many jobs.
- Sixth form, 16-18. The two-year baccalaureate (*bachillerato*), is preparation for higher education. Vocational training (*formación professional*) prepares students for the world of work.
- Higher education. There are universities (*universidades*) across Spain; the equivalent of an undergraduate degree (*licencia*) takes three years.

BANKING AND FINANCE

Banking

Spanish banks are either clearing banks (*bancos*), which usually offer cheque books (*talonarios*), or savings banks (*cajas de ahorras*), which typically record your transactions in a savings book (*libreta de ahorras*). Both types will usually offer a bank card for use at cashpoints. Accounts (*cuenta*) are either current (*corriente*) or savings (*ahorra*) accounts. A passport, address, NIE (*Número de Identificación de Extranjero*), initial deposit and a residence permit or evidence of employment in Spain should suffice for you to open a resident's account. Note that a certain number of credit card, cheque, standing order and direct debit transactions are usually granted for an annual fee, but beyond this threshold there is typically a charge per transaction.

Taxation

The Spanish tax year runs from 1 January to 31 December, and as a resident it will be your responsibility to file an annual tax return with the *Agencia Tributaria* (tax office). Income tax, *impuesto sobre la renta de las personas físicas* (IRPF), is divided into four bands ranging (in total with combined national and regional taxation) from 24 per cent to 43 per cent of your annual income. Savings, including capital gains are taxed at a single flat rate of 18 per cent. Dividends are also taxed at 18 per cent over allowances.

Wealth tax (*impuesto sobre el patrimonio*) is levied on total assets amounting to more than €108,182, and ranges from 0.2 per cent to 2.5 per cent, although the average family is unlikely to pay more than 0.5 per cent per annum. If you own property, you will also be subject to property tax, which is normally levied locally. Spain has a double taxation agreement with the UK, ensuring you will not be taxed twice on your income.

PROPERTY MARKET

Driven by thousands of overseas buyers snapping up residences and holiday homes every year, Spain's property market has achieved phenomenal growth over the last decade. As a result, many of the areas popular with British people moving to Spain – in particular, the Balearic Islands and the province of Malaga – now have some of the highest property prices in the country, although the Basque country, Madrid and Barcelona have the highest prices of all.

Concerned that overseas buyers might be losing confidence in the Spanish property market, in early 2008 the government announced plans to increase regulation and reform wealth and inheritance taxes.

The Spanish government has increasingly become involved in areas concerning property. For example, it is currently considering the retroactive application of a law passed in 1988 that made it illegal to build anything within 495 metres of the shoreline. According to a recent report by Spain's Environment Ministry, 40 per cent of the country's Mediterranean coastline is built up.

 Property prices in many regions of Spain are stalling or decreasing. The International Monetary Fund has warned that an overall drop in prices of 15–20 per cent is possible.

Mortgages

Mortgages (*hipotecas*) are available from most Spanish banks, almost all of which are repayment mortgages. The typical term of a *hipoteca* is 15 years, and banks will usually lend a maximum of 80 per cent of the value of the property.

How to buy

There are several types of contractual agreements with the seller, such as a reservation contract (*documento de reserva*), deposit agreement (*contrato de arras*) and option to buy agreement (*contrato de opción de compra*), but the most secure agreement is a properly negotiated bilateral private sale agreement (*contrato privado de compraventa*).

This contract specifies the agreed price, date and conditions under which the transaction will take place. As this contract is binding, ensure that it is checked by a lawyer and that escape clauses (*condiciones resolutorias*) are in place. When the contract is signed, a deposit (*arras*) of 10 per cent is generally payable.

Off-plan purchases may require a bigger deposit, and a commitment to pay instalments of up to 33 per cent of the purchase price as the building work takes place. As there is a risk of the developer being unable to complete the project, ensure you have appropriate guarantees or insurance in place.

Those buying a property that is part of a complex will more than likely become part of a community of owners (*comunidad de proprietarios*). If so, you must check the rules (*reglementos*) attached to this, such as maintaining the swimming pools, gardens and communal spaces.

The document that legally transfers the property into your ownership is the deed of sale (*escritura de compraventa*). This must be signed in the presence of a notary (*notario*), who is responsible for recording your ownership in the property register (*registro de la propriedad*) and the tax register (*registro catastral*).

Fees and taxes

- **Estate agents' fees** typically range from 6 per cent to 10 per cent of the property's value. Clarify with an agent who pays these fees and how much should be paid.
- **VAT** (*impuesto sobre el valor anadido*) is payable on new-builds and those sold on before completion at 7-8 per cent.
- **Property transfer tax** (*impuesto sobre transmisiones patrimonial*) is charged at 6-7 per cent on resale properties (excluding those sold before completion).
- **Stamp duty** (*impuesto sobe actos jurídicos documentados*) of 0.5 per cent to 1 per cent is payable on properties subject to VAT.

Property issues in Valencia

A law passed in the autonomous region of Valencia in 1994 means that land classed as *suelo rústico* (rural land) can be redesignated as *urbanizable* and therefore built on. Some British property owners have already had their land repurchased by developers as a result, often at well below market value, and the properties of others are still very much under threat until the issue is resolved.

- **Notary fees** are approximately 0.5 per cent.
- **Legal fees** are typically 1 per cent to 1.5 per cent.

Property taxes

- **Property tax** (*impuesto sobre los bienes inmuebles urbana/rústica*) is payable to the local council by whomever is resident in the property on 1 January, and ranges from 0.3 per cent to 1.7 per cent. Variables are the size of the property in square metres, location, quality of construction and the rates charged by the municipality itself.
- **Refuse and drainage tax** (*basura y alcantarillado*) can range from €50 to €450 per annum.

UTILITIES

Electricity

If you have a new property, it must be connected to the electricity supply, which can be arranged through an electrician or the energy supplier. You will need a connection certificate (*boletin de enganache*) and a first occupation licence (*licencia de primera ocupación*), available from the town hall.

If your property isn't new, ask the electricity supplier to take a special meter reading so you don't pay the previous owner's bill, and sign the contract over into your name. In order to carry out this task, you'll need your NIE, passport and bank details. When setting up a contract, you have to estimate how much electricity you think you need, and are then billed on a bi-monthly basis.

Most properties in Spain are connected to the standard 220v supply, but some older properties may still be wired to run on 110v. You will need to convert such a property – an undertaking that is expensive.

Gas

Most of Spain's major cities are now connected to a mains gas supply, in which case the procedure for connection is similar to electricity outlined above. However, many homes still use bottled gas (*butano*). Arranging a regular supply of gas will require a safety check of the property by your local authorised distributor, a deposit and the signing of a contract with your supplier.

Water

Water supply is generally metered, and a monthly or quarterly standing charge is common. To register the contract in your name, you generally have to visit the local council taking property deeds and proof of identification. If the property is new, you'll need an official water installation certificate (*boletin del aqua*) as well. In some properties, the developer retains control over the water supply and can charge well over the cost price for this service.

 A growing challenge for Barcelona is providing enough water for its residents. In early 2008, Spain's Water Agency reported that reservoirs in Catalonia are less than 20 per cent full, and in order to address the situation desalination plants are being built and water is being imported from elsewhere in Spain.

Telephone

If your property is new, you will need a landline installed by Telefónica, which can be organised at one of the company's offices or a telephone shop. You will need to prove your address with property deeds and a utility bill. Once this is done, there is plenty of choice of tariffs.

Television

There is no TV licence in Spain. There are a range of free and subscription services including digital and analogue terrestrial, cable and satellite channels.

FINDING PROFESSIONALS

- The British Embassy in Spain provides a directory of English-speaking services, such as lawyers – www.britishembassy.gov.uk/spain
- The British Chamber of Commerce in Spain has a directory of members working in a range of fields, such as translation and building services; it can also provide help for those setting up a business – www.britishchamberspain.com
- Estate agents should be members of the *Gestores Intermediarios en Promociones de Edificaciones* or the *Agentes de la Propriedad Inmobiliaria* – www.gipe.es and www.consejocoapis.org
- To find a surveyor contact the Professional Association of Valuation Companies (*Asociacion Profesional De Sociedades De Valoracion*) at www.atasa.com
- For an architect see the General Council of Technical Architects (*Consejo General De La Arquitectura Técnica De España*) at www.arquitectura-tecnica.com

Web resources

- Information on residency paperwork is available at the Spanish Interior Ministry website – www.mir.es The site also contains links to provincial police headquarters.
- For information on Spain's health service, see the Spanish National Institute of Health website – www.ingesa.msc.es
- Details on social security benefits can be found on the website of the Spanish Institute of Social Security – www.seg-social.es
- For information on confirming the equivalence of your qualifications, visit the Spanish Ministry of Education and Science – www.mec.es
- To access fact sheets on various aspects of buying property in Spain, visit the National Association of European Citizens at www.c-euro.org
- A list of English-speaking schools in Spain is available at www.spain.english-schools.org
- Visit www.bbc.co.uk/languages or www.learndirect.co.uk to find out about Spanish courses online and in the UK.
- For information about property problems in Valencia, visit www.abusos-no.org

France

Fiercely proud and protective of its own culture, France will appeal most to those who want to become completely immersed in another way of life.

Factfile

Area: 674,843 square kilometres
Population: 61.6 million
Capital: Paris
Number of British nationals resident for a year or longer: 200,000
Gross Domestic Product (per head): US$33,275

OVERVIEW

France has many geographical, architectural, gastronomic and cultural faces. Wherever you choose to live, you'll be surrounded by a culture with a pronounced regional flavour – but will still be in easy reach of a national health service that ranks among the best in the world. Recently, the proliferation of low-cost flights to almost every area of France means that more areas of the country are being discovered by British holidaymakers, many of whom go on to dream of making a permanent move across the Channel.

At two-and-a-half times the size of the UK, there is certainly plenty to discover. Mainland France is divided into 22 regions, which are themselves divided into a total of 96 *départements*.

In terms of culture shock, you may find the closure of shops and offices takes some getting used to. France takes its food seriously and that usually means providing a long-enough lunch hour for everyone to take a proper meal in the middle of the day. This in turn means that many shops, particularly those outside big cities, and most businesses shut down for two hours in the middle of every day. Most shops, including supermarkets, also stay closed on Sundays.

COASTAL FRANCE

The regions facing the Channel – Pas-de-Calais, Normandy and Brittany – all have attractive coastlines, but share a climate that's the coolest of the French coastal areas. Away from the ports and memorials of the Second World War, these regions offer picturesque harbours, rolling countryside, medieval architecture, quiet villages and strong regional products such as Camembert and Calvados.

The Atlantic coastline becomes progressively warmer as it runs from western Brittany down through the Pays-de-Loire, Poitou-Charente and reaches Aquitaine. Blessed with great beaches and seafood, Atlantic France is scattered with chateaux and bisected by rivers winding through attractive countryside. It is home to Bordeaux and the classic French wine, claret.

The Mediterranean coastline is the warmest of the three coastal areas. Nice, for example, enjoys several months of temperature above 20°C, and the Côte d'Azur in general has fantastic beaches. Those looking for the sunniest areas of France to move to should set their sights on Languedoc-Roussillon and Provence-Alpes-Côte d'Azur, although property prices here are among the highest in France.

 In March 2008, Environment ministers of 14 countries agreed in principle to ban the construction of commercial and residential developments within 100 metres of the Mediterranean's 29,000-mile coastline.

MOUNTAINOUS FRANCE

These areas are dominated by two great ranges – the Alps, to the southeast, and the Pyrenees in the southwest. The Jura mountains in the east also make their mark on French landscape and identity. Besides offering some of the best winter sports, summertime hiking and alpine scenery in Europe, the tectonic folds of the Rhône-Alpes, Midi-Pyrenees and Franche-Comté regions are also home to some of the most spiritedly independent manifestations of French culture. The culture of neighbouring countries is also evident in many border areas, such as the German-influenced Alsace and the fact that Catalan is spoken in some areas of the southwest.

Global warming and the Alps

In 2007, the Organisation for Economic Co-operation and Development (OECD) published a report entitled *Climate Change in the European Alps*. This report looked at how many ski areas are naturally snow reliable and likely to remain so under various climate change projections. Based on a rule of thumb that 100 days of 30 centimetres of natural snow cover per season makes a resort snow reliable, the report projected that up to one third of Alpine ski resorts may no longer be naturally snow reliable by 2050.

THE INTERIOR

The French interior, with its rolling pastures, beautiful valleys and lakes, is often referred to as *France Profonde* and is where those seeking a rural idyll come to start over. Dominated by the Loire, Burgundy, Limousin and Auvergne regions, here culinary tradition is found side-by-side with historical riches and pockets of an avowedly traditional way of living. This combination of stunning scenery and provincial lifestyle can also be found in the inland *départements* of the southern coastal regions – particularly Aquitaine, Languedoc -Roussillon and Provence-Alpes-Côte d'Azur.

Village life under threat?

One of the most appealing features of French life is that it retains a strong local character, right down to the independent retailers found on village high streets. However, in April 2008 the French government outlined plans to cut through regulation it believes is restricting the growth of the retail market. This prompted concerns that such a move would lead to big international retailers flooding France – which would, in turn, sound a death knell for small village shops. These form the heart of the rural communities that many Britons find irresistible.

POPULAR DESTINATIONS

Dordogne

Offering beautiful countryside, great wines, truffles and fois gras, the Dordogne was one of the first areas of France to capture the imagination of Britons looking to make a home outside the UK. Alluringly rural, and with affordable property (at that time), the first wave of Britons to move to France got to work restoring properties and opening *gîtes* (small holiday homes) as a way of making a living.

Provence

The charms and challenges of moving to rural France were highlighted by Peter Mayle's book *A Year in Provence* (1989), which triggered an influx of Britons into the south of France. However, this popularity led to rocketing property prices in Provence as it had in the Dordogne, and as a result those chasing a similar dream are now heading into neighbouring regions such as Limousin and Languedoc-Roussillon – a process greatly aided by ever-improving transport links between the UK and France.

Normandy, Brittany and the big cities

Improved transport links have also opened up northern France to those who want to live south of the Channel but continue their career in the UK. Technological developments have also increased our choice of destination. Internet connections mean that Britons in a range of professions have been able to live in France whilst working remotely for companies based elsewhere.

Those moving to France to further their career are drawn to the big cities, such as Nantes, Lyon and – especially – Paris.

> **❝ The Dordogne was one of the first areas of France to capture the imagination of Britons looking to make a home outside the UK. ❞**

Paris

Paris is situated in the Ile-de-France region, which is home to 11 million people and boasts the highest wages in the country. The base for France's biggest enterprises, as well as branches of many multinational companies, Paris also has a preponderance of communication and administration-based companies. Twenty-five per cent of the French workforce is employed in the public sector – and the Parisian workforce is no different. Of course, the city also offers world-class cuisine and culture.

IMMIGRATION

France no longer insists on EU nationals obtaining residency cards (*cartes de séjour*); you can live and work in France using your EU passport. Although in theory, applying for a *carte de séjour* is optional, it is worth checking the rules in your area in case the departmental *préfecture* in question still fines those who are unable to produce one when requested. If you need or decide to apply for a *carte de séjour*, you must find out where you need to make the application. This is generally made to the district police station (*préfecture de police*), in towns that have them, or the local town hall in small towns or the police station (*gendarmerie/commissariat de police*) in large towns and cities.

Within three months of living in the country, you should register as a resident (*enregistrement des citoyens européens*). To register, you must report to the town hall (*Mairie*) with your passport and proof of address. This information is recorded and a receipt issued (*attestation d'enregistrement*). This procedure also applies to family members (including children under 21).

Which permit you apply for depends upon your status: working and receiving an income in France (*actif*) or retired or studying (*inactif*). The permit for *actif* residents is the 'EC all occupations' (*CE toutes activités professionnelles*). An application requires the following:

- Valid passport.
- Employment contract or a declaration of employment from the employer. The self-employed require proof of

registration in a trade or profession from the Chamber of Trades (*Chambre de Métiers*), Chamber of Commerce (*Chambre de Commerce*), or proof of registration as self-employed (*Profession Libérale*) from the main social security office (*Union de recouvrement des cotisations de sécurité sociale et d'allocations*).

The permit for *inactif* residents is the *carte de séjour* for a retired person and an EC Student (*CE étudiant*); an application requires the following:

- Valid passport.
- Proof of medical insurance.
- Proof of sufficient financial resources for the applicant and their dependent family members in France.

Additionally, and in the case of both applications, family members require valid passports, documents proving the family relationship and, in some cases, proving financial resources. Note that some documents may need to be translated by a notarised translator or public notary.

Once you have provided all the required documentation you will be given a date to collect your permit. In the meantime you will be issued with temporary authorisation (*récipissé de demande de carte de séjour*)

Customs and money

The maximum amount of cash and traveller's cheques you can bring into France without declaring it is €10,000.

or an attestation of residence application (*attestation d'application de residence*). This should be kept as evidence you have applied for your residence permit.

DRIVING

In theory, a 1996 EU directive means that driving licences (*permis*) issued in the UK will suffice in France. However, there are three good reasons to obtain a French driving licence:

1 Many French officials either do not know about the directive or do not act in accordance with it.
2 If you commit an offence, you'll need a French licence to continue driving.
3 It's easier to obtain insurance.

To obtain a French driving licence, apply to your local *préfecture*.

HEALTHCARE AND SOCIAL SECURITY

A European Health Insurance Card becomes invalid when you become a resident. Therefore, those who live and work in France must pay into the French social security system (*sécurité sociale*). This is funded by taxes on income.

If you have salaried employment or are earning a sufficient amount through self-employment you must, after 12 months, start to contribute to this system. An E106 form (available from the Department for

Work and Pensions in the UK and valid for two years) covers you until this point.

If your employer doesn't register you, go to your local primary sickness insurance office *Caisse Primaire d'Assurance Maladie* (CPAM) with your passport, French residency document, proof of residence and documents proving family relationships where applicable (these certificates might need to be translated first). You will then receive a health card (*carte vitale*), which will show your name and social security number.

Under France's universal health cover system, *Couvreture Maladie Universelle* (CMU), you pay the majority of healthcare providers upfront and are then reimbursed via your health card. The French social security system defines the cost of virtually every type of medical treatment using the official or conventional rate (*tarif de convention*) and reimburses medical expenses at an average of 70 per cent of this rate. However, this is only the case where you are seen by doctors and treated in hospitals that are part of the state healthcare system: look for the word *conventionné*, this refers to doctors and hospitals that have an agreement with the state. Private clinics are unlikely to have such an arrangement, so refunds will be lower and even additional private insurance may not cover you. Most people take out what is known as a 'top-up' policy (*complémentaire* or *mutuelle*) to cover the amount not reimbursed by the state. With many policies you will be given a top-up insurance card (*carte blanche*),

For France's web portal, *Portail de la Sécurité Sociale*, which contains information on its social security system and links to related government departments, see www.securite-sociale.fr

through which your treatment will be recorded and the appropriate balance reimbursed.

If you are not working or are on a low income and you have been resident in France for more than three months you can apply for CMU coverage.

British retirees resident in France who have reached the state pension age are also eligible to use the state healthcare system under the same terms, but must provide their local CPAM with form E121, available from the UK Pensions Service. Retirees under the state pension age must have private health cover.

The French social security system offers such benefits as healthcare, occupational cover, unemployment benefit, family benefits and pensions. You must normally contribute to the French social security system for a certain period of time before you are eligible.

BANKING AND FINANCE

Banking

French banks are either commercial, co-operative or savings. To obtain a mortgage or loan from a co-operative bank you'll need to become a member and buy shares. The post office (*La Poste*) offers a cheap form of banking.

Current (*comte courant*) or cheque (*compte de cheques*) accounts don't accrue interest. To open a current account, a passport and proof of your address in France should suffice, but those in employment may also have to provide proof of this. Request a bank card, which can be used to pay bills throughout France. Bank cards (*carte bancaire* or *carte bleue*) in France combine cash and debit functions; this will cost you approximately €30 per annum. There is no equivalent of a credit card offered by banks in France. You will also receive a cheque book

EDUCATION

School years

- Pre-school (*écoles maternelles*), ages 2-6 broken into 3 cycles; ages 2-4 attend *petite*, ages 4-5 attend *moyenne* and ages 5-6 attend *grande*.
- Primary school (*école primaire*) ages 6-11.
- Secondary school (*collège*), ages 11-16.
- Sixth form (*lycée*), ages 16-19. At the age of 18 or 19, the student must pass a final exam called the *baccalauréat* – which can have a general, technological or vocational bias.
- Higher education (*enseignement* *supérieur*) is available across France. Traditional universities accept anyone who has passed a *baccalauréat*, but it can take years to graduate from these institutions. The universities called *grandes écoles* are run by individual ministries and tend to have the most imposing entry requirements and the most respected qualifications – the *licence, maîtrise* and *doctorat*, are roughly equivalent to bachelors, masters and doctorates.

(*chéquier* or *carnet de cheques*). Some banks charge for cash withdrawals.

A savings (*compte d'éparngne* or *compte rémunéré*) or deposit (*compte à terme*) account can be opened with commercial, co-operative and savings banks.

Taxation

French income tax has seven bands in total, ranging from zero to 40 per cent. A number of rebates and exemptions are granted on gross income, which can greatly moderate the tax. Although plans to introduce a pay as you earn system have been discussed in parliament, as a resident you'll be responsible for filing your own income tax return (*impôt sur le revenu des personnes physiques*). An annual tax return (*declaration des revenues*) is sent to you in the first quarter of the year, followed by a bill in the second half of the year. You have the option of paying in three instalments or monthly instalments.

Wealth tax (*impôt sur la fortune*) is levied on assets totalling more than €760,000 and includes several bands ranging from 0.55 per cent to 1.8 per cent.

PROPERTY MARKET

Property prices in France have risen steadily in recent years and are widely believed to be less susceptible to a price crash than the UK and Spain. Changes to the inheritance tax system in 2007, such as the abolition of inheritance tax between spouses and civil partners, were designed to persuade the French of the merits of property ownership.

Nonetheless, the French property market is slowing, and in 2007 the *Federation Nationale des Agents Immobiliers et Mandataires* (FNAIM) reported price increases of 3.8 per cent nationally – half as high as the figure for 2006, and just a quarter of the increase reported in 2004.

Mortgages

Mortgages (*hypothèque*) are available from most French banks. The typical home loan is a repayment mortgage, with a term of 15 years. Banks will lend to a maximum of 80 per cent of the cost of the property in most cases – although 66 per cent to 75 per cent is more common. Note that banks cannot lend you an amount that would exceed more than 30 per cent of your net disposable income to repay per month.

How to buy

Once an offer is made, a price is agreed upon and a promise to sell is made, the sales agreement (*compromis de vente*) commits both parties to the transaction and the date by which the transfer of ownership will take place. On signing you pay a deposit of around 10 per cent, which you forfeit if you default: the seller must pay you twice as much if they pull out. There is, however, a seven-day cooling off period (*période de rétractation de sept jours*) during which either party can pull out without penalty. Furthermore, your lawyer can negotiate appropriate 'get out' clauses (*conditions suspensive*), to allow you to walk away from the deal under pre-defined circumstances, such as being unable to obtain a mortgage.

If you buy an unfinished property you will need to sign a reservation contract (*contrat de reservation*), and make payments in stages. Through a lawyer, attempt to secure an 'extrinsic' guarantee, through which a bank or insurer pledges to complete the development if the developer goes bust.

If you are planning a renovation project, you will need a planning advice certificate (*certificat d'urbanisme*). It is an 'in principle' planning consent and you will need an architect or surveyor to apply for the *certificat*, and should make the purchase conditional on a positive response from the town hall. Bear in mind, however, that this is not planning permission, which will still need to be sought.

The final stage of the buying process is the signing of the deed of sale (*acte authentique de vente*), which must be done in the presence of a notary (*notaire*) – who registers your ownership with the land registry (*cadastre*).

Leaseback

The 'leaseback' model is a unique French scheme, and is often used a way of encouraging investment in tourism infrastructure. With a leaseback, the buyer leases the property back to a rental company who lets it out. The rental company provides the owner with a guaranteed income for a set period, usually between 3 per cent and 6 per cent of the asking price. Leases generally last nine years, but the developer may retain a right to renew. Benefits of buying a leaseback property include VAT reimbursement.

Fees and taxes

- **Estate agents' commission** varies from 5 per cent to 10 per cent; this is generally paid by the seller. See the selling agent's letter of authority to sell (*mandat*) for details.

- **VAT** (*taxe sur la valur ajoutée*) on a property less than five years old and being sold for the first time, or an older property that has been renovated within the last five years is 19.6 per cent.
- **Stamp duty** (*droits d'enregistrement*) for properties over five years old is 4.8 per cent.
- **Mortgage registration fees** are 1 per cent to 3 per cent for the arrangement of the loan.
- **Notary fees** are approximately 1 per cent to 2 per cent.

Property taxes

- **Land tax** (*taxe fonciére*) is based on a property's theoretical rental value, but can be waived for two years if the property has been recently renovated.
- **Occupancy tax** (*taxe d'habitation*) is paid by whoever is resident on 1 January. Both taxes amount to no more than a few hundred euros.
- **Rubbish tax** (*taxe d'enlèvement des ordures ménagères*) may be charged separately or as part of the land tax.

UTILITIES

To set up a contract you should contact each service provider and produce identification, proof of address and bank account details if you intend to pay by direct debit.

Electricity and gas

Electricity and gas provision is nationalised in France: EDF deal with electricity and Gaz de France, gas. In both cases, there are a range of tariffs. If your house is not connected to the mains gas supply, bottles (*bouteilles*) are widely available and can also be delivered. Many rural properties have wood-fired central heating; wood is available by the cubic metre.

Solar power

Solar power is becoming popular, both with energy providers such as the French electricity company EDF which is increasingly using photovoltaic technology for energy production, and with some homeowners who are choosing to power their homes though their own solar panels. For information, contact the Agence de l'Environnement et da la Maîtrise de l'Energie (ADEME).

Water

Water is supplied by private companies, such as Générale des Eaux, Ondeo and Groupe Ruas. To find out which company or companies supply your area, contact your local town hall. Water is metered and can be expensive in France, although costs vary between regions.

Refuse

Rubbish collection services are co-ordinated locally. Contact your local town hall to find your designated providers.

Telephone

To arrange the installation of a telephone line or to transfer the contract into your name, contact your local branch of France Télécom.

Television

There is an annual TV licence (redevance sur les postes de television), which is usually added to your annual occupancy tax and can be paid on a monthly or annual basis.

FINDING PROFESSIONALS

- The British Embassy in France provides contact details for English-speaking services – www.britishembassy.gov.uk/france
- The Franco-British Chambers of Commerce and Industry has a directory of members working in a range of professions. It can also provide advice to those setting up a business – www.francobritishchambers.com
- Estate agents should be a member of the Fédération National des Agents Immobiliers et Mandataires – www.fnaim.fr, the Syndicat Nationales des Professionels Immobilier www.snpi.com, or the Union Nationales de l'Immobilier – www.unit.fr
- You can find an *expert immobilier* (the French equivalent of a surveyor) via the online database of the Chambres des Experts Immobiliers at www.experts–fnaim.org
- Architects can be searched for via the Conseil National de l'Ordre des Architectes – www.architectes.org; the Syndicat d'Architecture – www.syndarch.com and the Union Nationale des Syndicats Français d'Architectes – www.unsfa.com
- Look for notaries at the French notaire's institute: www.notaires.fr

Web resources

- **Town halls – www.mairiesdefrance.org**
- **French ministry of education (Ministére de L'Education Nationale) – www.education.gouv.fr**
- **French Embassy in London – www.ambafrance-uk.org**
- **French tax office – www.impots.gouv.fr**
- **To find out about private schools, contact the Annuaire National Officiel de l'Enseignement Privé at www.enseignement-prive.info or the Council of British International Schools: www.cobisec.org**

Portugal

With medieval and Moorish-influenced towns, an inviting and
largely undeveloped coastline, and world class golf courses,
many Britons are attracted to Portugal.

Factfile

Area: 92,345 square kilometres
Population: 10.8 million
Capital: Lisbon
**Number of British nationals resident
for a year or longer: 38,000**
**Gross Domestic Product (per head):
US$21,719**

OVERVIEW

A comparatively small country,
mainland Portugal lies to the west of
Spain on the Iberian Peninsula;
Portugal also has two Atlantic island
groups – Madeira and the Azores,
which are approximately 500 and
1,500 kilometres from the mainland.
Little more than 150 kilometres wide,
Portugal nevertheless offers
considerable diversity with culturally
and geographically distinctive areas.

In a similar way to the French and
Spanish, the Portuguese often enjoy
long lunch breaks or siestas which are
offset by working late into the
evening. Be prepared to have a daily
work schedule that differs greatly to
what you were used to in the UK.

NORTHERN PORTUGAL

Home to the Costa Verde and Trás-os-Montes,
northern Portugal is the coolest and least
developed of the country's regions. Mixing
wooded hills with rugged wilderness and
fantastic beaches, the area is home to many
fishing villages, vineyards and Oporto – the
country's charming, river-cleft second city.

CENTRAL PORTUGAL

Central Portugal has great beaches,
historic cities with cobbled streets (such as
Óbidos and Coimbra) and rolling, wooded
countryside, but also boasts Portugal's only
ski resort, Serra da Estrela. Home to the
romantic, tree-lined streets of the café-
crowded capital, Lisbon, central Portugal
has a wide range of golf courses, the most
exclusive coastal resorts in the country and
the unspoilt Costa do Prata (Silver Coast).

Alentejo

Sandwiched between Portugal's most
developed areas, Alentejo is the largest
region in the country and is almost entirely
undeveloped along its 160-kilometre
coastline. An agricultural region, Alentejo
has huge oak forests and acre upon acre
of olive groves, but also houses some
beautiful towns and many villages with
whitewashed buildings. It is this combination

of charm, tradition and relative lack of modern development that provokes some to pronounce Alentejo the 'new Tuscany'.

The Algarve

The southernmost region of mainland Portugal, the Algarve has an excellent year-round climate – which includes over 3,000 hours of sunshine a year and 160 kilometres of golden, sandy, predominantly south-facing beaches plus 30 golf courses (many of which are championship standard). Despite being the most popular area of Portugal with expatriates and holiday home owners, and featuring large towns and big resorts, the Algarve is not saturated with property developments. Here, marshlands, sand flats, pine forests and vast orchards of fruit trees all have room to breathe.

❝ The Algarve is a home from home for many Britons in Portugal. ❞

Madeira and the Azores

Portugal's two island groups, Madeira and the Azores, are both volcanic in origin and green and floral in appearance. The former is famous for wine and the appealing capital Funchal. The latter is strong on watersports and golf developments are underway. Both have pleasant climates, with summer temperatures in the region of 25°C.

POPULAR DESTINATIONS

Although the Lisbon area, the Costa Verde and the Costa da Prata all have pockets of expatriates, and Alentejo is being marketed by property agents as the next great destination, the Algarve is the undoubted focal point. As with any concentration of expats, English is widely spoken and English-speaking schooling is available, making the Algarve a home from home for many Britons in Portugal. This, in turn, means that those unable to speak Portuguese do have a chance of finding work in the Algarve, whether in tourism, estate agency or self-employed in a construction-related trade; beyond this, information technology also features significantly on the list of regional employers.

As a whole, the Portuguese economy is dominated by the service sector (especially tourism), while industry, the building trade and utilities are also important.

IMMIGRATION

For the first three months of residence, a passport suffices. Within 30 days of the end of this period, you must register with the local immigration service office *Serviço de Estrangeiros e Fronteiras* (SEF) and will receive a registration certificate (*certificado de registro*), which is valid for up to five years. To obtain the certificate you need a valid passport, along with a sworn declaration that you:

- Work under a contract of employment or are self-employed in Portugal.
- Have sufficient resources for yourself and for your family (if applicable).
- Are registered in a public or private education establishment and have sufficient resources for yourself and your family (if applicable).

Family members must ask for a registration certificate, and will need to provide a valid passport, a document in evidence of the family relationship and the registration certificate of the EU national they are accompanying or going to join. You must also apply for a tax number, a *número de identificação fiscal* (NIF), which is required to receive an income and buy a house or car. Applications can be made at the local tax office (*finanças*), on presentation of a valid passport. A temporary tax number will be given until the permanent card (*cartão de contribuente*) is issued several weeks later.

Customs and money

Amounts of cash and traveller's cheques above €12,470 must be declared.

HEALTHCARE AND SOCIAL SECURITY

In order to benefit from the Portuguese national health system, *Serviço Nacional de Saúde* (SNS), you first need to obtain your registration certificate and start work, then apply for a national insurance card (*cartao de utente*) at your local health centre (*centro de saude*). Until you have a national insurance card, you will only be eligible for free emergency treatment. The exception is if you receive a UK state pension, in which case you can apply for the card on arrival. The health centre will inform you who your family doctor is. Under the Portuguese health system, some if not all hospital treatment is free, although you must pay upfront and are then reimbursed for 50 per cent to 100 per cent depending on the treatment received. Beneficiaries pay a small charge (*taxa moderadora*) for each appointment or

treatment provided in the SNS. Pharmacists are a popular means of obtaining basic, free health advice.

To start making social security contributions, you must get in touch with the Regional Centre of Social Security (*Centro Regional de Segurança Social*). Between 10 per cent and 15 per cent of an employee's salary is deducted to cover national health insurance – this figure is then topped up by the employer by about 20 per cent. The self-employed have to pay monthly contributions at a rate of 25.4 per cent or 32 per cent depending on which scheme they opt for.

EDUCATION

Most English-language and international schools are based in and around Lisbon and the Algarve.

School years

The Portuguese education system is structured as follows:
- **Pre-school (*jardin de infância*), ages 3-5 (optional).**
- **Compulsory schooling (*ensino básico*), ages 6-15; broken into three cycles.**
- **Secondary education (*ensino secundário*), 16-18; this can be preparation for higher education or work.**
- **Higher education (*ensino superior*) – universities (*universidades*) and polytechnics (*escolas politécnicas*). Bachelor, masters and doctorate degrees can be studied. Admission depends on the number of vacancies available and passing a national entrance exam.**

DRIVING

An EU directive means that your UK licence should be recognised in Portugal, however in practice exchanging it for a Portuguese licence (*carta de conduçao*) will make dealing with the authorities much easier.

BANKING AND FINANCE

Banking

Portuguese banks (*bancos*) offer current accounts (*cartão de crédito*) and savings accounts (*conta da poupança*). Interest is paid on both types of account, but it is also taxed. A passport, tax number card, residency certificate and proof of residence should suffice for you to open an account. Once an account has been opened, a card (*cartão multibanco*) will be sent to your home address. The cards can be used as credit cards but also work in cash machines and as chip and pin cards. Note that cheques are not common in Portugal, and must be ordered separately.

Taxation

Portugal's tax year runs from January to December and includes a Pay As You Earn (PAYE) system for employees. Personal income tax, *imposto sobre os rendimentos de pessoas singulares* (IRS), is broken down into six categories ranging from 10.5 per cent to 42 per cent and assessed annually. You will need to submit an annual tax return for income received, and this must be filed in the first four months of the following year. A taxpayer's card is required. Once a valid passport is presented to the local tax office (*reparticao de finanças*), a provisional document (*documento provisório de identificação fiscal*) is allocated. It is up to you to file a tax return and there are penalties for non-compliance, so it is worth seeking professional advice.

PROPERTY MARKET

A law passed in 1993 enforcing strict development controls on the Algarve means that its property market has been characterised by moderate growth. As a result, property in the area tends to be bought to be holidayed or lived in rather than sold on – something which helps foster a sense of community. With prices in the Algarve around the 3,500 euros-per-square-metre mark, the property market is considered to be on firm ground.

❝ Strict development controls on the Algarve mean its property market has enjoyed moderate growth and is considered to be on firm ground. ❞

For further information on tax in Portugal, see the government tax office (*Direcção-Geral dos Impostos*) website: www.dgci.min-financas.pt

Mortgages

Mortgages (*hipotecas*) are available from most banks and will be based on the lender's valuation of the property; this may be less than the purchase price. Banks will typically lend no more than 80 per cent of the value of the property, with 15 years being the average but by no means the only term on offer. Repayment mortgages are the most common, but endowment and pension-linked products are also available. Note that mortgage fees are extremely high – they can be as much as 15 per cent of the purchase price.

❝ Repayment mortgages are the most common, but endowment and pension-linked products are also available. ❞

How to buy

Both parties agree a legally binding promissory contract (*contrato de promessa de compra e venda*), detailing the conditions of sale. At this point a deposit (*sinal*) will be paid – typically 10 per cent to 30 per cent of the purchase price. Any conditional clauses (*clàusula de anulação*) must be fulfilled, or the contract is void. Your lawyer (*advogado*) must check that any plans held by the local council (*camara municipal*) referring specifically to the property agree with the existing construction, and confirm the details about planning permission and plans for future

construction nearby. The property must have a habitation licence (*licença de habitação*), a title deed (*certidao do registo predial*) and a detailed 'property ID' (*caderneta urbana* or *caderneta rustica*). The *caderneta* is like an identity card for the property. It gives the number, size, location and borders of the plot, and gives a rateable value for the property.

The formal transfer of the property takes place at the signing of the final deed (*escritura de compra e venda*), which must be witnessed by a notary (*notario*). Registration at the land registry (*conservatória do registo predial*) then takes place, but not always immediately. Note, if you are buying off-plan, expect to pay in stages and ensure that the developer has insurance in place to protect your investment in the event that he ceases to trade before construction is complete.

Fees and taxes

- **Estate agents commission** ranges from 3 per cent to 6 per cent and is usually included in the asking price.
- **Transfer tax** (*imposto municipal sobre as transmissões*) is only paid on resale properties and varies from 0 per cent to 8 per cent depending on factors such as the property price, intended use and location; 5 per cent to 6 per cent is typical.
- **VAT** of 21 per cent is charged on new properties.
- **Registration fee** (stamp duty) are usually no more than 1 per cent.
- **Legal fees** for conveyance are around 1 per cent to 2 per cent.
- **Notary fees** generally amount to no more than €200.

Property taxes

- **Council taxes** (*imposto municipal sobre imoveis*) are levied at different rates according to the value and the age of the property. Allow 0.2 per cent to 0.8 per cent depending on the type of property.

UTILITIES

If you are unable to sign up online or by telephone, you'll need to go to the local office with your passport, tax number, contract of the previous owner and property deeds.

Electricity

Electricity is supplied by Electricidade de Portugal (www.edp.pt) and charged at various tariffs.

Gas

Gas mains supply is available throughout most of the country; where it isn't (such as parts of the Algarve), bottled gas is available.

Water

The water supply is the responsibility of your local council (*camara*); you will need to register.

Telephone

Telephone installation is dealt with by Telecom Portugal (www.telecom.pt); several companies offer services.

Television

There is no licence fee for terrestrial TV. Both cable and satellite channels are available for a fee.

FINDING PROFESSIONALS

- The British Embassy lists English-speaking lawyers, translators, healthcare professionals and many other services at www.britishembassy.gov.uk/portugal
- Search for qualified estate agents on the website of the *Associação dos profissionais e Empresas de Mediação Imobiliária de Portugal*: www.apemip.pt
- To search for lawyers, visit the Portuguese Law Society website: www.oa.pt
- To find a qualified notary, visit: www.notarios.pt
- British-Portuguese Chamber of Commerce: www.bpcc.pt

Web resources

- **For business advice, contact The Business Development Agency (*Investimento, Comercio e Turismo*) via www.icep.pt**
- **If you encounter property ownership difficulties, visit the Association of Foreign Property Owners in Portugal website at www.afpop.com**
- **Portuguese government: www.portugal.gov.pt**
- **The national tax office publishes information on the tax system. Visit www.dgci.min-financas.pt**
- **To find your local Portuguese immigration service, visit: www.sef.pt**

Italy

Famous for *La Dolce Vita* but equally celebrated for its regional cuisine, Italy has the landscape, lifestyle, renovation projects and culture to attract Britons in search of a better life abroad.

Factfile

Area: 303,318 square kilometres
Population: 59.3 million
Capital: Rome
Number of British nationals resident for a year or longer: 26,000
Gross Domestic Product (per head): US$ 36,103

OVERVIEW

Bordering France, Switzerland, Austria and Slovenia in the north, the rest of Italy juts out into the Mediterranean – its Adriatic coastline is little more than 100 kilometres from Croatia, while southwestern Sicily is just a short boat ride from Africa.

The country enjoys a varied geography including the mountains of the Alps in the north, to the massive Po River Valley plain and, further south, the only active volcano in mainland Europe, Vesuvius. Italy's major industries include tourism, fashion, ceramics, mechanical machinery, metals, transport equipment and chemicals.

In terms of culture shock, you may find that different examples of Italian etiquette differ markedly to what you were used to

in the UK. For example, Italian shopkeepers frown on customers who handle their goods. Picking something up out of a window display is especially regarded as the height of bad manners.

NORTHERN ITALY

Geographically dominated by the Alps (known as the 'Dolomites' in Italy), which give way to the lake district (home to Lake Como, Lake Lugano and Lake Maggiore) northern Italy also includes major cities such as Milan and the tourist magnet of Venice.

Chic yet industrious, northern Italy has the coolest climate in the country, but in Liguria, which borders France and its Côte d'Azur, it has a distinctively Mediterranean feel with its pine-clad coastline.

CENTRAL ITALY

Central Italy is famous for its historical importance – Florence, the cradle of the Renaissance, and Rome, the Eternal City – but it's varied enough to offer gentle, rolling countryside and remote, mountainous getaways, too. If you're searching for a corner of Italy with a British accent, this is the area to come to. In fact, the Chianti area of Tuscany was dubbed 'Chiantishire' as long ago as the 1970s on account of the British influx.

SOUTHERN ITALY
The warmest of the three mainland areas, southern Italy offers stunning cities such as Naples and a beauty typified by the dramatic cliffs along the Amalfi coast. Here, summer and autumn temperatures regularly hover in the mid 20s, a climate that helped make the island of Capri a star-studded destination of choice for the past century. Southern Italy is also home to Italy's economic backwaters of Calabria, Puglia and Basilicata. The relative remoteness of these regions has left their local character mostly intact, although Puglia and Basilicata have low rainfall and can look quite barren as a result.

ISLANDS
Italy's main islands are Sicily and Sardinia, which lie to the west of mainland Italy. Sicily is a fertile island, home to the active volcano Etna, and also boasts a largely unspoilt coastline. Sardinia is the more developed for tourism, and attracts well-heeled visitors to its glitzy coastal resorts; much of the remaining coastline is undeveloped, though.

POPULAR DESTINATIONS
Not unlike the Dordogne in France, Tuscany first became popular with British expats in the 1970s. Its popularity quickly blossomed, as did its property prices. As a result, an English-speaking population is spreading into Marche and Umbria, both of which are largely rural, artisanal regions. Those with limited knowledge of Italian have a better chance of finding work here than in the rest of the country, due to the many tourist-related businesses. All three regions have high employment compared to the national average, so those with a good level of Italian might find these regions full of employment opportunities. Tuscany's economic strengths are its fashion and furniture industries; Umbria has a predominance of wholesale and retail traders, real-estate businesses and metal manufacture; while construction, light engineering, timber, furniture and crafts are important to Umbria's economy.

IMMIGRATION
British nationals must obtain a residence certificate (*Certificato di residenza*) from the local town hall's registry office (*Anagrafe*) within three months of arrival. You can do this by providing a valid passport, proof of address, and evidence of employment or financial resources, which can be in the form of bank statements or tax returns. A residence certificate is needed to carry out such acts as buying a car and opening a bank account. The authorities can defer a decision on your application for up to six months.

❝ The authorities can defer a decision on your application for up to six months. ❞

Although it is no longer necessary for EU citizens residing in Italy for more than three months to acquire a residence card (*Carta di Soggiorno Cittadini, UE*) the card is useful as you legally have to carry some form of photo-ID with you at all times. Although not obligatory, EU nationals can also obtain an EU citizen's permanent residence card. In most cases, you can make an application at a post office (if it has a *Sportello Amico* counter) by filling in an application called a **blue kit**. Such applications may also be made at the local town hall. In support of your blue kit application, you will need:

- A valid passport and four recent passport photographs.
- Your date of arrival in Italy and reason for stay.
- Certification proving the relationship of family members to you who have moved to Italy with you.

If you are in employment you will also need a declaration from the employer or a copy of the job contract, and if you are self-employed you will need authorisation from the Chamber of Commerce (*camera di commercio*).

Jargon Buster

Blue kit Set of forms issued by some post offices and town halls in Italy for members of the EU who wish to apply for the issue or renewal of a residence permit

Customs and money

Amounts of over €12,500 (in cash, traveller's cheques or a combination of both) have to be declared.

DRIVING

If you have a UK driving licence, you may use it for up to one year after you arrive. Unless you already have the EU standard licence (which must be validated at your local *Automobile Club d'Italia*), you should exchange your old UK licence for an Italian one.

HEALTHCARE AND SOCIAL SECURITY

As an employed or self-employed person living in Italy you will need to pay Italian national insurance to fund the national insurance system (*Instituto National Di Prevideza Sociale*).

Health cards (*tessera sanitaria*) can be obtained by registering with your local health authority (*unita sanitaria locale*). It will entitle you to low cost or free treatment. Hospital services are normally free and you can get as much as 75 per cent off some outpatient and dental treatments. If you are unemployed or retired but not yet at the state pension age, you will have to prove you have sufficient funds or health insurance. Once you've obtained your card you can register with a doctor (*medico convenzionato*).

As an EU citizen, you will also be eligible for other social security benefits such as sickness and maternity benefits and pensions.

EDUCATION

Most English-language and international schools are based in and around Rome, although some are dotted around Italy.

School years

The Italian education system is divided as follows:
- **Pre-school (*asilo nilo*), ages 0-3.**
- **Infant school (*scuole materne*), 3-5.**
- **Junior school (*scuola elementaire*), 6-11.**
- **Secondary school (*scuola media*), 11-15.**
- **High school (*liceo*; there are many options at this level), 16-18.**
- **University, 18 onwards.**

BANKING AND FINANCE

Banking

Banks (*banchi*) are either commercial (*commerciale*), co-operative (*popolari cooperative*) or co-operative credit (*credito*). The co-operatives were first established to provide mortgages for their customers and the credit co-operatives tended to be in rural areas. A current account is called a *conto corrente*. Debit and credit cards, and cheques are common in Italy, though banking charges tend to be high. To open an account you may be asked to provide the following documents:

- Valid passport, or birth certificate, or both.
- Valid residence certificate, proof of address in Italy.
- Proof of income, for example a tax return or contract.
- Reference from your home bank.

Taxation

Income tax (*Imposta sul Reddito delle Persone Fisiche*) is generally deducted at source from salaried workers. This is not the case with self-employed workers, who will need to file their own tax return and organise their own tax payments. The tax rate for an individual ranges between 23 per cent and 43 per cent. A tax code (*codice fiscale*) can be obtained by presenting your passport at the local tax office (*Agenzia delle Entrate*); a temporary document is issued and the permanent plastic card arrives in the post several weeks later. A tax code is required for you to open a bank account, register a car, pay bills, start paid employment and register with the national health service (*Servizio Sanitario Nazionale*).

PROPERTY MARKET

In percentage terms, the Italian property market has seen single digit growth from 2005 onwards, and as such isn't expected to experience a dramatic price correction.

Mortgages

The typical home loan is a repayment mortgage (*mutuo ipotecaria*), with a term of 15 years. Banks will lend a maximum of 60 per cent to 80 per cent of the cost of the property. Banks cannot lend you an amount that would exceed more than 30 per cent to 33 per cent of your net disposable income to repay per month.

How to buy

A written offer (*proposta d'accquisto irrevocable*), which is binding for up to 15 days, can be made before the contract is drawn up. The preliminary purchase contract (*compromesso*) sets out the terms of the deal, and on signing you must pay a deposit up to a third of the purchase price. There are two types of deposit; a *caparra confirmatoria* and a *caparra penitenziale*. With the former, legal action can be taken against you if withdraw from the contract. With the latter, you avoid legal action but lose your deposit. The completion date (*data del rogito*) is typically two to three months from the signing of the contracts. The deed or public sale contract (*rogito* or *atto pubblico di compravendita*), whereby title to the property is officially transferred to you, must be administered by a notary (*notaio*). Staged payments may be necessary for off-plan properties. A *geometra* – a cross between an architect and a surveyor – can handle pre-purchase searches (as can a lawyer and a notary) and any planning applications for restoration work.

Fees and taxes

- **Estate agents' commission** (*provvigione*) around 3 per cent each from buyer and seller.
- **Registration tax** (*imposta di registro*) ranges from 0 per cent to 10 per cent depending on whether the property is new, if it is your first house and where it is situated.
- **Stamp duty/land registry tax** (*imposta catastale*) and **Mortgage tax** (imposta impotecaria) is either a small fixed fee or 1 per cent each, depending upon your circumstances.
- **VAT** (*imposta sui valore aggiunto, IVA*) is 10 per cent if you bought new from a developer; 4 per cent if it will be your main home (*prima casa*); and

20 per cent if it is designated as deluxe (*di lusso*).
- **Legal fees.** Conveyance is typically done by a lawyer, who will charge 1 per cent to 2 per cent.
- **Notary fees.** This is fixed in bands by law, and usually less than 1 per cent.

Property taxes

- **Council tax** (*imposta comunale immobili*) is charged at 4 per cent to 6 per cent of the land registry value (*valore catastale*).
- There are separate taxes for rubbish disposal (*nettezza urbana*).

UTILITIES

If you have bought a new property, you typically have to pay to be connected to utility services. For existing properties, arrange for the meters to be read (where appropriate) and transfer the contracts into your name at the local office of your utility company; note that town halls sometimes deal with water supply, for which there is often a separate tax, *aquedotto comunale*.

Electricity and gas

Mains gas is widely available, although bottles (*bombole*) are often used in rural areas. For mains electricity information, contact Enel (www.enel.it).

Telephone

For installation contact Telecom Italia (www.telecomitalia.it). Other landline providers include Infostrada, Tele2 and Tiscali.

Television

There is an annual subscription fee payable to the state TV company via the post office.

FINDING PROFESSIONALS

- The British Embassy lists English-speaking lawyers, doctors and dentists in Italy at www.britishembassy.gov.uk/italy
- Also see the British Chamber of Commerce in Italy www.britchamitaly.com
- Estate agents should be a member of the *Federazione Italiana degli Agenti Immobiliari Professionali* or the *Mediatori e Agenta in Affari*, which are contactable via www.fiaip.it and www.fimaa.it
- Lawyers should be verifiable through their national representative body, the *Albo Nazionale Avvocati*. See the website at www.albonazionaleavvocati.it
- Notaries' credentials are listed on the website of the *Consiglio Nazionale Del Notariato;* www.notariato.it
- For surveyors (*geometri*) see www.cng.it

Web resources

- The *Centro Informazione Mobilita Equivalenze Accademich* deals with the equivalence of qualifications. See www.cimea.it
- Italian government: www.italia.gov.it
- Italian Ministry of Foreign Affairs: www.esteri.it
- National Insurance Institute: www.inps.it
- Health Ministry: www.ministerosalute.it
- Treasury: www.dt.tesoro.it
- To find your relevant local council, visit: www.comuni-italiani.it

Germany

Germany promises a high standard of living and its southern city of Munich regularly rates highly on surveys of cities with the highest quality of life in the world.

Factfile

Area: 357,021 square kilometres
Population: 82.2 million
Capital: Berlin
Number of British nationals resident for a year or longer: 115,000
Gross Domestic Product (per head): US$33,994

OVERVIEW

From its beer gardens and medieval town squares to its fairytale castles and Alpine heights, Germany has much to offer. The third-largest country in Europe, Germany borders nine other countries – Denmark, Poland, the Czech Republic, Switzerland, Austria, France, Luxembourg, Belgium and the Netherlands. However, it is the country's division into 16 semi-autonomous states (*länder*) which lends Germany its strong regional character and diverse appeal.

When acclimatising to German culture, be aware of being 'proper' in your manner and approach. German punctuality is more than a stereotype – it is regarded as impolite and inappropriate to be late for both business and social meetings.

Another area where it is possible to offend some inadvertently is through the use of the word *Fräulein*. It is regarded as old fashioned and many German women today find it offensive. Use *Frau* when speaking to women, it is the equivalent of Ms and gives no indication of marital status.

NORTHERN GERMANY

This area is the lowland, a fertile plain with beaches and mudflats along the Baltic coast. Although temperatures aren't exactly Mediterranean, this is Germany's summer playground. Northern Germany is also home to Hamburg, a friendly port city, and Berlin, the capital, with its riverside cafés, sprawling parks and cutting-edge architecture.

CENTRAL GERMANY

Central Germany sits on a plateau and is characterised by huge forests. The eastern side is cleft by the mighty Rhine, which flows down from the Alps and rushes past the vineyards in Rhineland-Palatinate. The skies of central Germany are punctuated by the financial towers of Frankfurt and the turrets of imposing castles.

SOUTHERN GERMANY

This region is dominated by the Alps, and although the winters are cold and white this provides residents of Munich with easy access to great skiing. Economically powerful but full of places in which to socialise, Munich demonstrates that working hard is compatible with an active leisure lifestyle.

POPULAR DESTINATIONS

The British expatriate community tends to be quite spread out in Germany, hence opportunities for English-speaking tourism work and construction-related jobs are limited when compared to Spain and Portugal. However, those with a good grasp of German have a much wider choice. Frankfurt is Germany's financial hub. Berlin's economy is dominated by the service sector, with health services, public administration and manufacturing also important. Tourism, technology and engineering predominates in Munich.

IMMIGRATION

Within seven days of moving into permanent accommodation, you should register with the police (*polizeiliche Anmeldung*) at the residency office (*Einwohnermeldeamt* or *Bürgeramt*) of the town hall (*Rathaus*). You will find your local office listed under the heading *Stadtverwaltung* in the telephone directory. You'll need a valid passport and proof of address, and will need to fill out a form. If you state that you are Christian or Jewish, you will be liable to pay a church tax, which varies according to the area in which you live, but is around 8 per

cent of your income tax. Once the formalities are complete, a registration card (*polizeiliche anmeldebestätigung*) will be issued. At the same time as registering, EU citizens can also apply for a certificate stating their right of residence – but must have a valid passport, proof of health insurance, evidence of employment, proof of monthly earnings (if self-employed), or evidence of pension, as applicable.

Customs and money

Amounts of over €12,500 (in cash, traveller's cheques or a combination of both) have to be declared and reported to the *Bundesbank* (German Federal Bank).

DRIVING

If you have a UK driving licence, an EU directive means you can continue to use it. However, you may find that exchanging your UK licence for a German one makes dealing with the police a little easier for you.

HEALTHCARE AND SOCIAL SECURITY

If you live and work in Germany, you must contribute to the social security system, which is overseen by the Ministry for Health and Social Security (*Bundesministerium für Gesundheit und Soziale Sicherung*).

Both the employed and self-employed are automatically enrolled (as well as their immediate family members living with them in Germany). In the case of the former, contributions are automatically deducted from taxable income, but the latter must pay their own contributions.

Unless you earn over a certain government-set threshold (approximately €50,000 per annum), you will be enrolled in the state health insurance scheme. Statutory health insurance schemes are run by several not-for-profit agencies. You have a large degree of choice, as you can choose exactly which of these agencies' funds (*gesetzliche krankenversicherungi*) to choose from. You also have a choice of doctor (*arzt*) and dentist (*zahnarzt*), but not all of them work in the state health system.

Besides healthcare, German social security covers sickness, maternity, unemployment benefits, pensions and also insures against several other eventualities. If you are in receipt of a state pension, you are also covered but those who've retired before the state pension age must obtain a E106 form to receive state healthcare for the first two years of their residence in Germany; after this point, and if you have not yet qualified for a state pension, you will have to take out private healthcare insurance.

EDUCATION

Private and international schooling is available in Germany; the latter is concentrated in the big cities.

School years

German education is dealt with at a federal level, hence each state has its own system. However, broadly speaking, the following applies:

- Pre-school (*Kindergarten*), ages 3-6 is voluntary and must be paid for.
- Primary schooling (*Grundschule*) ages 6-10.
- Secondary school, ages 11-16/18, is divided into four forms; *Hauptschule* has a vocational bias, *Gymnasium* has an academic focus, *Realschule* provides apprenticeships and *Gesamtschule* are comparable to comprehensives in the UK.
- Higher education at universities (*universitäten*) or colleges (*hochschulen*) take 4-6 years to complete. There are effectively three undergraduate degrees (broadly speaking, one for the arts, one for science and one for teachers).

BANKING AND FINANCE

Banking

Banking comes in three main forms: public savings (*sparkassen*), private commercial (*kreditbanken*) and credit co-operatives (*genossenschaftsbanken*). In practice, there is little difference between them as all generally offer current (*girokonto*) and

❝ Unless you earn over a set threshold you will be enrolled in the state health insurance scheme. ❞

savings (*sparkonto*) accounts. Cash, debit and credit cards are widely used in Germany, but there is often an annual charge. To open an account, proof of registration and address and passport are required.

Taxation

If you plan to enter employment, you should ask for an income tax card (*lohnsteuerkarte*) when you register as a resident. At this point your tax class (*steuerklasse*) will be allotted, and is based on your current marital, familial and employment status. When you start work, give your employer the card.

If you plan to be self-employed, you'll need a tax number (*steuernummer*); apply at the tax office (*finanzamt*) and the number will be posted to you.

Income tax (*einkommensteuer*) is deducted at source by your employer for the period 1 January to 31 December, and if you have no other source of income you don't need to file an income tax return.

Your tax card displays your taxpayer reference number, which must be quoted on all correspondence with the tax authorities, and your tax class – of which there are five. Income tax rates range from 15 per cent to 45 per cent.

PROPERTY MARKET

Germany's property market is typified by an extremely low level of home ownership. Most people rent, and apartments dominate the housing stock. As there are few transactions to drive the market upwards, investors have largely stayed away.

Mortgages

Mortgages (*hypothec*) are based on the value assigned to a property (*beleihungswert*) by the bank or mortgage bank (*kreditbank*) in question. Moreover, they tend to lend no more than 60 per cent to 70 per cent of this valuation. Fixed and variable repayment mortgages are common, and 30 years is usually the maximum term.

How to buy

The commission you pay to a property agency (*immobilienmakler*) is negotiable – including how the payment is split between buyer and seller. The first step is to make an offer via your agent. If accepted, deposits (*eigenkapitals*) can be anything from 10 per cent to 25 per cent.

If having a property surveyed, use an official surveyor (*amtlich vereidigter sachverständiger*) from the local building office (*bauamt*). A notary (*notar*) acts neither for the buyer nor the seller; rather, he or she checks that the conditions of the contract of sale (*caufvertag*) have been met.

A notary will also check to see if there are any restrictions on the sale and use of the property. When both parties agree to the terms of the contract, the notary submits the change of ownership to the government and the transaction is noted in the land register (*grundbuch*). The notary will send a copy of the contract to the Finance Office (*finanzamt*) and the buyer will then be asked to pay the property purchase tax (*grunderwerbssteuer*). Once this has been paid, the tax office will issue a clearance certificate (*unbedenklichkeitsbescheinigung*), this completes the transfer.

Fees and taxes

- **Estate agents' fees** are generally 3 per cent to 7 per cent of the purchase price, often split between buyer and seller.
- **Property transfer tax** is 3.5 per cent.
- **Stamp duty** ranges between 0.2-0.5 per cent.
- **Notary fees** are usually 1-1.5 per cent.

Property taxes

- **Incidental charges** (*nebenkosten*) are paid on a monthly basis and can include water costs and refuse collection.

UTILITIES

Electricity

Electricity is provided by a choice of companies. Electricity brokers (*strombrokers*), offer a range of tariffs. No matter which option you choose, get the meter read when you take possession of the property. Setting up an account will require proof of identity and address.

Gas

Gas is not available countrywide, with bottles being used in remote areas.

Water

Water costs are incidental charges (see above).

Telephone

For line installation, visit a Deutsche Telekom office and fill in an application form. Services are available from several companies.

Television

A licence fee must be paid annually to the Central Office for Licensing Fees for Radio and Television (*Gebühreneinzugzentrale*). There is an additional charge for cable and satellite channels.

FINDING PROFESSIONALS

- The British Embassy lists English speaking lawyers, doctors and dentists in Germany at www.britischebotschaft.de
- The British Chamber of Commerce in Germany has a membership list on its website www.bccg.de which includes accountants, architects and notaries.
- For estate agents and surveyors, visit the German Real Estate Association (*Immobilien Verband Deutschland*) website: www.ivd.net
- The German Bar Association, *Deutscher Anwaltverein*, has more than 66,000 members. See www.anwaltverein.de

---

Web resources

- **Federal Ministry for Health and Social Security: www.bmg.bund.de**
- **Federal Ministry of Transport, Building and Urban Affairs: www.bmvbs.de**
- **The website www.krankenkasseninfo.de lists many of the different healthcare funds.**
- **The website of the British–German Association features useful information on moving to Germany. See www.britishgermanassociation.org**
- **Information on private schools can be found at: www.privatschulberatung.de**

Cyprus

Cyprus is popular as a retirement destination, especially with Britons who welcome the opportunity to settle into a Mediterranean country where English is widely spoken.

Factfile

Area: 9,251 square kilometres
Population: 788,457
Capital: Nicosia
Number of British nationals resident for a year or longer: 59,000
Gross Domestic Product (per head): US$23,739

OVERVIEW

Rich in history and blessed with consistent sunshine, southern Cyprus has the beaches, golf courses and expatriate communities needed to tempt those looking to wind down in a warm climate. The north of the island is controlled by Turkey, and is not yet part of the EU. The south is under Greek control.

A former British colony, Cyprus gained independence in 1960 and became a Commonwealth republic in 1961. One of the newer members of the European Union, Cyprus adopted the euro as its currency in January 2008. The economy is dominated by services and tourism, with some agriculture and manufacturing.

COASTAL CYPRUS

Coastal Cyprus basks in daily summertime temperatures that often settle at 35°C, and winter temperatures regularly break the 20°C barrier. Here, you'll find resorts that cater for either end of the age spectrum. Agia Napa in the east is a summer hotspot for British partygoers, and resorts such as Kamares in the west are popular among older people. In between, golf courses, historic attractions, citrus groves and hills provide a backdrop for beaches both sandy and rocky, fishing harbours and marinas, and residential areas both old and new.

CENTRAL CYPRUS

Towards the centre of the island is a vast plain rising up into mountains in the north, south and west. Chief amongst these is the Troödos mountain range, which is densely forested in its valleys and rises to the island's highest point, Mount Olympus (1,952 metres).

Due to the elevation, summers in central Cyprus are mild and dusty, while winters are chilly and snowy enough at the higher altitudes for a ski resort to operate. Those looking for a rural retreat in need of renovation have plenty of villages to explore in this area.

POPULAR DESTINATIONS

Britons have long been present in southern Cyprus, initially at the two military bases, but are slowly and surely populating the western end of the island. Pafos, in particular, is a focal point. A town of some 50,000 people, Pafos mixes old and new buildings.

The west of the island is also where you'll find extensive developments tailor-made for foreign buyers, such as Aphrodite Hills, Coral Bay and Peyia, often referred to as 'Little Britain' locally on account of its popularity among British expats.

Those limited to looking for work in an English-speaking environment will find the greatest choice of employment both in the west of Cyprus and in Agia Napa at the opposite end of the island. Beyond tourism-related work and offering services specifically within the British expat community, the Cypriot labour market is dominated by the government and banking.

IMMIGRATION

If you plan to stay in Cyprus for longer than three months, or begin working there, you must register at the local Immigration Branch of the Police for an *Alien Registration Certificate (ARC)*. This is a small booklet issued for a fee. You must also make an application for a residence certificate (commonly known as the pink slip) within four months of your entry into Cyprus. You can make this application at the same time as the ARC.

Proof of employment or adequate finances is needed, and if not employed, proof of health insurance is essential for your application. Applicants who are employed or self-employed will need to take with them a passport, two recent passport photos and proof of employment. Family members also moving to Cyprus must have passport and photos and the family relationship must be proven via birth certificates, and if applicable, marriage certificates. Those who are retired must show the following: adequate income, proof of funds and proof of health insurance (although an E121 should suffice for those who are receiving a state pension, and form E106 for the first two years of residence for those who aren't).

Customs and money

Amounts of over €10,000 (in cash, traveller's cheques or a combination of both) have to be declared.

DRIVING

Exchanging your UK or EU licence for a Cypriot equivalent is not necessary but can be done via the Department of Road Transport.

HEALTHCARE AND SOCIAL SECURITY

If you are employed and pay social insurance contributions in Cyprus, you will be covered by the country's social insurance scheme. Participation in social insurance gives the possibility of benefit cover for contingencies such as unemployment, sickness, maternity, occupational disease, and several other eventualities.

If you are a pensioner you must apply for a Cyprus medical card via the Ministry of Health. You will need supporting documents, among them proof that your pension is being paid in Cyprus, and an E121 or E106 as appropriate.

In Cyprus, patients pay towards the cost of appointments and hospital stays. In addition, they pay the fees for all examinations and tests. Depending on your age, income and medical condition, you may be entitled to free or half-price treatment.

EDUCATION

The education system in southern Cyprus is in Greek, although special lessons are available to help speakers of other languages adapt.

School years

- **Pre-school, age 3-5 years and 8 months; attendance from the age of 4 is compulsory, although there is normally a fee.**
- **Primary education, age 5 years and 8 months to 11 years and 8 months. Lower secondary, age 11 years and eight months until 15.**
- **Upper secondary, age 15 to 18.**
- **University. Cyprus's colleges and universities offer the same sort of range of bachelor, master and doctorate degrees that UK universities do.**

BANKING AND FINANCE

Banking

Banks in southern Cyprus offer similar accounts and terms to their UK equivalents. Note that deposit accounts are good for short-term savings and long-term saving and investment accounts offer a higher return but tie your money up for a specified period. To open a resident account, a passport and proof of address should suffice.

Taxation

Income tax is charged on a scale between 20 per cent and 30 per cent which relates to how much you earn. Cyprus operates a Pay As You Earn (PAYE) system, which deducts tax from employees at source. If you are self-employed you need to complete a tax return.

PROPERTY MARKET

Development continues apace in Cyprus, as developers attempt to cash in on the boom in owning property overseas. The western end of the island is the focus for this activity, but Lanarka and Limassol are also being developed, with moderate growth expected to continue in the short term.

Mortgages

These typically cover only 70 per cent of the property's value; repayment mortgages with terms of 10 to 25 years are the most common.

How to buy

The legal system is based on English law, but it is essential that you enlist the services of a lawyer nonetheless. Use a reputable estate agent to put in an offer for you. If accepted, you will have to pay a small reservation fee. If a survey is required, this is the time to organise one. Before you sign the contract, your lawyer should check it thoroughly, and negotiate on any key points when buying a resale property. (If buying off-plan, you will have to commit to several staged payments; it is imperative that there is a guarantee in place protecting your investment in the event of the project failing.) When you sign, a deposit of between 10 per cent and 30 per cent is payable and the contract is registered with the Land Registry Office. When necessary checks have been carried out, the balance is payable, and the deeds registered. However, it can take years for the deeds to be made available to you.

Fees and taxes

- **Estate agents' fees** are typically paid for by the sellers, which can be 5 per cent or more.
- **VAT:** 10 per cent is payable on a new-build property.
- **Real estate transfer fees** range from 3 per cent to 8 per cent and are payable to the Land Registry.
- **Stamp Duty** is 2 per cent.

Property taxes

- **Local authority taxes** are annual taxes based on property size and range from 0.1 per cent to 0.5 per cent of the property's value. They are used to pay for refuse collection, sewerage and street lighting.
- **Immoveable property tax** is an annual tax ranging from 2.5 per cent to 4 per cent of a property's value, although those valued under €170,860 are exempt.

UTILITIES

Electricity

Electricity is managed by the Electricity Authority of Cyprus (www.eac.com.cy). You may have to pay a deposit to set up an account. The Cyprus government provides financial incentives to homeowners who use renewable energy resources. As a result, as much as 90 per cent of the housing market uses solar power to heat water.

Gas

Gas can be mains or canisters depending on the region you are in.

Telephone

Telephone line installation is dealt with by Cyprus Telecommunications (www.cyta.com.cy).

Television

There is no TV licence fee; public broadcasting is paid for via your electricity bill. You also have the choice of paid for satellite and cable channels.

FINDING PROFESSIONALS

- The British High Commission lists English speaking lawyers in Cyprus. Visit www.britishhighcommission.gov.uk/cyprus
- The Cyprus Real Estate Agents Association: +357 22 889759.
- The Cyprus Architects Association: www.architecture.org.cy
- Cyprus Chamber of Commerce and Industry: www.ccci.org.cy

Web resources

- **To find out about the equivalence of qualifications, click on the Cyprus link at: www.enic-naric.net**
- **Cypriot government: www.cyprus.gov.cy**
- **Ministry of the Interior: www.moi.gov.cy**
- **To find immigration offices, visit: www.police.gov.cy**
- **Department of Road Transport: www.mcw.gov.cy**
- **Ministry of Health: www.moh.gov.cy**
- **Minstry of Labour and Social Insurance: www.mlsi.gov.cy**
- **Central Bank: www.centralbank.gov.cy**

Antipodes

On the other side of the world are two English-speaking
nations boasting a generally better climate than the UK
and a greater emphasis on leisure time spent outdoors.
These qualities, more perhaps than any other, have made
Australia and New Zealand favoured locations among
many people who wish to start afresh.

Australia

Rich in natural resources and alive to the influences of its multicultural population, Australia's major cities offer UK-level salaries and cosmopolitan attractions.

Factfile

Area: 7,741,220 square kilometres
Population: 21,225,000
Capital: Canberra
Number of British nationals resident for a year or longer: 1,300,000
Gross Domestic Product (per head): US$37,091

OVERVIEW

Blue skies, bronzed surfers, golden beaches, red rocks, green parks, exotic fish – Australia offers those moving abroad the chance to start afresh in an environment saturated with vibrant colour. Boasting a climate that reaches over 20°C month after month, Australian life makes a virtue of being outdoors – whether relaxing by the pool or ocean, lazing in the park, or exploring the beautiful surroundings.

Although it has a surplus of space, Australia's roasting red centre means that 80 per cent of the population live in only 5 per cent of the landmass – a broad, ocean-cooled coastal fringe that snakes all the way from Brisbane in the east to Perth in the west.

This mere slither of Australia is still one and half times the size of the UK, and far less populous.

As residential areas are typically just a short walk from a green or sandy space, Australia's cities provide residents with all the ingredients needed to enjoy a high quality of life.

Although Australia is an English-speaking country, it's English with a twist – and this requires some adjustment. Another factor that could cause culture shock is not so much Aboriginal culture but the way in which it exists – uncomfortably in many cases – on the margins of modern Australia.

Australia is actively recruiting a range of skills including computing, plumbing, nursing and teaching.

EASTERN AUSTRALIA

Sydney and Brisbane are situated on the east coast. Famous for its sail-roofed opera house and enjoying international prominence when it hosted the Olympic Games in 2000, Sydney is a truly global city. Home to 4.2 million people living in more than 400 suburbs draped over the surrounding hills, Sydney has an immense natural harbour at its heart. This, combined with the skyscrapers of the central business district, and the nearby Pacific coastline, make the capital of New South Wales (NSW) one of the world's most striking cities. The home of fusion cooking, Sydney has al fresco dining off to a fine art, and exemplifies the outdoor, t-shirt-and-sandals lifestyle the country is famous for. Other coastal cities of note are Newcastle and Wollongong, and away from the coast NSW boasts the vineyards of the Hunter Valley and the country's highest mountains.

North of NSW, the state of Queensland basks in a sub-tropical climate. Laid-back, beachfront Brisbane is the state's focal point, and is growing quickly due to immigration – both from other states and countries. When it comes to spare time, the residents of Queensland have world-class natural leisure opportunities to enjoy – from reefs to rainforests.

South of NSW is the Australian Capital Territory (ACT); a purpose-built state for a purpose-built capital, Canberra. In addition to the Australian parliament, the city houses most of the country's bureaucrats and civil servants.

SOUTHERN AUSTRALIA

The south coast of Australia where Melbourne, in Victoria, and Adelaide, in South Australia are located, is a few degrees cooler than the east coast, but still warmer than the UK. Even though less rain falls on the south than the east coast, the skies aren't always so clear. Indeed, Melbourne has a reputation for being cloudy and dull. With a population of 3.8 million, it is the second-biggest city in Australia – and proud residents make a habit of favourably comparing their city's sporting and cultural calendar to Sydney's own range of annual events.

Climate change

Australia's sunny climes carry an increased risk of skin cancer, but there are also significant environmental factors to take into account. In recent years, the area around Sydney has suffered from serious forest fires, and a drought has afflicted the Murray-Darling basin – Australia's agricultural centre - since 2002.

A recent United Nations report on climate change predicted that droughts will become more frequent, agricultural production will continue to decline, and that Queensland will suffer a loss of biodiversity.

WESTERN AUSTRALIA

The modern, booming west coast city of Perth exists in glorious isolation to Australia's other cities. It is undoubtedly the centre of Western Australian life, which is concentrated in the south-western corner of the state. Western Australia has sweeping beaches, a stunning marine environment and a wild, rugged interior.

NORTHERN AUSTRALIA AND TASMANIA

Rounding off the options are the Northern Territory, which has a humid tropical climate and a frontier feel, and the island state of Tasmania, which is a green and scenic gem nurtured by Australia's mildest climate.

The biggest city in the Northern Territory is Darwin. It is geographically closer to Jakarta than it is to Sydney, and closer to Singapore than Melbourne. Such proximity to its overseas neighbours is evident in its multicultural outlook.

POPULAR DESTINATIONS

Although New South Wales remains the unrivalled destination for immigrants from around the world, it ranks only third in terms of British immigration – behind Western Australia and Queensland. Of the 23,223 Britons who made a permanent move to Australia in the 2006/07 migration year, 7,286 relocated to Western Australia, 5,569 to Queensland and 4,192 to New South Wales.

House prices, employment rates, specific immigration policies (see below) and concerted efforts to attract skilled workers to specific areas of Australia all play a part in this shifting pattern of British emigration to the country.

IMMIGRATION

Australia's immigration programme is overseen by the Department of Immigration and Citizenship (DIAC) and is designed to help the Australian economy by bringing suitably skilled workers and investors into the country, as well as reuniting families. As such, visas leading to permanent residence are available in three different streams – skilled, business and family.

The skilled visa stream and its many subclasses dominate the immigration programme. Of the 140,000 visas available for the year 2007/08, 95,000 were skilled visas. Although these visas vary greatly – for example, the Skilled-Independent visa allows you to settle anywhere in Australia, while other visas are specifically designed to attract skilled workers to a region of Australia, on a temporary basis – qualification for all of them is based upon the same points grid. This means you score points for different factors, such as relevant work experience and having an occupation in demand, and bonus points in specific cases.

In all of the above cases, both the health and character of the applicant must be proven to be satisfactory by way of medical and police certificates.

Prove your language ability

Even those applicants whose mother tongue is English must take an IELTS English Test if they want to score the maximum 25 points for the language factor. If you don't take the test, you will score only 15 points – these ten points could be the difference between your success or failure in qualifying for a skilled visa.

Skilled stream visas

To qualify for one of the visas available in the Australian immigration system's skilled stream, you must:

- Be under 45 years of age.
- Have sufficient English-language ability.
- Possess a skill on the Skilled Occupation List (SOL) – this is your 'nominated occupation'.
- Have recent work experience in an occupation on the SOL. If you intend to apply for a skilled visa, your skills and qualifications in this nominated occupation must first be assessed by the relevant authority – either Trades Recognition Australia or VETASSESS.

There are three key subclasses within the Skilled stream:

- **The Skilled-Independent visa** has a pass mark of 120 points, leads directly to permanent residence and enables you to settle anywhere in Australia.
- **The Skilled-Sponsored visa** has a pass mark of 100 points, requires sponsorship from a relative in Australia or a state government (assuming you have an occupation on the state's 'high demand' occupation list), and that you live in a particular state for a certain period of time (usually two to three years) before qualifying for permanent residence.
- **The Regional-Sponsored visa** is similar to the Skilled-Sponsored visa, but the applicant must reside in a designated area of the country and is initially granted on a temporary basis.

Family stream visas

Australia's family stream of visas enables spouses, prospective spouses, partners, parents, dependent children, aged dependent relatives and remaining relatives to join their sponsoring relative in Australia, who must be an Australian or eligible New Zealand citizen or an Australian permanent resident. In some cases an 'Assurance of Support' (whereby the relative in question commits to supporting the applicant financially, if necessary) and a 'balance of family' test (which stipulates that at least as many children belonging to the family in question must be residing in Australia as elsewhere) will be required.

Business stream visas

The business visa programme has two distinctive goals: to help businesses recruit workers with specific skills, and to attract talented business owners, senior executives, senior managers and investors to Australia. Most of the nine business visas available are temporary, but some offer a springboard to permanent residence.

Among the other visa options are the Investor Retirement visa (wherein each investment enables the recipient to stay in Australia for four years), and the Working Holiday Maker visa.

Whichever visa you apply for, you'll have to pay a fee to get it processed. This can range from a few hundred Australian dollars for temporary visas to several thousand for permanent visas.

Customs and money

If you are carrying more than A$10,000 or more in cash and traveller's cheques, or both, you must declare this on arrival.

DRIVING

You can use your UK licence (assuming it is a photocard licence; if not, it's advisable to obtain an International Driving Permit from post offices at £5.50 plus processing fee and postage where applicable) for the first three months in Australia, but after that point you'll need a licence issued by the state or territory where you live. This requires an eyesight test and for a fee to be paid. You may also be required to pass a knowledge test and a practical driving test.

SOCIAL SECURITY AND HEALTHCARE

The Australian social security system is financed from general taxation. You must wait two years to be eligible for many benefits, and have been a permanent resident for 10 years to be eligible for a state pension.

 If you are on a temporary visa, you will not have access to the Australian social security system, including Medicare.

However, three exceptions worth noting are family tax benefits, child care benefits and Medicare cover – which you can claim as soon as you register. For the former, you must register with Centrelink shortly after arrival with your passport, address and bank information.

Medicare is Australia's version of the National Health Service; it is funded by a 1.5 per cent levy on income. Medicare offers subsidised healthcare, but doesn't cover prescriptions or ambulance charges, and if you receive hospital treatment you will have to pay for accommodation, nursing and the cost of medicines. To enrol, you will need to take your passport and visa to the nearest Medicare office. The Australian government recommends that you do this seven to ten days after your arrival. Even if you haven't enrolled before you need treatment, you'll be able to claim reimbursement once you've registered. As Medicare typically covers 75 per cent of medical costs, private insurance is taken out by some – but by no means all –

Australians to cover the remaining 25 per cent. If you emigrate on a visa that requires an Assurance of Support (see Immigration section, above), you will not receive social security benefits because your assuror has undertaken to support you financially.

EDUCATION

School years

- Pre-school – ages 3–5 (this is optional, not always easily available and must be paid for).
- Primary school – ages 5/6–12/13.
- Secondary school (high school) – ages 12/13–17/18. In most states students take the School Certificate (SC) at the age of 15/16 and the Higher School Certificate (HSC) at the age of 17/18.
- Higher education – Australia has a wide range of universities. The age of admission is normally 18 and undergraduate courses last an average of three years. Degrees reflect the same system of bachelors, masters and doctorates as the UK.

Each state and territory is responsible for its own education system. From the age of five or six, depending on the state or territory in question, until the age of 15, full-time education is compulsory. School terms run from late January or early February to December. Vocational Education and Training (VET) or Technical and Further Education (TAFE), is undertaken by many young Australians who don't want to study at HSC level. A VET/TAFE course will usually last for two years.

158

Going private

About one-third of Australian children attend a private – or 'independent' – school. They offer the same qualifications as state schools, but academic achievement is usually higher. It is fairly common for children to switch from a state school to a private school when secondary education begins, despite fees being several thousand dollars a year. In fact, some state schools ask for 'voluntary' contributions from time to time in order to bridge perceived shortfalls in funding.

BANKING AND FINANCE

Banking

A cheque (or transaction) account is the Australian equivalent of a current account, while a savings account offers higher interest but more limited access to your money. Most building societies and credit unions (effectively building societies) offer many of the services provided by banks, such as bank cards, cheques, transaction and savings accounts. Many Australian post offices also offer banking services.

Most cheque accounts will provide an Electronic Funds Transfer at Point of Sale (EFTPOS) card, which works like a switch or debit card in the UK, and a chequebook. It is usual to have a savings account for long-term saving as well as a current account. Australia doesn't have cheque guarantee cards, hence cheques are not widely used, but credit cards and stored value cards (effectively credit cards charged or 'topped up' with a certain amount, and which have to be in the 'black' to be used) are commonplace. New arrivals to Australia can open a bank account during their first six weeks with only a passport for identification. When choosing a bank, look for one that belongs to the Australian Bankers' Association. This has a code of practice and provides a banking ombudsman for the resolution of disputes.

Taxation

Income tax is deducted by employers at source (called 'Pay As You Go' in Australia), but paid in arrears by the self-employed. However, anyone who earns over A$6,000 in an Australian tax year (1 July to 30 June) must file a tax return, although most people employ an accountant to do this for them. There are four tax bands above this threshold: 15 per cent, 30 per cent, 40 per cent and 45 per cent. Each band has a flat rate of tax, on top of which the relevant percentage of each dollar earned is taxed.

You will need a tax file number (TFN) to file a return, but also to claim benefits and ensure that you aren't automatically taxed at the highest rate as you would with an emergency tax code in the UK. A TFN is available from your local Australian Tax Office; alternatively, you can request an application by telephone or apply via the Australian Taxation Office website.

PROPERTY MARKET

Mortgages

There are a wide range of lenders and mortgages to choose from, and plenty of brokers available to help you make a choice. Housing loan insurance is payable when the mortgage is more than 80 per cent of the value of property, and although 25 years is the typical term, if you've been in employment in Australia for at least six months you can qualify for a 30-year mortgage.

How to buy

Although each state and territory has specific regulations for buying land and property, the following steps apply universally. After the making and acceptance of an offer, the estate agent prepares a contract of sale with a specific settlement date, which is signed by both parties. Between acceptance and settlement, all necessary searches and surveys, conveyancing and financial aspects are undertaken. You can employ a solicitor or conveyancing specialist (also called a land broker, land agent or settlement agent) to do the conveyancing for you, although this varies depending on the state. In some cases, lenders provide property conveyance as a free service to borrowers.

Fees and taxes

- **Stamp Duty** is paid on a sliding scale based on the value of property; the scale ranges from 1.25 per cent to 6.75 per cent.
- **Registration fees** are 0.01 per cent to 0.6 per cent depending on the location of the property.
- **Legal fees** range from approximately A$1,000 to A$2,000 depending on which state you are buying property in.
- **Conveyance fees** are not fixed by law and range from 0.5 per cent to 2 per cent.

- **Other costs** including government taxes, termite and pest inspections and surveys could, if applicable, all add to the cost of buying a property in Australia.

Property taxes

- **Council rates** are paid on a quarterly basis for local services such as maintenance of pathways and roads and refuse collection. This is determined by the value of the property, and also by each state or territory's own tax rates. Expect to pay at least A$2,000 a year for the average family property.
- **Land tax** is payable everywhere apart from the Northern Territory, and ranges from 0.6 per cent to 1.7 per cent.

UTILITIES

Electricity and gas

These are supplied by local state providers and are paid for on a quarterly basis. To get connected or transfer the supply into your name, you'll need to contact the supplier. In most cases, you'll have to pay a fee to establish an account, make a deposit and, if necessary, pay a connection charge.

Solar power

Although expensive to install, this is growing in popularity. For information on solar power in Australia, including the Solar Cities Initiative, see www.environment.gov.au

Water

Usage is metered, but there is also an annual charge – as there is for sewerage.

Telephone

Any local provider can connect a phone line to your home, but a connection fee and deposit will be required. A range of tariffs are available.

Television

There is no licence fee in Australia. There are several free channels and a range of paid-for cable and satellite services.

FINDING PROFESSIONALS

In Australia, immigration lawyers and agents are regulated by the same organisation: the Migration Agents Registration Authority (MARA), a division of the Migration Institute of Australia. To become members, lawyers need to prove that they have a current legal practising certificate in an Australian state or territory, but agents – who must be Australian passport holders but can be based overseas – must complete the Graduate Certificate in Australian Migration Law and Practice. Both must possess professional indemnity insurance, which will cover the costs of any actions brought against them. It is only these two different types of MARA members that can represent you in dealings with the Department of Immigration and Citizenship and its overseas offices. When searching for lawyers or agents to help you, a good starting point is the MARA website: www.themara.com.au. In addition, migration lawyers are listed on the membership directory of the Migration Institute of Australia at: www.mia.org.au

There are many relocation and settlement services available, but unless you are being resettled as part of a corporate relocation, there are no organisations regulating the activity of these providers. Many companies can help with both the physical and the financial aspects of moving abroad.

- To search for a mortgage broker, visit the website of the Mortgage and Finance Association of Australia: www.mfaa.com.au
- To find an estate agent, visit the Real Estate Institute of Australia website, www.reiaustralia.com.au, and click on the relevant state link.
- To find out about the various regional conveyancing institutes, visit the Australian Institute of Conveyancers at: www.aicnational.com.au

Web resources

- **The Department of Immigration and Citizenship provides free Welcome to Australia online publications specific to each state or territory. The site also includes the Skilled Occupation List and a Skill Matching Database. See www.immi.gov.au and click through to the links you require.**
- **Centrelink has produced a *Recently Moved to Australia* booklet. To obtain a copy, visit: www.centrelink.gov.au**
- **Medicare's website is: www.medicareaustralia.gov.au**
- **To find out more about tax in Australia see the website of the Australian Taxation Office at: www.ato.gov.au**
- **To find out about land tax in the state or territory you are moving to, visit: www.business.gov.au**
- **The Australian Bankers' Association publishes a guide entitled *Smarter Banking – Make the Most of Your Money*. To download a copy, visit: www.bankers.asn.au**
- **To find a certified financial planner, see the Financial Planning Association of Australia website: www.fpa.asn.au**

New Zealand

With its mountainous backdrop and ocean vistas, sparsely populated New Zealand is a popular choice with Britons looking for more space and time in which to enjoy life.

Factfile

Area: 268,680 square kilometres
Population: 4.2 million
Capital: Wellington
Number of British nationals resident for a year or longer: 215,000
Gross Domestic Product (per head): US$26,608

OVERVIEW

New Zealand is, geographically at least, the most extreme escape possible from the UK; even the nearest neighbour of any size (Australia) is a gaping 2,200 kilometres away.

This remoteness has its drawbacks, though. So far from the rest of civilisation, New Zealand isn't particularly fashionable, hi-tech or cutting edge. The built environment leans towards the basic and the functional, and the transport infrastructure isn't exactly world class. Yet those who make a success of moving to New Zealand see this remoteness as a blessing, something of a buffer from the stresses of the modern world. Many British emigrants claim that moving to New Zealand is like going back in time, a time when British life

was less stressful, family life took centre stage and everyone had time to foster a community spirit.

New Zealand's landmass is a little bigger than the UK, but the country only has one fifteenth of the population. This almost guarantees you won't be tripping over your fellow countryman at every turn. Many Kiwis enjoy an outdoor and sports-focused lifestyle, whether enjoying barbecues on the beach, surfing, rugby or snowboarding down a picture-perfect peak.

Divided into 18 regions across two main islands and ridged by a volcanic spine that runs almost the entire 1,300-kilometre length of the country, New Zealand offers three broad types of environment for the emigrant: large cities, smaller cities and towns, and rural areas.

Like many English-speaking countries, New Zealand has its own take on the English spoken in the UK. You may find it takes some adjusting to get used to alternative words, as well as the rural, underdeveloped feel of much of the country – such as seeing children walk to school barefoot in some rural areas.

Large cities

Auckland is New Zealand's biggest city, and yet still manages to feel like a town. Home to one-third of the country's population, many of whom live in sprawling shoreline suburbs, Auckland is New Zealand at its most cosmopolitan. The widest range of jobs is available in the education, finance, manufacturing and distribution sectors.

Wellington, the capital, has 430,000 people, who live sandwiched between hills and beaches. Government, IT and education are among the biggest employers, and the city's mix of culture and cafés makes it a firm favourite with emigrants.

Christchurch, on the South Island, combines a mixture of lush gardens with neo-gothic architecture. It is a great place to base yourself if you wish to head off on ocean and mountain-based activities. Home to 340,000 people, Christchurch has a broad economy, ranging from viticulture to software.

Small cities and large towns

Dunedin, one of New Zealand's many mid-sized cities, attracts a fair share of Britons with its vibrant student life and Victorian architecture. From Nelson and Blenheim in the sunny, wine-growing Marlborough region to booming Tauranga, New Zealand has a wide range of smaller urban areas with 20,000-120,000 residents.

Rural areas

Those preferring a smaller, more remote settlement could, for example, explore the Gisborne region in the extreme east of the country, or the west coast of the South Island. The former has one of the warmest climates in New Zealand, great beaches, a strong Maori presence and just 1 per cent of the country's population. The latter is separated from the rest of the South Island by the majestic Southern Alps, and offers a beautiful, if damp, hideaway.

Transition towns

Several New Zealand cities, towns and districts have signed up for the Transition Town initiative, which is aimed at lowering their dependence on oil and reducing their carbon footprint. Transition towns are given funding to raise awareness of the impact that small-scale community changes have on sustainability in the face of global warming. Nelson, for example, is developing a plan for the impact such changes could have over a period of 50 years. Further information is available at: www.transitiontowns.org

❝ Auckland is New Zealand's biggest city, and yet still manages to feel like a town. ❞

POPULAR DESTINATIONS

No matter how much you might want to settle in a rural paradise, chances are that you'll be living in a town or city. After all, 80 per cent of the Kiwi population lives in an urban environment, because this is where the jobs are and Kiwis are unwilling commuters. Unless you have a family connection in New Zealand, you'll probably need a job to qualify for residence in the country (see below). It is for this reason that New Zealand's three biggest cities are also the three most popular destinations for Britons moving to the 'Land of the Long White Cloud'. However, the saving grace of almost all of New Zealand's cities and towns is that they offer easy access to the great outdoors, so you should never be too far away from some dramatic scenery.

IMMIGRATION

You must qualify for a visa via the country's immigration system, which is overseen by Immigration New Zealand (INZ).

With a growing economy and a number of young Kiwi workers living and working in Europe, New Zealand is in need of suitably skilled workers from overseas to plug the shortages in its home-grown labour force. Therefore, of the four categories that make up New Zealand's immigration system – Skilled Migrant, Work to Residence, Family and Business – it is the first that takes precedence. In fact, of the 52,733 immigrants admitted to New Zealand in the 2006/07 migration year, 30,898 were classed as skilled workers – almost 60 per cent of the intake.

The Skilled Migrant category (SMC)

This is a points-based system that takes into account qualifications, work experience, employment, family connections and age – it is only open to those aged 20 to 55. Those scoring 100 points or more in the four factors listed above can lodge an 'Expression of Interest' (EoI). This is an initial application containing basic details conforming to the above factors. These EoIs are placed in a pool and, every two weeks, INZ picks the highest-scoring and invites a full application. The top score possible is 240, although an applicant scoring 140 points or more is likely to be successful. Additional points can be scored for having experience in, or a qualification relating to, an occupation listed on the 'Skill Shortage List' or 'Long Term Skill Shortage List'. These lists are wide-ranging, with healthcare, teaching and trade skills to the fore. Certainly, those with a relevant job offer have a much greater chance of scoring the necessary points and are therefore more likely to be selected from the SMC pool by INZ and invited to make an application.

> ❝ New Zealand is in need of suitably skilled workers from overseas to plug local shortages. ❞

The Work to Residence category

This option allows those with qualifications in a highly specialised occupation, an

Are your qualifications recognised?

As part of the application process, overseas qualifications are checked by the New Zealand Qualifications Authority to make sure that a recognised institute has awarded them and that documents submitted by applicants are authentic. The overseas qualifications are compared against New Zealand qualifications and a report is issued that states the nearest New Zealand qualification the overseas one can be compared to. When the report is needed for immigration purposes, it also sets out the level of the qualification.

occupation that is in high demand, or those with exceptional talents in sport or the arts, to work temporarily in New Zealand as a step towards gaining permanent residence. After two years you can apply for permanent residence.

The Family category

This enables those with a family member who is already a New Zealand citizen or resident to move to the country, but your relationship to this person must be either:

- Conjugal partner (including same sex partners).
- Dependent child.
- Parent.
- Brother, or sister.
- Adult child.

The Business category

Those looking to set up a business in New Zealand should investigate the Investor and Entrepreneur categories. Although both routes offer permanent residence, the applicant must make a substantial investment in New Zealand. In the former case, this is currently NZ$2.5 million. Another business option, the Long-Term Business Visa, is initially a temporary visa, but could present the opportunity to pursue residence through the Entrepreneur Visa.

There are application fees for all of the above visas, and you'll need medical and police certificates to prove you have a clean bill of health and good character. In most cases, applications should be submitted to INZ in London. Applications are typically processed within a year, with skilled visa applications often taking just a matter of weeks.

New Zealand also offers several temporary options: the Working Holiday Visa Scheme, the Student Visa Permit and the Work Permit.

Customs and money

On arrival, if you are carrying currency of more than NZ$10,000 you must declare it.

DRIVING

You can drive for up to one year with a current and valid driving licence from another country or an International Driving Permit. Before this period has elapsed, you should apply for a New Zealand driving licence at any AA office, which will involve passing a theory test.

HEALTHCARE AND SOCIAL SECURITY

As a permanent resident of New Zealand you aren't required to make social security contributions (but you must contribute to the Accident Compensation Corporation – see below). You, your partner and dependants are automatically entitled to state healthcare – which in large part is funded through taxation. Hospital treatment is free, but you must pay a charge for each outpatient consultation or treatment, such as visiting a GP (subsidies are available in some cases). Once you decide where you are going to live, you should register with a GP in your area. This is your first point of contact with the medical system for everything other than an emergency. Prescription medicines are subsidised but most dentists and optometrists run private practices.

Although New Zealand offers a full range of social security cover, such as sickness, maternity and family benefits, there are two aspects to be aware of. Firstly, the rules state that unemployment benefit is only available to those permanent residents who have worked in the country for two years. Secondly, ten years of employment is necessary before you qualify for a state pension, with at least five of those after the age of 55.

Compensation for accidents at work, socially (such as playing sport), domestically, or in road traffic incidents are covered by the Accident Compensation Corporation. Those in employment and self-employment have a small percentage deducted from their earnings towards this scheme, but the self-employed have the option of contributing to a private scheme instead.

Due to the reciprocal agreement between the UK and New Zealand, UK nationals can apply for benefits sooner than is the norm.

EDUCATION

School years

- **Pre-school (kindergarten) – ages 3–5 (private options are available, state kindergartens are subsidised).**
- **Primary school – ages of 5/6–12/13.**
- **Intermediate schooling – ages 11/12–12/13 two years of 'intermediate schooling' that precedes secondary school. Such schools will tend to be set in rural locations.**
- **Secondary school – ages 13–18, is based around the National Certificate of Educational Achievement (NCEA). Students must attain a sufficient amount of credits in the four levels of the NCEA to go on to study in higher education.**
- **Higher education – known as tertiary or post-compulsory education it normally lasts three to four years and includes a range of universities, institutes of technology, polytechnics, colleges of education, wananga (tertiary organisation focused on Maori culture) and private training establishments.**

Frozen pensions

On leaving the UK, all pension benefits get frozen. However, while a British state pension cannot be transferred to New Zealand, all company and personal pensions can.

New Zealand schooling is compulsory for children between the ages of six and 16, but many start school when they turn five and can legally leave school at the age of 15. The school year starts in February and runs until November or December depending on the level of education in question.

Most state schools are co-educational, although some state secondary schools offer single-sex education. NCEA levels 1, 2 and 3 are broadly the equivalent of GCSE, AS level and A level respectively; level four is effectively a higher education pre-entrance exam. For those not proceeding to higher education, 'industry training' – effectively an apprenticeship – is offered by a range of employers.

BANKING AND FINANCE

Banking

Banking services are available at registered banks, credit unions and building societies. Current accounts typically come with a cheque book (for which there's a charge), and a debit card – called an 'electronic funds transfer at point of sale' (EFTPOS) card. Banks also have regular savings accounts which pay slightly higher interest than current accounts but give ready access to your money. If you want to aim for the highest interest rates then you would need a 'term deposit' account which usually ties your funds up for a pre-defined period, and you typically have to give notice before withdrawing cash. Almost all transactions for both types of account carry a small charge.

To open an account, you will need an opening balance (usually no more than NZ$500), photo identification (your passport, for example), and proof of your permanent address, but references are not usually required. If you open an account after you become a permanent resident of New Zealand you'll also need an Inland Revenue Department (IRD) number. If you don't have this, the higher rate of Resident Witholding Tax – equivalent to an emergency tax code – will be deducted from the interest accrued. Therefore, it is advisable to open an account before you move to New Zealand.

Taxation

There are just three tax bands and no personal allowances in New Zealand, and employers usually deduct tax from your salary or wages. An IRD number (similar to the UK national insurance number) is also needed for you to start a job. In order to obtain this number, visit an IRD office with your passport and complete the relevant form for each member of the family. Contact Inland Revenue Department to find out what tax rules apply to your business. In some cases, a tax return must be filed at the end of the tax year (runs from 1 April to 31 March), but in others (such as sole traders, for example) tax must be paid progressively throughout the year – and this may alter the date on which tax payment is due.

PROPERTY MARKET

No matter where you buy, most New Zealand residential properties are stand-alone wooden buildings. Newer houses are insulated but older houses may have minimal insulation. Central heating and double glazing are not common (although as of September 2008, all new-build properties must have double glazing).

Mortgages

Mortgages are available from banks but also brokers and from companies offering loans over the telephone or via the internet. The standard term is 25 years, and lenders will typically offer a maximum mortgage of 95 per cent of the property's value, but repayments will generally not be permitted above 30 per cent of your net income. Repayment mortgages, called 'table' mortgages in New Zealand, and interest-only mortgages are the prevalent types; fixed-rate mortgages have become very popular in recent years. Interest rates tend to be higher than in the UK, and a fee of approximately 1 per cent will be charged by the lender.

How to buy

Most New Zealanders buy property with the help of an estate agent, known as a 'real estate agent'. The first step is a formal written offer, often 5 per cent to 10 per cent below the asking price, and is conditional upon such things as mortgage approval. If the offer is accepted, a 10 per cent deposit is required. Next, a contract specifying the settlement date is signed.

At this point you will lose your deposit if you pull out for a reason not covered by a specific clause. A real estate agent can provide a legally binding contract. The process takes on average three to four weeks, but can take as little as a week.

Many people use a lawyer to assist with the purchase process, although it isn't mandatory and even conveyance can be undertaken by the buyer. However, it is certainly advisable for a newcomer to New Zealand to use the services of a lawyer – who is the only professional who can charge for conveyancing, although the charges are negotiable. Buying houses by auction is more common in New Zealand than it is in the UK, as is buying a section of land and having a house built on it, and even buying a pre-fabricated house and having it transported to land you own.

Fees and taxes

Mortgages aside, purchase costs can be low in New Zealand.

- **Registration fees** for resale properties are fixed. In 2008 these are NZ$21 via electronic submission, NZ$50 by post and NZ$106 for a new property.
- **Lawyer's fees** can range from NZ$600 to NZ$2,000.
- **Real estate agent's fees** are typically around 4 per cent, but are usually paid by the seller, who is often also required to pay for marketing the property.

Property taxes

Every property owner in New Zealand pays taxes, which are paid to both the district council and the regional council, and covers such services as refuse collection, street lighting, water and sewerage. However, Auckland residents pay separate water rates – resulting in a higher overall bill. Each house is assessed annually by the local Government and given a 'Qualitative Value' on the basis of what the inspector thinks the property and land is worth; this is used in determining the rates.

UTILITIES

Electricity and gas

The supply of power is privatised in New Zealand, hence to connect your property to the electricity or gas supply you'll need to call a local company. Bills are typically sent out on a bimonthly basis. Note, though, that there is no mains gas supply on the South Island. Instead, canisters of liquid petroleum gas (LPG) are widely available, as are gas bottles to run small appliances such as cookers.

Water

This is supplied by the local council, but in rural areas properties have water tanks and septic tanks. See 'Property taxes' for billing information.

Utility companies

These are listed in the *Yellow Pages*; it is possible to arrange a connection via the telephone.

Telephone

Following deregulation, there are many telephone companies in New Zealand. To have a telephone connected, contact a local telephone company and provide proof of identity. Besides a line rental fee, there will also be a charge for a specific package.

Television

There is no licence fee in New Zealand. Besides six freely available terrestrial stations, there are also cable and satellite channels available for a fee.

FINDING PROFESSIONALS

Under the Immigration Advisers Licensing Act, anyone who provides advice about New Zealand immigration matters and practice in New Zealand will have to be licensed from 4 May 2009; advisers who work offshore will need to be licensed by 4 May 2010.

Before the Act was passed, anyone in New Zealand could call themselves an adviser, whether or not they were competent to give immigration advice. An official report identified complaints about immigration advisers such as inaccurate advice leading to serious financial loss and unsuccessful settlement in New Zealand. The new licensing procedures mean that people who wish to provide immigration advice will have to prove their expertise by meeting

For updated information concerning New Zealand's immigration legislation, see the Immigration Advisers' Authority website, www.iaa.govt.nz or the government's immigration website, www.immigration.govt.nz

competency standards. Licensed advisers will also have to adhere to a code of conduct, which should increase industry-wide professionalism and ethical behaviour.

Licensed advisers who breach the code of conduct can have their licence revoked or be fined up to NZ$10,000. Unlicensed people who are caught providing immigration advice can be sentenced to seven years in prison, fined up to NZ$100,000, or both. Providing publicly available information, pointing an immigrant to a website, directing someone to Immigration New Zealand or to a licensed adviser, translation or interpretation, or settlement services, is not considered chargeable advice.

There are many relocation and settlement services available, but unless you are being resettled as part of a corporate relocation, there are no organisations regulating the activity of these providers (removals companies excluded). Many companies can help with both the physical and the financial aspects of moving abroad.

- Estate agents must complete a course approved by the Real Estate Institute of New Zealand or obtain a recognised degree in property, as well as holding a current Certificate of Approval from the Real Estate Agent's Licensing Board. For details, visit: www.reinz.org.nz
- To find a qualified mortgage broker, visit the Mortgage Brokers Association website: www.nzmba.co.nz
- To search for a property lawyer,

visit the property law section of the New Zealand Law Society at: www.propertylawyers.org.nz
- There is no regulating body for surveyors in New Zealand.

Web resources

- **Immigration New Zealand's website is www.immigration.govt.nz Follow the relevant links to find out about settlement support and a free magazine for newcomers. You will also find links to the Skilled Shortage List and Long Term Skilled Shortage List there.**
- **For information about early years, primary and secondary education, go to: www.teamup.govt.nz**
- **To find a GP and a range of other services, visit: www.whitepages.co.nz**
- **To apply for an IRD number and for more information on tax, go to: www.ird.govt.nz**
- **Department of Building and Housing's website is at: www.dbh.govt.nz**
- **You can find information from the Ministry of Health at: www.moh.govt.nz**
- **For the New Zealand Qualifications Authority, visit: www.nzqa.govt.nz**
- **For information on pensions, see the Ministry of Social Development's website: www.msd.govt.nz And for information about pensions and family benefits, visit: www.workandincome.govt.nz**
- **The Land and Transport Safety Authority's website is www.ltsa.govt.nz**

North America

North America comprises a complete and varied range of relocation opportunities. Whether you want your new life abroad to look out onto warm seas or have a snow-capped mountain range as a backdrop, America and Canada provide an environment where choice is king.

America

Whichever climate, culture, landscape or leisure opportunities are on your wish list, the chances are you can tick them off by relocating to America.

Factfile

Area: 9,826,630 square kilometres
Population: 303.5 million
Capital: Washington DC
Number of British nationals resident for a year or longer: 678,000
Gross Domestic Product (per head): US$45,818

OVERVIEW

From the sandy fringe of Florida all the way across the mountains, plains and lakes to the spectacular wilds of Alaska, America boasts a plethora of environments in which to make a fresh start. There are also a bewildering range of cities and towns to choose from, but this choice will, of course, be constrained by factors such as employment opportunities and property prices.

Although similar to the UK in several ways, some differences may come as a surprise and could cause a degree of culture shock. For example, outside of the biggest cities, the entire nation is heavily reliant on the car. Poor public transport and scant few public footpaths could make life difficult for you if you don't drive. On the plus side, most cities are built on a grid system, making orientation much simpler than in the UK's cities. Despite having a separation of church and state written into the constitution, America has high levels of faith and a large proportion of the population regularly attend church.

Geographically, mainland America can be divided into seven regions: New England; Atlantic Seaboard; Gulf Coast; Southwest; Pacific Coast; Rocky Mountains; and Midwest.

NEW ENGLAND

Comprising six states, New England has a temperate climate and is famous for its autumnal colours. With its picturesque coastline, clutch of Ivy League universities and pleasant towns and cities, New England remains perennially popular with migrants from the UK. Popular holiday destinations such as the dune-dotted curl of Cape Cod, the ski resorts of Vermont and Boston's redbrick architecture and European-style layout mean that New England is always popular with tourists, too. As such, tourism plays a big part in the region's economy, but paper and book production are also significant, while Hartford in Connecticut is known for its concentration of insurance companies.

ATLANTIC SEABOARD

The Atlantic Seaboard is separated from the Great Lakes and the Midwest by the ridges of the Appalachian mountain chain and sweeps down from the snowy winters of upstate New York through Washington DC all the way to the 'Sunshine State' of Florida. Britons are drawn to everything from the cultural and commercial epicentre that is Manhattan to the constant warmth and expat communities of Florida.

Unsurprisingly given its length, the Atlantic Seaboard is dotted with big cities such as New York, Philadelphia, Baltimore, Washington DC, Atlanta and Miami. Manufacturing and tourism are the predominant industries, but the economy of the region is as varied as the lifestyle opportunities it offers – everything from the go-getter buzz of Manhattan to the backwoods feel of much of Virginia.

GULF COAST

Western Florida, Mississippi, Louisiana and Texas, make up the Gulf Coast. They offer a coastline lapped by warm waters – although Mississippi and Louisiana are still recovering from the damage wrought by Hurricane Katrina in August 2005, which caused 90 billion dollars of damage, caused nearly 2,000 deaths and displaced thousands of people. Rich in oil and big on ranching, Texas has three big city skylines – Houston, Dallas and Austin.

SOUTHWEST

The Southwest is America's most barren corner, but its deserts and mountain landscapes are home to the popular emigrant cities of Phoenix, Arizona, and Las Vegas, Nevada – with the latter beginning to draw in more Britons than ever before.

PACIFIC COAST

California, Oregon, Washington State and Alaska are the four states that make up the Pacific Coast. Home to Hollywood, Silicon Valley, San Francisco and the Sierra Nevada mountains, California is one of the most sought-after destinations for those moving abroad. Oregon and Washington State are temperate, verdant and home to the progressive, liberal cities of Portland and Seattle.

Alaska, the biggest of the 50 states and home to perhaps America's hardiest residents, boasts a pristine, glacier-gouged landscape which brings in the tourists and their much-needed dollars and a growing oil industry.

Not to be forgotten, the volcanic chain of Hawaiian Islands lies 1,600 miles to the west of the Pacific coast and offers a sub-tropical blend of culture which is two parts American and one part Polynesian.

❝Britons are drawn to the cultural and commercial epicentre of Manhattan, and the constant warmth of Florida. ❞

THE ROCKY MOUNTAINS

The Rocky Mountain states of Idaho, Montana, Wyoming, Utah and Colorado all offer fantastic outdoor activities in summer and winter (think world-class mountain sports and excellent trekking by horseback), desirable addresses such as Boise and Boulder which typically feature strongly in 'quality of life' surveys, and the 'Mile High' city of Denver. The economy of the Rocky Mountain states is dominated by agriculture, cattle ranching, mining, petroleum, gas and timber, although Montana has a growing tourism sector and Denver, the capital of Colorado, is strong in storage and distribution.

MIDWEST

Spanning the distance between the Rocky Mountain states and the Atlantic seaboard is the Midwest. Of particular appeal to immigrants in this great swathe of land is Illinois, which mixes the big, cosmopolitan city of Chicago with numerous small lakeside communities. Illinois is just one of the states which borders the Great Lakes – Minnesota, Wisconsin, Indiana, Michigan and Ohio also boast miles of shoreline, while Missouri, Iowa, Kansas, Nebraska and South Dakota offer a similarly flat but much drier landscape.

As the largest of the regional groupings covered in this chapter, the Midwest offers a range of economic opportunities to match its geographic scope. From the 'Motor City' of Detroit in Michigan to the pharmaceutical industries of Indianapolis and endless acres of farmland in the breadbasket states, the Midwest evades easy characterisation – perhaps fitting for a region spread across the centre of America.

❝ California offers high wages and big cities. ❞

POPULAR DESTINATIONS

California

When it comes to Britons making a permanent move to America, it is California – the most populous state in the United States – which comes out on top. In 2006, 2,593 Britons became permanent residents of California (out of a total of 17,207 moving to America). The state abounds with opportunities for those with high-level IT, engineering and design skills. Relaxed, liberal and wealthy enough to deserve its 'Golden State' tag, California offers high wages and a choice of big cities (Los Angeles, San Diego and San Francisco).

Florida

A temporary home to tens of thousands of Britons every year, Florida also attracts a significant annual flow of permanent residents from these shores. Featuring a more dependable climate than the foggy notoriety of San Francisco, in California, and a range of opportunities for those setting up in business, Florida has the beaches, leisure attractions and the sun-kissed lifestyle to turn visitors into would-be residents.

New York

New York state encompasses everything from the economic might and 24/7 entertainment blitz of New York City to the sleepy towns and farmsteads ensconced in the lakeland scenery of upstate New York.

Texas

Home to numerous company headquarters, Texas tends to attract executives transferred from sister branches in Europe. But the state is full of scenic surprises such as the verdant hairpin valley of Big Bend and an impressive cultural mix, so has much more to offer than corporate relocations.

IMMIGRATION

The American immigration system is overseen by the United States Citizenship and Immigration Services (USCIS). In the UK, the USCIS works in conjunction with the US Embassy in London.

USCIS processes all immigrant and most non-immigrant applications. The US Embassy in London has responsibility for processing some non-immigrant applications and – once medical and police checks have been completed – issuing visas for UK residents. In total, USCIS issued 1,052,415 immigrant visas in 2007 and 65.5 per cent of these were family-based visas. Other significant categories are employment-based, investment, student and visitors.

America's immigration system grants two main types of visa: immigrant (or permanent) and non-immigrant (or temporary). It is only the former which allows permanent residence and therefore provides a Permanent Residence Card (PRC); this is also known as a **Green Card**.

Immigrant visas

The immigrant classification has two main categories: employment-based and family. These are often divided into further classifications, (which are, in turn, often further subdivided). For example, there are five principal 'employment-based' (EB) visas:

- **EB-1** is for 'priority workers' – those with extraordinary abilities in the sciences, arts, education, business or athletics.
- **EB-2** is for those professionals with advanced degrees or exceptional ability in the sciences, arts or business.
- **EB-3** is for 'professional', 'skilled' and 'other workers'.
- **EB-4** is for religious workers and ex-government workers.
- **EB-5** is a 'job-creation' visa (though there is no work requirement) for those with at least $500,000 to invest; sometimes also used as an option by those looking to retire to the States.

In some cases where a job offer is required before immigration can be granted, a process called **labor certification** is involved. This requires the prospective employer to prove that no suitably qualified US citizen or permanent resident is available to take the job instead of the 'alien' worker. This situation is then ratified by the Department of Labor.

Jargon Buster

Green cards The informal name for Permanent Residence Cards. The name came from the original colour of the document and, despite the fact they are now pink, the name has stuck

Labor certification In order to prove to the Department of Labor that no suitably qualified US citizen or permanent resident is available to take a given job over an immigrant, the prospective employer is required to advertise the position for a predetermined period of time

Family visas provide a means of spouses, parents, step-parents and children or step-children under the age of 21 to join their American relative on a permanent basis. A preference system of family visas also exists for biological siblings, the married children of US citizens, and the spouses and children of permanent residents. However, these visa applications can take one to seven years to be granted.

Jargon Buster

Escrow A legal arrangement in which an asset (such as cash) is deposited with an escrow agent (a neutral third party), in a trust account pending the completion of a contractual contingency or condition

Non-immigrant visas

The non-immigrant class of visa is required by people who are visiting America on holiday or for business, as well as a list of other reasons including temporary employment.

Working in the States on a non-immigrant employment visa sometimes makes the process of obtaining an EB visa more straightforward in that you are in a better position to capitalise on any opportunities that arise. In fact, a significant number of would-be immigrants find that they have to obtain a temporary visa first (this is true of 60 per cent of those who were granted an immigrant visa in 2007).

Non-immigrant employment visas such as the speciality worker visa can be used by those with specialised technical knowledge and are a popular choice for those working in IT and software development, but the number of these visas made available every year is capped. Temporary intra-company transferee visas are used by international businesses to transfer managers, executives and specialised knowledge workers to branches in the US. If you have a business in the UK, you could also use this visa if you want to open a sister company in America and effectively transfer yourself to manage the US operation.

Another popular non-immigrant visa is the treaty investor visa, which enables the purchase or setting up of a business – even for those with no business experience. This is a popular option for those who have been unable to find another immigration route to America. Visas for both academic and non-academic students are also available, as well as a range of exchange, work and visitor visas. Follow the links given in the 'Web resources' section of this profile to find out more information.

Many temporary visas offer no obvious path to permanent resident status, although some can be renewed if the conditions of the visa have been met. In addition to the risk of failing to qualify for a visa renewal, any children you have will not be granted residence once they turn 21 unless they qualify for their own visa.

Customs and money

On arrival you must fill out an Arrival-Departure Record (I-94) form and have this checked and stamped by a customs officer. A customs officer will also check an inventory of your goods being imported in to the country. If you are bringing more than $10,000 into the country in cash or traveller's cheques, or both, you must declare this. If you are moving to an address not yet specified to USCIS, you will need to inform them within ten days of arrival.

DRIVING

Driving licence laws differ by state. In some cases, your British licence can be exchanged, and in others up to 90 days is given to obtain the relevant state licence. You can check the exact requirements with the Department of Motor Vehicles, Department of Transportation, Motor Vehicle Administration, or Department of Public Safety in the state you are moving to.

SOCIAL SECURITY AND HEALTHCARE

Those who live and work in America must contribute to its social security system, which provides benefits such as pensions, disability and low-income support, and a wide range of services grouped under the 'welfare' banner. Employee contributions to the Social Security Administration (SSA) are deducted at source, but the self-employed must make their own contributions.

The US government keeps track of these contributions via a Social Security Number (SSN), which functions in exactly the same way as a British National Insurance number, but is also used by banks and other organisations, such as schools, to identify you. There are two ways to obtain an SSN. You can ask for one when you apply for an immigrant visa. Within three weeks of your arrival the SSA should mail your SSN card to the same address where USCIS sends your Permanent Resident Card (PRC). If the address in question changes before you receive the card, inform the SSA.

You can also obtain an SSN by visiting

a social security office with a birth certificate and passport with visa inside or PRC, and filling in the relevant form. You should get your social security card about two weeks after this point.

Those with UK pensions can claim them in America when they reach state retirement age and, unlike, Australia, New Zealand and Canada, the amount will not be frozen on the day you leave the UK. Those who have contributed to America's social security system for at least ten years before they retire will also be eligible for American retirement benefits.

Although social security contributions are used to fund Medicare, America's equivalent of the National Health Service, this funding is minimal. In fact, Medicare and the associated Medicaid programme only pay for the hospital treatment of the elderly, disabled and those with low incomes. Everyone else pays for their own medical care through taking out private health insurance, although some employers may offer health insurance as a benefit to their employees. It is up to you to find a family doctor (or primary care practitioner), but you don't have to register with a dentist. When you are treated, you must show your medical cards and doctors will send the bill to the health insurance company. It is worth noting that, depending both on the cover you have and the treatment involved, you might still have to pay something towards the overall cost.

❝ You can claim your UK pension in America. ❞

EDUCATION

School years

- **Pre-school (kindergarten) – ages 3-5, this is widely available, though provision and cost varies greatly.**
- **Primary school (elementary) – ages of 5/6; in states where elementary school starts at the age of five, the first year of education is spent in kindergarten.**
- **Intermediate schooling (junior high) – ages 12-14.**
- **Secondary school (high school) – ages 15-18, at the end of the 12th (final) grade, students take a high school diploma, which reflects their overall Grade Point Average (scored out of 4).**
- **Higher education – Those with high school diplomas can proceed to higher education in a community college, technical college or university. Students choose a specific subject to study in depth (their 'major'). A bachelor's degree takes four years to obtain; masters and doctorates are also available. Depending on the college, tuition fees will run to several thousand dollars a year, but scholarships are available for those with outstanding abilities.**

Each state is responsible for its own education system, although in most states compulsory education starts from the age of five and lasts until the age of 16. These stages of schooling are paid for through local taxation. Call or visit your local school district's main office to find out which school your child should attend. The school year begins in August or September and ends in May or June. Your child might be tested to determine what class (or grade) they should be in.

Pupils can stay in high school until the age of 21 in most states. If they have not graduated from high school by then, they can enrol in adult education classes to obtain a General Educational Development (GED) certificate instead. Private schooling is also available in many areas.

BANKING AND FINANCE

Banking

American banking institutions are either commercial or savings banks, or savings and loan associations. There are also credit unions, which provide similar services to banks but are run on a not-for-profit basis. Two main types of accounts are offered: checking (the equivalent of a current account) and savings. Checking accounts come with cheque books, but seldom with cheque guarantee cards as these are not common in America. Bank cards – for use in ATMs and for debit purposes – are standard with a checking account, but you'll only be issued cards with savings accounts offering some form of instant access.

When choosing a bank, make sure it is a member of the Federal Deposit Insurance Corporation (FDIC), which provides banks with insurance to protect their clients' deposits of up to $100,000.

To open an account, take your PRC, driver's licence and deposit to the bank of your choice (there are few nationwide banks in America – they tend to be far

more localised). As some banks also require proof of residence and your SSN to set up your account, it makes sense to open a US bank account before you move to America; then, when you have accommodation arranged and your SSN is available, you can open a resident's account.

Obtaining a credit rating can be a challenge to new arrivals in America and can take years to achieve, even with excellent references from a UK employer or bank. A good way to build up credit rating is by obtaining credit from local businesses and stores and paying your bills on time. Once you have established a good credit rating you can obtain credit from a number of lenders.

Taxation

In most states, you will have to pay more than one form of income tax: every employee is liable for federal income tax and some states also have state income tax; additionally, a number of cities and counties tax locally as well.

The agency responsible for the collection of taxes is the Internal Revenue Service (IRS). The tax year runs from 1 January to 31 December. Federal tax rates are divided into six bands; the lowest band has a tax rate of 10 per cent and

North America: America

179

the highest band 35 per cent. Taxpayers file federal income tax return Form 1040 with the IRS each year by 15 April, which informs the government how much you earned and how much you were taxed. These bands apply to each filing bracket: Single, Married Filing Jointly or Qualified Widow, Married Filing Separately, and Head of Household. However, the bands of income taxed differ for each of these brackets.

In addition state income tax is payable in 41 states, (with New Hampshire and Tennessee limiting state income taxes to dividends and interest earned only). Rates range from 1 per cent to 10 per cent depending on which state you live in and how much you earn. The seven states that impose no income tax are: Alaska, Florida, Nevada, South Dakota, Texas, Washington and Wyoming.

Federal law prohibits two states taxing you on the same income, although if you live in one state and work in another, you will still need to file a tax return for both. For example, if you live in New Jersey and work in New York, you will get a credit in your home state for the taxes you paid in your work state. This means you will pay no tax in New Jersey, but you will pay tax in New York.

❝ If you live in one state and work in another you'll need to file a tax return for both. ❞

PROPERTY MARKET

From 2008, property prices started stagnating after having enjoyed years of double-digit percentage increases. It is in such conditions that buyers often find bargains.

Mortgages

Mortgages are available from most American banking institutions, but the majority of these will require information on your US tax returns and credit rating. Some banks, though, will accept a UK credit rating. Repayment and interest-only mortgages are available in America, with banks typically lending up to 75 per cent of the value of the property over a 30-year term.

How to buy

Procedures differ from state to state, so the following acts as a general guide only. Once you have found a property, a verbal offer will be made through your real estate agent, realtor or realtist (see 'Finding professionals', opposite). Following any negotiations necessary, the seller's lawyer will prepare a contract of sale specific to the state you are in, and your lawyer checks the deed and title (not all states stipulate that an attorney must undertake this work). Make sure the contract contains all the conditions that must be met before it becomes binding, including home inspections. The seller is under obligation to disclose any defect the property might have. On making the offer you may have to pay a 'good faith' deposit, typically of 10 per cent. If your offer is accepted, the contract will be signed by you and the seller and becomes binding. Once various costs and fees are paid, the relevant documents should be filed at a public recording office.

Fees and taxes

- **Real Estate Broker's fees are** in the region of 6 per cent but are generally paid by the seller.

- **Title search and insurance** is typically 0.5 per cent to 1 per cent of the purchase price.
- **Recording fee** will be a maximum of 0.5 per cent.
- **Legal fees** should be no more than 1 per cent.

Property taxes

State and local taxes will be levied on your property, usually in order to fund local state schools and other services. Water rates are also often included in property taxes. The value of your property will be assessed and you will be charged a certain percentage of every $1,000 of that value. Depending on the state and size of property, taxes can range from a few hundred dollars to several thousand.

UTILITIES

Electricity and gas

This is often supplied by the same company – which will tend to have a local monopoly. Contact the supplier at least a week in advance of your moving in date and ask for a contract to be set up in your name. For this, you will need proof of address, a deposit and – ideally – a social security card; if you are yet to obtain one, use your passport instead. Electricity and gas meters are typically read, and bills sent out, on a monthly basis. Your first bill will include a connection or set-up fee.

Telephone

There is a choice of several telecoms companies in most locations, so you'll have a number of tariffs to choose from.

To set-up a contract, call the company of your choice with details of your address, SSN number, and information on the number of phone jacks and services you require. Billing is carried out on a monthly basis.

Television

There is no TV licence in America. Several channels are available free of charge, but cable and satellite services must be paid for.

FINDING PROFESSIONALS

- Immigration attorneys are members of the bar association in the state in which they reside. For example, the Florida Bar website, www.floridabar.org, lists members and gives details of any disciplinary history. Attorneys are the only professionals who can deal directly with US Citizenship and Immigration Services on your behalf.
- Immigration consultants, who work mainly in the field of business visa applications made to the US Embassy in London, are not regulated.
- To learn more about how business brokers are regulated in America, visit the website of the American Business Brokers Association at: www.americanbusinessbrokers.org
- To find a Certified Public Accountant, visit the website of the American Institute of Certified Public Accountants: www.aicpa.org
- Real estate agents, brokers or salespeople in America should be licensed by the state in which they work. This means they will have passed exams and are covered by indemnity insurance. Only real estate licensees who are

members of the National Association of Realtors can use the name 'realtor'. They must adhere to a code of conduct. For details, visit: www.realtor.com. Members of the National Association of Real Estate Brokers are known as 'realtists'. For more information, visit: www.nareb.com

- To find out about professional property inspectors, who fulfil a similar role to pre-purchase surveyors in the UK, visit the website of the International Association of Certified Home Inspectors: www.nachi.org
- To find out more about the Real Estate Settlement Procedures Act, visit the US Department of Housing and Urban Development at: www.hud.gov
- See also the Mortgage Bankers Association of America website (www.mbaa.org) and the National Association of Mortgage Brokers website (www.namb.org)

Web resources

- To find out more about America's immigration system, see the website of the United States Citizenship and Immigration Services: www.uscis.gov
- The US Embassy in London's website contains useful immigration and general information: www.usembassy.org.uk
- For information about buying a home and getting a mortgage, visit the Federal Citizen Information Center at www.pueblo.gsa.gov
- America's tax department is the Internal Revenue Service. Its website is www.irs.gov
- Social Security Administration: www.socialsecurity.gov
- To find a clinic or doctor near you, visit the Health Resources and Services Administration at http://ask.hrsa.gov/pc/
- To find your local Department of Motor Vehicles, visit www.anydmv.com

Canada

The second-biggest country in the world, Canada provides those in search of a vaunted quality of life, filled with a variety of outdoor activities, with a vast array of landscapes and cityscapes to choose from.

Factfile

Area: 9,984,670 square kilometres
Population: 33.2 million
Capital: Ottawa
Number of British nationals resident for a year or longer: 603,000
Gross Domestic Product (per head): US$38,453

OVERVIEW

Canada is impossible to encapsulate in one sweeping statement. What's easier to understand is why Britons want to move there. A wide range of jobs are available in clean, efficient cities that feature impressive, and often large, parks and convenient access to some of the most spectacular leisure landscapes in the world. Offering world-class wildlife-watching, kayaking, hiking, biking, surfing, sailing, fishing and skiing, Canada is a showcase for outdoor activities.

While its weather may chill the bone in winter, this is merely a chance for its communities to demonstrate how well they can work together. It is this sense of society, sustained by friendly, open people, that helps Canadians achieve such a high quality of life.

Canada's ten provinces and three territories each have a strong identity of their own, from the Francophone festivals of Quebec to the laid-back lifestyle of the west coast. They are also economically diverse – a wide variation of house prices reflects this. All, however, share a common theme: harnessing the raw power of nature. From hydro-electric industries to forestry, fisheries, agriculture and mining, Canada has an abundance of natural resources.

Causes of culture shock may include the extremes of weather. Winter normally brings heavy snowfalls across most of the country, causing some cities including Toronto, for example, to build a network of underground pedestrian 'streets' so that you can still go shopping or get around despite adverse weather conditions.

THE ATLANTIC PROVINCES

Comprising Newfoundland and Labrador, Nova Scotia, New Brunswick and Prince Edward Island, the Atlantic provinces combine picturesque coves with major harbours, historic streets with hiking trails, brisk springs with colourful autumns, and summer sunshine with deep winter snowfalls. Home to some of the oldest buildings – and the cheapest housing –

in Canada, the Atlantic provinces suffered from the decline of the fishing industry but are slowly and surely beginning to find new ways, particularly in the manufacturing sector, with which to reinvigorate their economies.

EASTERN CANADA

The provinces of Quebec and Ontario, situated in eastern Canada, are as vast as they are varied. To the east, French-speaking Quebec is dotted with towns and villages oozing French culture, as well as the larger cities of Montreal and the province's capital, Quebec City. The next door state, Ontario, is the location of the functional capital Ottawa, and Canada's biggest city, Toronto, with its five million residents. Southern Ontario is surrounded by lakes, so its urban environments are within easy reach of various water sports.

❝ Quebec and Ontario are as vast as they are varied. ❞

CENTRAL CANADA

Central Canada is home to the prairie provinces of Manitoba and Saskatchewan, which boast wide, open spaces, cheap housing, high employment and civic pride. The labour market of the central provinces is dominated by agriculture, manufacturing, trades and healthcare; although employment is high, the range of jobs available tends to be quite narrow.

WESTERN CANADA

In Western Canada, the prairies rise up into the majestic Rockies, enabling the residents of Alberta and British Columbia (BC) to enjoy hiking in summer and skiing in winter virtually on their doorstep. Economically, both provinces are enjoying record levels of prosperity, but climatically Alberta feels the fuller force of winter while BC's towns and cities see less snow and enjoy milder temperatures.

NORTHERN CANADA

Considering its size, Northern Canada – the Yukon, Northwest Territories and Nunavut – is sparsely populated, and its deep-freeze climate limits lifestyle opportunities.

POPULAR DESTINATIONS

Toronto

In terms of international and British migration to Canada, three cities tower above the rest: Toronto, Vancouver and Calgary (Montreal is the most popular destination for Francophones). Toronto has the broadest economy, the most employment opportunities and the greatest range of cosmopolitan attractions. It is surrounded by smaller cities and towns, which are also popular with British immigrants.

Vancouver

Vancouver continues to attract large numbers of newcomers. Enjoying an enviable coastal location and offering a high quality of life, Vancouver's only downside is its sky-high property prices. This situation has resulted in more immigrants looking to nearby locations such as Vancouver Island in search of cheaper property.

Calgary

Calgary is growing at a phenomenal pace and its seemingly unstoppable sprawl across Southern Alberta has set the city's leaders a challenge in providing sufficient infrastructure for the influx of new residents. Still, rich in oil, it has the money to solve any shortfall – and to pay its workforce well.

IMMIGRATION

Canada's federal immigration system is overseen by Citizenship and Immigration Canada (CIC) and its missions around the world – such as the Canadian High Commission in London. In total, a quarter of a million permanent residence visas are granted to successful applicants worldwide every year, and many temporary residence permits besides. Visas granting permanent residence are divided into three categories:

- **Economic Class** (skilled workers, business immigrants, provincial nominees and live-in caregivers).
- **Family Class** (spouses and partners, children, parents and grandparents of the sponsors).
- **Protected Persons** (refugees and those admitted on humanitarian grounds).

In 2006, 40 per cent of the 251,649 visas granted went to tradespeople and professionals – collectively known as 'skilled workers'. Applicants for the Skilled

Worker visa are initially assessed through a points-based selection grid. This grid is divided into six selection factors – education, language, work experience, age, arranged employment and adaptability. As Canadian occupational requirements can differ from their apparent UK equivalents, you may find that you need to have your credentials assessed in Canada or pass licensing exams.

At the time of writing, the pass mark is 67 points. Anyone who matches or exceeds this score, who also proves that they are in good health and have good character (via medical and police certificates), and who has the necessary settlement funds (approximately C$20,000 for a family of four), qualifies for a Skilled Worker visa.

Visa changes

In March 2008, CIC announced that changes to Canada's Skilled Worker visa system had been proposed to the Canadian parliament. If accepted, it would appear that CIC, and the Minister of Citizenship and Immigration in particular, would have the right to pick Skilled Worker applicants for fast-tracking if the Canadian labour market was suffering from an acute shortage of their specific occupational skills.

One of the challenges for those applying for the Skilled Worker visa is the processing time – which averaged 44–48 months in 2007, but began to shorten in 2008. There are, however, two ways to drastically reduce this waiting time: secure an Arranged Employment Offer from a Canadian employer, or be selected for the Provincial Nominee Programme. In both cases, processing times should drop to less than 12 months, and you will still receive a permanent resident visa. Alternatively, obtaining a work permit in a suitably skilled occupation could reduce processing times to a matter of weeks, but a **Labour Market Opinion (LMO)** – which shows that the skill in question is needed in Canada – is required and the permit does not directly lead to a permanent residence visa. It is the prospective employer's responsibility to obtain an LMO: as a prospective employee you are not able to arrange this yourself.

Canada's immigration system also offers two business visas – Investor and Entrepreneur. Both of these visas require business experience and a minimum net worth of C$800,000 and C$300,000 respectively; in addition, the former requires an investment of C$400,000. Note that CIC also offers a Self-Employed Person's visa, for those with farm management experience or world-class participation in cultural or athletic activities. All Business Class applications are, at the time of writing, taking two years or more to process.

Jargon Buster

Labour Market Opinion (LMO) A legal requirement needed by employers who wish to employ foreign workers in Canada. It involves confirmation from Human Resources and Skills Development Canada that the occupational skill in question is considered to be in short supply

Canada's Family Class of visas is designed to reunite family members in Canada. A wide range of family members can qualify for a visa via this route, with spouses, partners and dependent children of Canadian citizens and permanent residents being the most common of these. However, the sponsoring family member must undertake to support those moving to Canada for a period of three to ten years. Many Family Class visa applications are processed within a year. Study permits are also available, and depending on the level and duration of study undertaken can help towards qualifying for a Skilled Worker visa.

Federal or provincial?

Besides the federal system, there is another tier to Canada's immigration structure: the Provincial Nominee Programme (PNP). The PNP system enables Canada's provinces and territories to devise their own immigration system in line with the needs of their economy. The regional governments can therefore specify which skills and what type of investments they are looking for, as well as offer an alternative route for those hoping to join family members in Canada. In the case of skilled and business immigration, these programmes can be easier to qualify for than the federal system – assuming you have the experience the provinces and territories are looking for, and that you intend to settle there.

Quebec, however, is neither part of the federal system nor does it have its own PNP; rather, the government of Quebec administers its own system, which leans heavily towards Francophones.

Customs and money

Upon landing in Canada, you must give the customs officer a list (or 'inventory') of all the household and personal items that you will be bringing into Canada, including those that are being shipped. The officer will sign your Record of Landing and Confirmation of Permanent Residence. The Canadian address you provide will be where your permanent residence card is sent, which usually takes approximately six weeks to arrive.

You will also need to declare any currency equal to or greater than C$10,000 that you are bringing into Canada.

DRIVING

Licences are issued by the province or territory where you live. Your foreign driving licence will be valid for a short time (usually 90 days) after you arrive in Canada, but eventually you will need to exchange your licence or take a Canadian driving test to remain licensed. If you are moving to British Columbia, Prince Edward Island, Nova Scotia or Newfoundland and Labrador, or Canada's three territories, you will need to take a test within three months of arrival. It is worth noting that when there is a reciprocal agreement to exchange a British licence it only applies to those from England, Scotland and Wales.

SOCIAL SECURITY

To work in Canada and receive government benefits available under the Social Insurance programme, you must have a Social Insurance Number (SIN) – which is the equivalent of the British national insurance number. SIN applications can be made at branches of Service Canada or via the Service Canada website. The SIN card will be sent to you in the mail, typically four to six weeks after your application. The SIN enables the government to keep track of taxes paid, pension plan contributions made, and any unemployment, childcare, disability or low income benefits paid out; it is also necessary for opening a bank account. Social insurance is funded through taxation on your gross salary.

A small percentage of your salary will be contributed to the Canada Pension Plan, which will provide you with a monthly income when you retire. Residents of Quebec pay into the Quebec Pension Plan, which works in the same way.

Unfortunately, if you have a UK state pension it will be frozen at the value it reached on the date of your departure from Britain, but you can transfer such a pension to a Registered Retirement Savings Plan in Canada, where it will accumulate interest.

As Canada is a federal country, whereby the different provinces and territories are semi-autonomous, it is important to avoid the assumption that laws and rules are identical across Canada. For example, healthcare, education and vehicle licensing are all dealt with at a provincial or territorial level, hence each province or territory you are considering as a destination should be researched separately.

HEALTHCARE

Every family member must obtain a health insurance card. This is necessary to access Medicare – which is how Canada's national health service is generally referred to. Medicare covers: visits to family doctors, many types of surgery, specialist treatment, hospitalisation, tests and most immunisations. Note that ambulance services, prescriptions, and dental and optical care are not covered.

Medicare is administered at provincial and territorial level. In this respect, there are two key differences to be aware of. In some regions you will have to pay a monthly fee; and in British Columbia, Ontario, Quebec and New Brunswick there is a three-month eligibility waiting period. To cover this period, you should obtain temporary private health insurance coverage. Note that some employers cover the cost of private health insurance.

No matter where you move in Canada, apply for your health insurance card as soon as possible. Visit the provincial ministry responsible for health with your birth certificate, passport, confirmation of permanent residence, or permanent residence card. It is then up to you to choose a doctor and dentist.

EDUCATION

Each province is responsible for its own education system. In the case of Francophone Quebec and bilingual New Brunswick, most classes will be taught in French – although **immersion classes** are designed to help pupils make a quick start in learning French.

Most children attend public schools, which are funded through taxation. The choice available is usually based on where you live, but there are also a number of Catholic schools and private schools.

Jargon Buster

Immersion classes A way of teaching a foreign language by the exclusive use of that language

School years

- **Pre-school (kindergarten) – ages 3–5, this is either voluntary, where nursery schooling must be funded by the parent; or compulsory, whereby children aged five on 1 September attend kindergarten for a year.**
- **Primary school (elementary) – ages of 6–11; in states where elementary school starts at the age of five, the first year of education is spent in kindergarten.**
- **Secondary school (high school) – ages 11–18, although education is only compulsory until the age of 16. In the final year of high school, students sit the General Educational Development Diploma (GED).**
- **Higher education – Those who do well enough and want to go onto university take a 'transfer course' at a college; those who choose not to go to university can study one- to three-year vocationally orientated qualifications at a community college. Canadian universities offer the same degree structure as British universities.**

BANKING AND FINANCE

Banking

Canada's version of the current account is the cheque account. It allows you to write cheques and comes with a debit card, although Canada doesn't have cheque guarantee cards. There is typically a monthly fee to cover the bank's costs.

One challenge faced by new arrivals is their lack of credit history. However, obtaining loans and store cards where necessary and always paying off the full amount by the due date will help build a credit profile in Canada. Given this situation, it is useful to keep one British credit card open to use until your Canadian credit rating is established.

When choosing a bank, look out for those that are covered by the Canadian Deposit Insurance Corporation, as this means your deposit is protected up to C$100,000. To open a bank account, you will need to provide two forms of identification, such as your passport and utility bill, and your SIN (this is necessary if you want to open a resident's account).

Taxation

All Canadian employees must file an income tax return each year, whether they earned any money or not. Employers will deduct a percentage of your salary to cover income tax; the self-employed are responsible for paying income taxes due. There are four federal tax bands (deducting anything from 15 per cent to 29 per cent of your gross income), which apply nationwide, and provincial taxes (which range from about 4 per cent to 18 per cent).

PROPERTY MARKET

In common with many property markets around the world, house prices in Canada began to level out towards the end of the first decade after 2000.

Mortgages

Mortgages are either **open** mortgages, which you can repay without penalty, or the more restrictive **closed** mortgage. By law, Canadian lenders cannot lend more than 75 per cent of the market value of the property in question, and will often lend no more than 65 per cent to newcomers. However, you might be able to take out Government-backed mortgage insurance run by the Canada Mortgage and Housing Corporation, which can increase the mortgage available to 90-95 per cent of the value of the property. Most lenders will also refuse an application to borrow a mortgage that will require more than 30 per cent of your gross monthly income to repay. However, there can be a great deal of flexibility in the term of the mortgage: 25 years is standard, but recently some lenders have been issuing mortgages with 40-year terms. Although it can take as long as 90 days for a lender to approve a mortgage, it generally takes less time.

> ### Jargon Buster
>
> **Open mortgage** A mortgage which can be paid off, often without penalty, before the full term has concluded
> **Closed mortgage** A mortgage with terms that are fixed for the duration of the loan

How to buy

Once you have found a property you like, your real estate broker (see 'Finding professionals' on page 191) will prepare an offer to purchase, possibly in conjunction with a lawyer, and may have to make subsequent offers depending on the response of the vendor. When a price is agreed, a 10 per cent deposit is made and a copy of the signed agreement is sent to a lawyer to examine any conditions placed on the sale; these conditions must be satisfied by the specified closing date.

Legal checks into the title of the property follow, and a legal document is prepared which states the asking price, the deposit and the amount outstanding; a certified cheque for this amount is then provided. When this is paid to the seller, the lawyer registers the home in the buyer's name and provides a deed. If you want to buy off-plan, ensure that any deposits and stage payments you make are protected in the event of the developer going bust.

Fees and taxes

- **Real estate agent's fee** – Realtors generally charge 7 per cent on the first C$100,000 of the sale price and 3 per cent on the rest. The seller usually pays the agent's fee, but in cases where there is a selling and a buying agent involved the fee may be divided between the seller and buyer. Note that a Goods and Services Tax of 6 per cent is payable on any amount the buyer pays in agency fees.
- **Legal fees** – There is a minimum charge of C$500.

- **Land/property/purchase transfer tax** – This is between 0.5 per cent and 2 per cent depending on the price of the property. In Alberta, Saskatchewan and parts of Nova Scotia this tax isn't levied.
- **Goods and Service Tax** – New property and resale property that has been extensively renovated have a GST of 6 per cent – although partial rebates are possible in some cases.
- **Estoppel certificate fee** – This certificate is required for those buying an apartment (Quebec excluded) and costs no more than C$100.
- **Other fees** could include an appraisal, home inspection and survey.

Jargon Buster

Estoppel certificate fee A fee paid to obtain a certificate which outlines the legal and financial state of affairs of a company managing an apartment block – known as a 'condominium' in Canada

Property taxes

In order to fund local services such as refuse collection and the emergency services, taxes are levied against each C$100,000 of the property's value. Rates vary between each province and territory and within them.

UTILITIES

Electricity, gas and oil

There are generally one or two main companies that provide these services in an area, all of which will be listed in the yellow pages of the telephone book. You'll need to visit the offices of the utility companies in question with your passport, property deeds or proof of address and a deposit. As part of the set-up procedure, for which there is a cost, the company in question will read the meter.

Water

You will either receive a regular bill for water rates from the municipal council or they will be included in your property taxes, depending on where you live.

Telephone

To get a phone line installed or a service connected, contact one of the local telephone companies listed in the telephone book. There will be a small charge and a deposit payable. Charges will typically be for monthly line rental and local calls, with an additional amount payable for a long distance call plan.

Television

There is no TV licence fee for the four basic nationwide channels; cable and satellite services are available on subscription.

FINDING PROFESSIONALS

- Professional assistance with immigration applications can only be legally offered by immigration lawyers and immigration consultants. For more information on the regulation of these professionals, visit the Canadian Bar Association website at www.cba.org and the Canadian Society of Immigration Consultants website at www.csic-scci.ca

&&Professional assistance with immigration applications can only be legally offered by immigration lawyers and consultants. 99

- There are many relocation and settlement services available, but unless you are being resettled as part of a corporate relocation, there are no organisations regulating the activity of these providers. Many companies can help with both the physical and the financial aspects of moving abroad, from picking you up at the airport to helping you establish a financial identity in Canada.
- The Canadian Association of Accredited Mortgage Professionals (CAAMP) is the professional body responsible for mortgage lenders, brokers, insurers and other industry stakeholders. To search for a professional, visit: www.caamp.org. Note that some provinces also have their own association.
- Real estate agents should be members of a provincial association or a local board, or both. To be known as a realtor, agents must be members of the Canadian Real Estate Association (CREA). To search for realtors, visit: www.crea.ca
- Property purchase procedures in Quebec include the use of notaries. To find out more about the role of the notary, visit the website of the Chambre des Notaires du Quebec at: www.cdnq.org

191

Web resources

- To find out more about Canada's immigration system, visit the website of Citizenship and Immigration Canada (CIC) at: www.cic.gc.ca. This also includes a section providing settlement information.
- To find out about Quebec's immigration system, visit: www.immigration-quebec.gouv.qc.ca
- To find out about getting your credentials assessed for work in Canada, visit: www.credentials.gc.ca
- The Financial Consumer Agency of Canada provides information on a variety of financial products and services such as bank accounts and mortgages. For details, visit: www.fcac-acfc.gc.ca
- To read the latest on a number of issues facing consumers in Canada, visit the Consumers Council website: www.consumerscouncil.com
- The website of the Canada Mortgage and Housing Corporation is at www.cmhc-schl.gc.ca
- See the Canadian Deposit Insurance Corporation website at: www.cdic.ca
- Printed health information is available from provincial ministries of health and from Citizenship and Immigration Canada. Free pamphlets on a variety of topics are also available from Health Canada.
- To find the nearest Service Canada office, where you can apply for a SIN, visit: www.servicecanada.gc.ca
- The Canada Revenue Agency's website address is www.cra-arc.gc.ca
- The Canadian Real Estate Association lists properties for sale across the country on its Multiple Listings Service, see www.mls.ca

Global round-up

With the world increasingly criss-crossed by flight paths, and the global economy bringing about ever-greater levels of migration, those moving abroad have an increasingly long list of countries to choose from. Here are ten more destinations with a great deal to offer.

Europe

It may be on our doorstep, but it is only in recent decades that significant numbers of Britons have started to move to other countries within Europe.

Europe is an evolving concept, both geographically and politically, and while its borders expand and the list of cities, towns and landscapes it encompasses grows, so too do the range of destinations opening up to British citizens. Although many Britons moving to Europe choose a European Union (EU) member state, and therefore do not have to qualify for a visa (Greece, for example), others set their sights on a country that has decided not to become a full member (Switzerland) or has yet to accede to the EU (Turkey).

GREECE

Factfile

Area: 131,957 square kilometres
Population: 11 million
Capital: Athens
Average daily temperatures: maximum 25°C, minimum 12°C (data for Heraklion, Crete)
Number of British nationals resident for a year or longer: 18,000
Key economic sectors: Administration and public services, shipping, tourism, food, drink, building materials, metallurgy
Gross Domestic Product (per head): US$29,565

Overview

Picture-postcard beaches, azure seas, white-washed villages, colourful flora, clean air, and a slower pace of life that follows the rhythms of traditional culture, the Greek islands offer a retreat from the stresses of modern British life.

With pristine coastline and an immense architectural heritage to consider, the Greek authorities have restricted coastal development – perfect for those looking to get away from it all, but less than ideal for those looking for an English-speaking community in the sun. Those looking to further their career are likely to find most opportunities – and indeed English-speaking communities, schools and services – in Athens, the capital.

Issues to consider are the dry heat of summer and the risk of forest fires, the challenges of learning a language based on a different alphabet, a patchy health system and just how quiet the smaller islands can be in winter.

Immigration

EU citizens are free to work in Greece, but must register with the police within eight days (or the 'Aliens Department' if in Athens) and obtain a permit for stays of more than three months.

Social security

Britain has a social security agreement with Greece, so a range of benefits are available, such as free healthcare. For those working in Greece, form E106 will suffice until you become a resident; for pensioners and those who have retired but have not yet reached state pension age, forms E121 and E106 will be needed respectively to access free healthcare provision. Leaflet SA22, available from the Department for Work and Pensions, provides a full breakdown of the benefits available.

Useful websites

- **British Embassy:**
  www.britishembassy.gov.uk/greece
  (the consular section lists English-speaking services).
- **Greek Embassy in London:**
  www.greekembassy.org.uk
- **Greek National Tourism Organisation:**
  www.gnto.gr
- **Greek chapter of the International Real Estate Federation (FIABCI):**
  www.fiabci.gr

❝ From a bureaucratic perspective, Switzerland is not the easiest country to move to. ❞

SWITZERLAND

Factfile

Area: 41,300 square kilometres
Population: 7.3 million
Capital: Berne
Average daily temperatures: maximum 17°C, minimum -1°C (data for Zurich)
Number of British nationals resident for a year or longer: 45,000
Key economic sectors: Finance, tourism, precision engineering, chemicals, pharmaceuticals
Gross Domestic Product (per head): US$39,642

Overview

Switzerland is famously neutral, offers world-leading public services, a high quality of life, and features lakeside cities with easy access to some of the world's most stunning mountains. Yet, despite being geographically in Europe, Switzerland has twice voted to stay outside the European Union. Therefore, from a bureaucratic perspective, multilingual Switzerland is not the easiest country to move to – and the fact that the country is divided into 26 autonomous or semi-autonomous 'Cantons' does nothing to alleviate this. However, from 2014 EU citizens will be able to live and work freely in the country, and in the meantime an agreement on the free movement of persons between Switzerland and the EU allows the right of entry, residence and access to employment to everyone with an EU passport.

Immigration

Those staying in Switzerland for longer than three months require a permit, (issued by each Canton's Migration Office) and health insurance cover with a Swiss provider. For those working in Switzerland, proof of employment is required to obtain a residents' permit; permanent residence can be secured after five years of living in the country. Retirees have to provide evidence of sufficient financial means.

❝ Most EU social security rules apply to Switzerland. ❞

Social security

EU rules on social security do, broadly speaking, apply to Switzerland. Although Switzerland is not a member of the EEA, it signed an agreement on 1 June 2002, resulting in certain benefits being available in Switzerland for a short period after arrival from another EU country. For details of the agreement, leaflet SA29 is available from the Department for Work and Pensions.

Useful websites

- Swiss Embassy in London:
  www.swissembassy.org.uk
- Federal Office for Migration:
  www.bfm.admin.ch
- British Embassy in Berne:
  www.britishembassy.gov.uk/switzerland
- Switzerland Tourism:
  www.switzerlandtourism.ch
- International Real Estate Federation:
  Swiss chapter, **www.fiabci.ch**

TURKEY

Factfile

Area: 783,562 square kilometres
Population: 70.5 million
Capital: Ankara
Average daily temperatures: maximum 28°C, minimum 9°C (data for Antalya)
Number of British nationals resident for a year or longer: 34,000
Key economic sectors: Finance, tourism, construction, automotive, electronics
Gross Domestic Product (per head): US$8,843

Overview

With a meandering Mediterranean coastline indented with idyllic beaches and peppered with bargain properties, it is no surprise that Turkey is becoming popular with Britons looking to retire overseas. From Antalya to Izmir, the Turkish coast has rapidly developed in recent years, and now offers the resorts, golf courses and marinas that Britons relocating within Europe often look out for. This rapid concentration of facilities has resulted in the growth of several expatriate communities along the coast, so those looking for an English-speaking enclave could certainly find Turkey's Mediterranean resorts to their liking. However, Turkey is still years away from joining the EU – when the bureaucracy of moving to the country will be eased considerably.

Moreover, whether Turkey will actually join the EU is difficult to predict at the present time. Progressive and European-looking politics have been in the ascendancy in Turkey in recent times, but more conservative politics could come to the fore once again – making it less likely that Turkey will become a member of the EU. This battle for control of Turkey's direction will also greatly influence how traditionalist the country's culture will remain, or whether it will open up more to the customs of Western Europe.

Immigration

Foreign nationals may not apply for a work permit directly, but must rely on an employer obtaining a work permit for them from the Turkish Ministry of Labour and Social Security. Only once they have been granted this may they apply for a work-based visa from the Turkish Embassy in London. On arrival in Turkey with the work permit, formal application for a residence permit must be made to the police authorities in the province in question. It is possible to retire to Turkey, but you must prove that you have the financial means to support yourself and your dependants.

Social security

Britain has a social security agreement with Turkey. This means that depending upon your circumstances, you may be able to access incapacity, maternity, industrial injury, widows and guardian's benefits for a short period following your relocation to Turkey. However, this agreement does not cover healthcare, hence private healthcare insurance will be required. For details of the agreement, see leaflet SA22, available from the Department for Work and Pensions.

Useful websites

- **Turkish Embassy in London: www.turkishembassylondon.org**
- **Turkish Consulate in London: www.turkishconsulate.org.uk**
- **Ministry of Labour and Social Security: www.csgb.gov.tr**
- **Turkish Culture and Tourism Office: www.gototurkey.co.uk**
- **International Real Estate Federation, Turkish chapter: www.fiabciturkey.com**

❝ Foreign nationals may not apply for a work permit directly, but must rely on an employer obtaining a work permit for them. ❞

Africa and the Middle East

Offering an abundance of sunshine and fascinating cultures, selected African and Middle Eastern countries are beginning to appeal to Britons in search of a different lifestyle – and booming cities are attracting a multinational workforce.

AFRICA

Unquestionably, Africa has the landscapes and the climate sought by Britons moving abroad, but thus far South Africa is the continent's only popular relocation destination. Many African countries simply do not offer the stability, infrastructure or opportunities required for a significant number of Britons to relocate to the continent on a permanent basis. However, with developments in countries such as Cape Verde, Morocco, Senegal, Botswana and Egypt now being marketed to second homebuyers from overseas, this picture could be about to change.

“ South Africa was one of the most popular retirement destinations for Britons. ”

SOUTH AFRICA

Factfile

Area: 1,219,912 square kilometres
Population: 47.6 million
Capital: Tshwane (formerly Pretoria)
Average daily temperatures: maximum 21°C, minimum 12°C (data for Cape Town)
Number of British nationals resident for a year or longer: 212,000
Key economic sectors: Textiles, chemicals, automotive, tourism, electronics
Gross Domestic Product (per head): US$9,810

Overview

For much of the twentieth century, South Africa was one of the most popular retirement destinations for Britons, but interest has slowly tapered off in the last two decades. Located on the southernmost tip of the continent, it offers incredibly verdant landscapes, a sub-tropical coastline, the beautiful city of Cape Town, welcoming people, and fantastic flora and fauna, as well as the opportunities offered by a developing economy.

However, the sometimes painful transition from apartheid to democracy, a high crime rate and rising property prices mean that fewer Britons moving abroad now consider South Africa to be a viable option.

Nonetheless, the country still has a tremendous amount to offer as the economic powerhouse of Africa, as well as a comparatively large population of British-born residents.

Immigration

The South African Department of Home Affairs offers a range of permits for those looking to work, set up a business, join immediate family or retire. Engineers, physicists, chemists, healthcare professionals, teachers and technicians have the best opportunities for those looking to work in South Africa, courtesy of a work permit quota. Retirees are required to have a monthly income of at least ZAR20,000 per person.

Social security

South Africa does not have a social security agreement with the UK. The South African Social Security Agency awards Old Age Grants to permanent residents (over the age of 65 for men and 60 for women) who also meet the requirements of a means test. Unemployment, illness and maternity benefits are available to workers who have paid into the government Unemployment Insurance Fund.

Useful websites

- **South African High Commission in London: www.southafricahouse.com**
- **Government of South Africa: www.gov.za**
- **South African Tourism Commission: www.southafrica.net**
- **British High Commission in South Africa: www.britishhighcommission.gov.uk/southafrica**
- **Estate Agency Affairs Board: www.eaab.org.za**

MIDDLE EAST

Until the late 1990s, British expatriates in the Middle East were likely to be diplomats or working in the oil or arms industries. However, with Dubai leading the way, many Gulf States are reinventing themselves as logistical hubs and tax-free havens, and thereby attracting companies and workers from overseas. Having built many facilities from scratch, the Gulf States offer a modern environment and the chance to be part of a fast-growing, largely English-speaking community.

❝Dubai is a major commercial centre and tourism destination.❞

THE UNITED ARAB EMIRATES

Overview

The United Arab Emirates (UAE) is a federation of seven emirates situated on the southern shore of the Persian Gulf. These seven emirates are now diversifying economically in order to break their dependence on oil revenues.

The largest of the emirates is Abu Dhabi. However, the emirate with the largest population is Dubai. Now a major commercial centre and tourism destination, Dubai has poured billions into developing everything from tax-free trade facilities to glitzy tourism attractions, as well as residential property development for its booming expatriate population. Although the heat can be stifling in summer, and the cost of accommodation is rising fast, Dubai and its taste for mega-projects will ensure that Britons with impressive managerial experience and commercial acumen will continue to pour into the emirate for the time being.

Still, Dubai and its rapidly changing skyline should not be mistaken for a utopia. Despite its 'tax-free' allure, rental costs and utilities charges have taken a greater chunk of attractive-looking salary packages in recent years. Besides this, the new residential areas are often some way from amenities, and lack a sense of community as a result. The heat and more traditional elements of Emirate culture will certainly not suit everyone.

Immigration

Dubai offers a quicker path to wealth than is possible in most countries, but it does not offer permanent residence. Instead, labour cards and residence visas valid for three years are available to those who have secured suitable employment and are under 50 years of age.

Social security

The UAE does not have a social security agreement with the UK. Social welfare, including unemployment benefit is only payable to UAE nationals.

The Caribbean, Central and South America

Laid-back living, colourful cultures and some of the biggest economic success stories of the twenty-first century, the Americas south of the United States are proving that the continent is full of tempting reasons to move across the Atlantic.

THE CARIBBEAN

If a consistently warm climate and an inviting coastline are what most Britons moving abroad are looking for, then the Caribbean islands certainly provide the raw materials. Although, due to the small size of many of the islands, the Caribbean region does not offer a great range of economic opportunities, thousands of Britons do reside on the islands that were once under British rule. Of these, Jamaica, Trinidad and Tobago, and – in particular – Barbados are the most popular. This is partly because significant levels of immigration from the islands to Britain in the wake of the Second World War have resulted in family ties crossing the Atlantic.

66 More Britons live in Barbados than any other Caribbean island nation. 99

BARBADOS

Factfile

Area: 431 square kilometres
Population: 280,000
Capital: Bridgetown
Average daily temperatures:
maximum 26°C, minimum 23°C
(data for Bridgetown)
Number of British nationals resident for a year or longer: 27,000
Key economic sectors: Sugar production, manufacturing, tourism
Gross Domestic Product (per head): US$17,610

Overview

More Britons live in Barbados than in any other Caribbean island nation. Turquoise seas, beaches of fine sand, a tropical climate cooled by Atlantic Ocean trade winds and a colourful, laid-back culture all help, but Barbados also offers the highest standard of living in the region and is English-speaking. In fact, Barbados is sometimes referred to as 'Little England' by its neighbours, and its culture still bears the influence of Britain. It is, however, quite an exclusive place, and this is reflected in the property prices.

Immigration

Financially self-sufficient individuals wishing to retire to Barbados and entrepreneurs wishing to invest in a business venture in Barbados, which would benefit the economy of the country and provide employment for Barbadian nationals, could be eligible for immigrant status. After five years of residence, an application for permanent residence is also possible.

Social security

Britain has a social security agreement with Barbados, so depending upon your circumstances you may be able to access incapacity, maternity, industrial injury, widows and guardian's benefits, as well as free healthcare, for the initial period of your residence in Barbados. For details of the agreement, obtain leaflet SA43 from the Department for Work and Pensions.

Useful websites

- **Ministry of Foreign Affairs:**
  www.foreign.gov.bb
- **Government of Barbados:**
  www.barbados.gov.bb
- **British High Commission in Barbados:**
  **www.britishhighcommission.gov.uk/
  barbados**
- **Barbados Tourism Authority:**
  www.barbados.org

CENTRAL AND SOUTH AMERICA

Culturally vibrant, blessed with warm weather, studded with fantastic archaeological sites and colonial architecture, and home to some of the most striking and diverse landscapes anywhere in the world, Central and South America have much to offer the expatriate.

An ability to speak Spanish or Portuguese (depending on the individual country) will be essential for those pursuing a career (except, perhaps, for teachers of English as a second language). Economic opportunities will almost certainly be limited in some of the poorer – and less politically stable – countries in the region. Chile and Argentina have the most developed economies, but it is Panama and Brazil that are beginning to attract a greater flow of Britons.

PANAMA

Factfile

Area: 75,517 square kilometres
Population: 3.3 million
Capital: Panama City
Average daily temperatures:
maximum 27°C, minimum 25°C
(data for Panama City)
Number of British nationals resident
for a year or longer: 1,000
Key economic sectors: Finance,
commerce, tourism
Gross Domestic Product (per head):
US$9,000

Overview

Less than one-third the size of the UK, Panama is a snaking strip of land that links Central America with its southern neighbour, and it is this location that affords Panama some of its significant advantages.

Situated in the tropics, Panama has a reliably warm climate, and is hemmed in by the Caribbean Sea to the north and the Pacific Ocean to the south. The Panama Canal is an important source of income for the country and many associated businesses. It was constructed as a result of the narrow landmass between these two bodies of water. Having recently taken over the running of the Canal from the United States, and investing $5.3 billion in its expansion, Panama's economic future is looking bright; the property market, in particular, is booming.

The Panamanian government has worked hard in recent years to attract expatriates to the country, with retirees in particular made welcome in the form of generous discounts for a range of services.

Immigration

The *Pensionado* (Pensioned Tourist) visa offers indefinite residence – in order to qualify, the applicant has to prove they will receive a monthly income of at least $500. Other visas include a spousal visa and a range of investment-based visas, requiring a minimum 'micro business' investment of $40,000, or $150,000 in a 'macro enterprise'. The National Directorate of Immigration and Naturalisation define a macro business as a company of industrial or wholesale

type that has an initial minimum payroll of three full-time Panamanian employees. Micro business investment is where an investor is a shareholder in the company, which must also employ a minimum of three Panamanians.

Social security

Panama does not have a social security agreement with the UK. All workers and employers pay a percentage of their earnings into the Panamanian special security scheme. This funds benefits such as unemployment and maternity benefit, as well as the country's state pension scheme.

❝ Panama's economic future is looking bright; the property market, in particular, is booming. ❞

BRAZIL

Factfile

Area: 8,514,877 square kilometres
Population: 180 million
Capital: Brasilia
Average daily temperatures:
maximum 26°C, minimum 23°C (data
for Maceio in north-eastern Brazil)
Number of British nationals resident
for a year or longer: 11,000
Key economic sectors: Mining,
manufacture, agriculture, services
Gross Domestic Product (per head):
US$9,695

Overview

The fifth-largest country in the world, with the tenth-biggest economy (and growing, fast), Brazil combines an increasing prosperity with a renowned carnival culture and fantastic geography. With the standard of living rising, more British tourists visiting the cities and towns on Brazil's Atlantic coast, and British property buyers investing in developments in the northeast of Brazil, the South American giant could be about to welcome a steady stream of migrants from the UK.

Those considering such a move should choose their destination carefully: Brazil's biggest cities have areas troubled by repeated gun crime, and those unable to speak Portuguese will find that tourism-related work or English-language work in Rio de Janeiro, Sao Paolo, Florianopolis, Brasilia and Natal are among what is a limited number of options.

Immigration

Brazil's government offers visas for those who are studying or training in Brazil, are in a stable relationship with a Brazilian, have secured a job offer from a Brazilian company, managers and directors of companies setting up a branch in Brazil, those investing a minimum of US$50,000 in a Brazilian business that will create jobs for at least ten Brazilian nationals, and retirees aged over 50 who have a monthly income of at least US$2,000 a month. Note that foreign nationals with no criminal record can apply for Brazilian citizenship when they have lived in Brazil for an uninterrupted period of at least 15 years.

Social security

Brazil does not have a social security agreement with the UK. Foreign nationals who work in Brazil are required to contribute to the social security scheme, and are eligible for the same benefits as Brazilian citizens.

Useful websites

- **Brazilian Embassy in London: www.brazil.org.uk**
- **Brazilian Consulate in London: www.consbraslondres.com**
- **British Embassy in Brazil: www.britishembassy.gov.uk/brazil**
- **International Real Estate Federation, Brazilian chapter: www.fiabcibrasil.com.br**

Asia

The Far East has long fascinated Britons looking to experience a different perspective on the world. Today, those in search of riches have the opportunity to catch an economic tiger by the tail.

Britain's colonial past has resulted in well-worn immigration trails across the globe – and one of the most established trails leads to India, where Kerala and Goa beckon those in search of a downshift. These are far from the only popular destination in Asia, however. Many Britons who teach English in Japan and Korea put down roots and take the opportunity to pursue a career in educational administration, while the high standard of living in tiny, prosperous Singapore and the tropical islands and resorts of Thailand encourage some British visitors to seek an indefinite stay. However, it is the economic potential of China and the retiree-friendly immigration programme of Malaysia that could prove to be the biggest Asian attractions for those moving abroad.

CHINA

Factfile

Area: 9,600,000 square kilometres
Population: 1,320 million
Capital: Beijing
Average daily temperatures: maximum 26°C, minimum -4°C (data for Beijing)
Number of British nationals resident for a year or longer: 36,000 (including Hong Kong)
Key economic sectors: Finance, industry, utilities
Gross Domestic Product (per head): US$5,478

Overview

Under British rule, until returned to Chinese control in 1997, Hong Kong once attracted many British diplomats, financiers and city workers with its economic dynamism and cultural differences. Now, though, with China currently bulldozing its way to superpower status, it is the Chinese mainland – and the cities of Beijing and Shanghai in particular – that is welcoming executives, salespeople, engineers and English teachers in increasing volumes every year. And with China's gross domestic product expected

❝China is welcoming increasing numbers of immigrants every year. ❞

to grow at pace in the short term, opportunities continue to arise for those who are prepared to learn Mandarin and are in search of investment opportunities, a new cultural experience and first-hand knowledge of a country set to reshape global power relations.

Still, rapid growth comes with its own set of problems – China's air pollution, for example, was well-documented in the run up to the Beijing Olympics. Culturally, the Chinese language will tax even the sharpest linguists, while the pervasive strength of Chinese state ideology could perplex the unprepared.

Immigration

The Chinese government offers a range of visas, all of which are assigned a letter. The two of most interest to those planning a permanent move to China are the Z and D visas. The former is for those with an offer of employment in China, and the latter permits residence in China for up to ten years but is typically granted only to those married to a Chinese national.

Useful websites

- **Chinese Central Government web portal: www.gov.cn**
- **Chinese Embassy in the UK: www.chinese-embassy.org.uk**
- **Chinese National Tourism Office: www.cnto.org**
- **British Embassy in Beijing: www.uk.cn**

Social security

China does not have a social security agreement with the UK, nor does it have any nationwide social security legislation yet. Provincial and city or county social insurance agencies and employers adapt central government guidelines to local conditions.

MALAYSIA

Factfile

Area: 77,000 square kilometres
Population: 26.6 million
Capital: Kuala Lumpur
Average daily temperatures: maximum 27°C, minimum 26°C (data for Kuala Lumpur)
Number of British nationals resident for a year or longer: 13,000
Key economic sectors: Rubber and palm oil extraction and processing, electronics, mining, timber
Gross Domestic Product (per head): US$13,152

Overview

Making its global mark with the Petronas Towers – once the world's tallest building – and a Formula 1 Grand Prix, Malaysia has economic potential, a tropical setting and a retiree-friendly immigration system.

Its two main regions, some 640 miles distant from each other, both offer great beaches and rainforest, but it is the capital, Kuala Lumpur, and its environs, as well as the island of Penang, which offer the most obvious employment and entrepreneurial opportunities.

In many ways, Malaysia is forward-thinking, but political machinations and proposed restrictions on the movement of women serve as reminders that Malaysian life should not be taken entirely for granted; it still clearly retains the capacity to surprise.

Immigration

The Government of Malaysia, through its 'Malaysia My Second Home' (MM2H) programme, is actively encouraging foreigners to stay in Malaysia for as long as possible on a multiple-entry 'Social Visit' pass. MM2H participants are required to place a mandatory fixed deposit of RM300,000 if they are under 50 years of age, or RM150,000 if they are 50 years or older, in any banking institution in Malaysia. After a one-year period, the participant can apply to withdraw part of the deposit. The Malaysian government also offers spousal visas to those married to a Malaysian citizen, and temporary visas for those taking up executive or managerial posts, those with highly technical skills, low-skilled and unskilled workers in certain economic sectors, and students at Malaysian institutions.

Social security

Malaysia does not have a social security agreement with the UK. It does have a social security scheme designed to provide benefits for certain categories of employees and their dependents in the event of death or disability from accidents at work, or occupational diseases. However, coverage is not extended to expatriate workers and there is no requirement to contribute to the scheme.

Useful websites

- Immigration Department of the Malaysian government: www.imi.gov.my
- Malaysia My Second Home programme: www.mm2h.gov.my
- Malaysian High Commission in London: www.kln.gov.my
- British High Commission in Kuala Lumpur: www.britishhighcommission.gov.uk/malaysia
- Tourism Malaysia: www.tourism.gov.my
- International Real Estate Federation, Malaysian chapter: www.fiabci.com.my

“ Malaysia has economic potential, a tropical setting and a retiree-friendly immigration system. ”

Glossary

Advance Payment Protection Scheme:
A scheme, run by the Overseas Group of the British Association of Removers (BAR), insuring customers against a loss of money or possessions, should their removals company cease to trade.

Alien: A non-nationalised resident or visitor to a country from overseas.

Basis point: 1 per cent of 1 per cent – there are 100 basis points to each cent or penny. So if the interbank rate is €1.3850 to every pound sterling, 100 basis points more would be 1.3950.

Blue kit: Set of forms issued by some post offices and town halls in Italy for members of the EU who wish to apply for the issue or renewal of a residence permit.

Carte de séjour: Identification card in France.

Client trust account: An account maintained at a bank for the purpose of holding client funds.

Closed mortgage: A mortgage with terms that are fixed for the duration of the loan.

Corporate relocation services:
An agency which largely focuses on transferring employees to overseas branches of their companies. This is more established than the relocation agent business and has clearer professional benchmarks.

E106: A certificate issued by the Department for Work and Pensions entitling you to an extension of the European Health Insurance Card cover for a period of up to two years.

E121: Like the E106 form, this is available from the Department for Work and Pensions, but is for people in receipt of a UK state pension.

EEA: An acronym for European Economic Area, which provides a single market for the free movement of labour and services, as well as most capital products. It comprises all the members of the European Union and the European Free Trade Association, with the exception of Switzerland.

Endowment mortgage: The monthly payment is used to buy stocks and shares. The hope is that when the term of the mortgage comes to an end the endowment policy will have increased to a level where it can be used to repay the original loan - and perhaps provide surplus cash.

Escrow: A legal arrangement in which an asset (such as cash) is deposited with an escrow agent (a neutral third party), in a trust account pending the completion of a contractual contingency or condition.

Estoppel certificate fee: A fee paid to obtain a certificate which outlines the legal and financial state of affairs of a company managing an apartment block – known as a 'condominium' in Canada.

Forward trades: Fixing an exchange rate in advance of currency purchase, usually for up to two years. Typically, you pay a 10 per cent deposit but don't pay the full amount until you make the full transfer.

Green cards: The informal name for Permanent Residence Cards. The name came from the original colour of the document and, despite the fact they are now pink, the name has stuck.

Immersion classes: A way of teaching a foreign language by the exclusive use of that language.

Interbank rate: The rate at which banks trade currency between themselves. In Europe, this is set by the European Central Bank.

International Labour Organisation (ILO): A United Nations agency that aims to promote rights at work and employment opportunities.

Job board: An online listing of job vacancies, often published by newspapers or by dedicated websites such as Monster.

Labor certification: In order to prove that no suitably qualified US citizen is available to take a given job over an immigrant, the prospective employer is required to advertise the position for a predetermined period of time.

Labour Market Opinion (LMO): A legal requirement needed by employers who wish to employ foreign workers in Canada. It involves confirmation from Human Resources and Skills Development Canada that the occupational skill in question is considered to be in short supply.

Landing card: Also known as an 'embarkation card' and an 'arrival-departure record card', this is a form requesting details such as contact addresses that all non-residents (or, in the case of the European Economic Area, non-EEA citizens) are required to complete on entry to a country.

Land Registry: A government agency that registers title to land in England and Wales and keeps records on dealings such as sales and mortgages.

Limit orders: An advance agreement to an upper or lower exchange rate whereby the currency purchase is triggered as either limit is reached.

Loan-to-value: The ratio of the mortgage loan amount to the property's appraised value or selling price, whichever is less.

Multiple: Mortgages calculated on the basis of your income. For example, in the UK, you might be able to obtain a mortgage that is three times your annual wage.

Net emigration: The total of British nationals leaving the UK in any given year, minus those returning.

Net monthly income: What's left of your monthly income after regular outgoings (such as taxation) are accounted for. Your maximum mortgage might be based on your ability to meet your monthly mortgage repayments with 30–33 per cent of your net monthly income.

Número de identificación de extranjero (NIE): Identification number for foreigners in Spain.

Open mortgage: A mortgage which can be paid off, often without penalty, before the full term has concluded.

Pension-linked mortgage: An interest-only mortgage where the borrower usually pays a monthly amount into a pension fund. When the borrower reaches retirement, the cash lump sum repays the outstanding balance on the mortgage.

Professional indemnity: A type of insurance (also known as 'errors and omissions insurance' in some countries), that protects a business against compensation sought by a client claiming it has made mistakes or has been negligent in some or all of the services provided.

Regional visa: An immigration opportunity provided by a region – whether a state, province or territory – within a country. Such schemes are used by regional governments to attract workers with particular skills.

Relocation agent: An individual or agency offering help in relocating to a certain country, or a specific region. Such services are often offered for free when the agent has a related service to sell, such as estate agency.

Spot trades: Buying the currency at the current price, and paying for it immediately.

Technical analysis: A method used to make investment decisions based on price movements in the market. Technical analysis studies supply and demand in a market in an attempt to determine its future direction.

VOIP: An acronym for voice over internet protocol, a technology for making telephone calls via the internet.

Useful addresses

UK/EU Government bodies

British Embassy
www.britishembassy.gov.uk

Foreign and Commonwealth Office (FCO)
King Charles Street
London SW1A 2AH
Tel: 0207 008 1500
www.fco.gov.uk

Pensions
Department for Work and Pensions
(DWP)
www.dwp.gov.uk
State pensions are administered
through the Pensions Service.

Tax
HM Revenue & Customs Centre
for Non-Residents
www.hmrc.gov.uk/cnr
for income tax/capital gains tax
Tel: 0845 070 0040 / 0151 210 222
for national insurance
Tel: 0845 915 4811 / 0191 203 7010

Work
The European Job Mobility Portal
Tel: 00800 4080 4080 (free phone)
or 00 32 16 271 216
www.europa.eu.int/eures

European Centre for the Development
of Vocational Training
PO Box 22427
Finikas
GR-55102
Thessaloniki
Tel: 00 30 23 10 49 01 11
www.cedefop.europa.eu

UK National Europass Centre
Oriel House
Oriel Road
Cheltenham
Gloucester GL50 1XP
Tel: 0871 330 8341
www.uknec.org.uk
An organisation that aims to make
your skills, training and qualifications
recognisable to European employers
and education institutions.

Non-EU government bodies

Australia
Department of Immigration
and Citizenship
Australian High Commission
Australia House
Strand
London WC2B 4LA
Tel: 0906 550 8900
www.immi.gov.au

Trades Recognition Authority
PO Box 9879
Canberra
ACT 2601
Australia
Tel: 61 2 6121 7333
www.workplace.gov.au

VETASSESS
PO Box 2752
Melbourne 3001
Australia
Tel: 61 3 9655 4801
www.vetassess.com.au

Canada
Canadian High Commission
Immigration Section
38 Grosvenor Street
London W1K 4AA
Tel: 0207 258 6600
www.canada.org.uk

Citizenship and Immigration
Canada
www.cic.gc.ca
An organisation that oversees
Canada's immigration programme,
and principally deals with processing
visa and citizenship applications.

Foreign Credentials Referral Office
365 Laurier Avenue West
Ottawa Ontario K1A 1L1
Canada
www.credentials.gc.ca
Tel: 00 1 888 854 1805

New Zealand
Immigration New Zealand
Mezzanine Floor
NZ House
80 Haymarket
London SW1Y 4TE
Tel: 0906 910 0100
www.immigration.govt.nz

The New Zealand
Qualifications Authority (NZQA)
PO Box 160
Wellington 6140
New Zealand
Tel: 00 64 4 463 3000
www.nzqa.govt.nz

USA
United States Citizenship
and Immigration Services
(USCIS)
Tel: 00 1 800 375 5283
www.uscis.gov
USCIS is responsible for
managing America's vast
immigration system. Among
its key tasks are processing
visa and citizenship applications.

United States Embassy
in London
The Consular Information Unit
United States Embassy
24 Grosvenor Square
London W1A 1AE
Tel: 0904 245 0100
www.usembassy.org.uk

Professional and regulatory bodies

The British Chambers of Commerce
65 Petty France
London SW1H 9EU
Tel: 0207 654 5800
www.britishchambers.org.uk

Council of British Chambers of
Commerce in Continental Europe
(COBCOE)
12 York Gate
London NW1 4QS
Tel: 0207 544 4852
www.cobcoe.org.uk

Immigration

Canadian Society of Immigration
Consultants
390 Bay Street
Suite 1600
Munich Re Centre
Toronto (Ontario) M5H 2Y2
Tel: 00 1 416 572 2800
www.csic-scci.ca

Migration Institute of Australia (MIA)
PO Box Q102
QVB NSW 1230
Australia
Tel: 00 61 2 9279 3140
www.mia.org.au

Legal services

International Bar Association (IBA)
10th Floor
1 Stephen Street
London W1T 1AT
Tel: 0207 691 6868
www.ibanet.org

Australia

Law Council of Australia
19 Torrens Street
Braddon ACT 2612
Australia
Tel: 00 61 2 6246 3788
www.lawcouncil.asn.au

Canada

Canadian Bar Association (CBA)
00-865 Carling Avenue
Ottawa Ontario K1S 5S8
Tel: 00 1 613 237 2925
www.cba.org/cba

Europe

European Lawyers Association
Gentsesteenweg 1154
B-1082 Brussels Belgium
www.european-lawyers.org

New Zealand

New Zealand Law Society
PO Box 504
Lambton Quay
Wellington 6145
Tel: 00 64 (4) 472 7837
www.nz-lawsoc.org.nz

UK

The Law Society
113 Chancery Lane
London WC2A 1PL
Tel: 0207 242 1222
www.lawsociety.org.uk

USA

American Bar Association (ABA)
321 N. Clark St
Chicago IL 60610
Tel: 00 1 800 285 2221
www.abanet.org

Property

Association of International Property
Professionals (AIPP)
94 New Bond Street
London W1S 1SJ
Tel: 0207 409 7061
www.aipp.org.uk

Confédération Européenne
d'Immobilier (CEI)
Sainctlettesquare 11-12
B-1000 Brussels
Belgium
Tel: 00 32 2 219 4008
www.web-cei.com

Conseil des Notariats de l'Union
Européenne (CNUE)
Avenue de Cortenbergh
52 B - 1000 Brussels
Belgium
Tel: 00 32 2 513 95 29
www.cnue.be

International Real Estate Federation
(FIABCI)
FIABCI Secretariat
23 Avenue Bosquet
75007 Paris
France
Tel: 00 33 1 4550 4549
www.fiabci.org

Royal Institute of British Architects
(RIBA)
6 Portland Place
London W1B 1AD
Tel: 0207 580 5533
www.riba.org

Royal Institution of Chartered
Surveyors (RICS)
RICS Contact Centre
Surveyor Court
Westwood Way
Coventry CV4 8JE
Tel: 0870 333 1600
www.ricsfirms.co.uk

Financial services

Financial Ombudsman Service
(FOS)
South Quay Plaza
183 Marsh Wall
London E14 9SR
Tel: 0845 080 1800 /
0207 964 0500
www.financial-ombudsman.org.uk

Financial Services Authority (FSA)
25 The North Colonnade
Canary Wharf
London E14 5HS
Tel: 0207 066 1000
www.fsa.gov.uk

Removals services

British Association of Removers
(BAR)
Tangent House
62 Exchange Road
Watford
Hertfordshire WD18 OTG
Tel: 01923 699 480
www.bar.co.uk

Fédération Internationale
des Déménageurs Internationaux
(FIDI)
69 Rue Picard B-5
1080 Brussels
Belgium
Tel: 00 32 2 426 51 60
www.fidi.com

Overseas Moving Network
International (OMNI)
Unit 2
Lawster House
South Street
Dorking
Surrey RH4 2EU
Tel: 01306 889 218
www.omnimoving.com

Translation services

Chartered Institute of Linguists
Saxon House
48 Southwark Street
London SE1 1UN
Tel: 0207 940 3100
www.iol.org.uk

European Union of Associations
of Translation Companies (EUATC)
c/o Fifth Floor Greener House
66–68 Haymarket
London SW1Y 4RF
www.euatc.org

Consumer bodies

UK European Consumer Centre
1 Sylvan Court
Sylvan Way
Southfields Business Park
Basildon
Essex SS15 6TH
Tel: 0845 604 0503
www.ukecc.net

Which?
2 Marylebone Road
London NW1 4DF
Tel: 0207 770 7000
www.which.co.uk

Index

Index

Which? Books

Other books in this series

NEW EDITION
Buy, Sell and Move House

Kate Faulkner
ISBN: 978 1 84490 056 5
Price: £10.99

This new edition of the Which? best-selling property guide covers the latest changes to HIPs and government initiatives to tackle house prices. From dealing with estate agents to chasing solicitors and working out the true cost of your move, this guide tells you how to keep things on track and avoid painful sticking points.

NEW EDITION
Renting and Letting

Kate Faulkner
ISBN: 978 1 84490 054 1
Price: £10.99

A practical guide for landlords, tenants and anybody considering the buy-to-let market. Written by an experienced property professional, this real-world guide covers all the legal and financial matters, including tax, record-keeping and mortgages, as well as disputes, deposits and security.

Buying Property Abroad

Jeremy Davies
ISBN: 978 1 84490 024 4
Price: £9.99

This is a complete guide to the legal, financial and practical issues of buying property abroad, providing down-to-earth advice on how the buying process differs from the UK, and how to negotiate contracts, commission surveys, and employ lawyers and architects. Practical tips on currency deals and taxes all ensure you can buy abroad with total peace of mind.

To find out more about Which? Books log on to www.which.co.uk or call 01903 828 557.